Effective Grading

Effective Grading

A Tool for Learning and
Assessment in College

Second Edition

Barbara E. Walvoord
Virginia Johnson Anderson

JOSSEY-BASS
A Wiley Imprint
www.josseybass.com

Published by Jossey-Bass
A Wiley Imprint
989 Market Street, San Francisco, CA94103-1741—www.josseybass.com

Jossey-Bass books and products are available through most bookstores. To contact Jossey-Bass directly call our Customer Care Department within the U.S. at 800-956-7739, outside the U.S. at 317-572-3986, or fax 317-572-4002.

Jossey-Bass also publishes its books in a variety of electronic formats. Some content that appears in print may not be available in electronic books.

Library of Congress Cataloging-in-Publication Data
Walvoord, Barbara E. Fassler, 1941–
    Effective grading: a tool for learning and assessment in college/Barbara E. Walvoord, Virginia Johnson Anderson.—2nd ed.
        p.   cm.— (The Jossy-Bass higher and adult education series)
    Includes bibliographical references and index.
    ISBN 978-0-470-50215-0 (pbk.)
    1. Grading and marking (Students)—United States.   2. College students—Rating of—United States.   3. Educational tests and measurements—United States.   I Anderson, Virginia Johnson, 1939-   II. Title.
    LB2368.W35 2010
    378.1'672—dc22
                                                                            2009029085

Printed in the United States of America

FIRST EDITION

PB Printing

10   9   8   7   6   5   4   3   2   1

The Jossey-Bass Higher and Adult Education Series

Contents

To our children: Lisa, Brian, Randy, Sherry, and Billy
To our grandchildren: Kristen, Bria, Lauren, Liana, and Madison,
and in loving memory of Kameryn
To our spouses: Sharon Grace and Cliff Anderson

Preface to the Second Edition

THE SECOND EDITION of *Effective Grading* has the same goals as the first: to help instructors in college classrooms use the grading process effectively for learning and to explore how it can be used for assessment and improvement in the classroom and in broader contexts, such as the department or the general education program

Much has happened since the first edition was published in 1998. New emphasis has focused on learning as the goal of teaching. Research on how people learn has more fully infused the teaching process and the teaching literature. The scholarship of teaching and learning movement has arisen to help faculty conduct systematic inquiry about learning in their classrooms and share that inquiry with others. The requirement by accreditors and others that institutions assess student learning has not gone away; instead, it has become stronger and more insistent.

This second edition addresses those changes. The most significant change is a wholesale rewriting of Part Two, on assessment in the department and general education, to reflect new realities about assessment and build on the latest developments in the field. We added a chapter on assessment for grant-funded projects, because many funding agencies now insist on assessment of learning. In addition, we have revised Part One of the book on classroom grading so that it builds on new research, theory, and practice that have emerged since the first edition and incorporates what we ourselves have learned in the ten years since we wrote the first edition.

Acknowledgments

Our greatest debt is to the hundreds of faculty members in our own institutions—the University of Notre Dame and Towson University in Maryland—and in the many workshops we have led at other institutions and conferences. Our colleagues are our greatest teachers. For whatever in this book is practical, realistic, down-to-earth, and sensible, we profited greatly from their insistence on usable suggestions. For the examples we use throughout the book, we drew from their experiences, generously shared. For the will to revise this book, we drew on their support and encouragement. For the vision that inspires this book, we drew on their hopefulness, gifted teaching, and enthusiasm for learning and for the students who flourish in their classes.

For this second edition, several faculty contributed new case studies that greatly enriched the book: John C. Bean of Seattle University; David F. Carrithers of Seattle University; Mary Elizabeth Camp of Indiana University; Trish Casey-Whiteman of Anne Arundel Community College in Maryland; Theresa Earenfight of Seattle University; Tara Eisenhauer Ebersole of The Community College of Baltimore County; Cindy Ghent of Towson University in Maryland; Joan Middendorf of Indiana University; Susan Robison, a private practitioner and faculty member at the College of Notre Dame of Maryland; and Colette M. Schrank of Moraine Valley Community College in Illinois. Thomas A. Angelo responded to the manuscript of the first edition at a number of points and contributed important ideas to its development, though we, of course, take full responsibility for the ways in which we used his suggestions. We are indebted as well to the anonymous reviewers who provided detailed, thoughtful suggestions for this second edition. Our heartfelt thanks to Sharon Grace for her work with permissions. Aneesa Davenport and Cathy Mallon at Jossey-Bass were attentive and helpful in bringing the book to production.

The Authors

BARBARA E. WALVOORD is professor emerita at the University of Notre Dame. She earned her B.A. degree in English and philosophy at Hope College in Holland, Michigan, and her M.A. degree in English from The Ohio State University. She received her Ph.D. degree in English from the University of Iowa.

Walvoord was named the 1987 Maryland English Teacher of the Year for Higher Education by the Maryland Council of Teachers of English Language Arts. For more than thirty years, she has taught courses in composition, literature, and interdisciplinary humanities at institutions both large and small, public and private.

Walvoord has consulted and led workshops on the campuses of more than 350 colleges and universities and at many national and regional conferences. Her topics are assessment, teaching and learning, and writing across the curriculum. She came to Notre Dame in 1996 as the founding director of the John Kaneb Center for Teaching and Learning, where she worked with faculty and graduate students across disciplines. In 2003, she coordinated the self-study for Notre Dame's reaccreditation by the Higher Learning Commission of the North Central Association of Colleges and Schools, and she continued to work on assessment at Notre Dame.

Before coming to Notre Dame, Walvoord founded and directed Writing Across the Curriculum programs at Central College in Iowa, Loyola College in Maryland, and the University of Cincinnati. She was founding codirector of the Maryland Writing Project (a site of the National Writing Project) and the Baltimore Area Consortium for Writing Across the Curriculum. All of those programs won national acclaim.

Her publications include *Teaching and Learning in College Introductory Religion Courses* (2008); *Assessment Clear and Simple: A Practical Guide for Institutions, Departments, and General Education* (2004; second edition in process); *Academic Departments: How They Work, How They Change* (2000); *In the Long Run: A Study of Faculty in Three Writing-Across-the-Curriculum Programs* (1997); *Thinking and Writing in College: A Study of Students in Four Disciplines* (1990); and *Helping Students Write Well: A Guide for Teachers in All Disciplines* (second edition, 1986). She has also published articles and book chapters about grading, assessment, teaching, learning, and writing. *Making Large Classes Interactive* (1995), a thirty-minute video of which she is co–executive director, has won two national awards.

• • •

Virginia Johnson Anderson is professor of biological sciences at Towson University (TU). A nationally known assessment activist and author, she has presented grading and assessment workshops at more than 180 community colleges, colleges, and universities across the country and abroad. She received her B.S. degree in biology from Lamar University and M.S. degree on a National Science Foundation (NSF) Outstanding Teachers Fellowship at the University of Georgia. While teaching general biology and microbiology for nurses at TU, Anderson earned her doctorate in science education at the University of Maryland—College Park in 1984. She routinely teaches eleven hour contact hours per semester: eight in life sciences and three in an upper-level scientific and technical writing course. She chairs her department's assessment committee and the university's subcommittee for undergraduate programs assessment, and she is actively engaged in general education assessment.

Widely published, Anderson has been the principal investigator for two major NSF urban science initiatives and a consultant or external evaluator on seven other national grants. Currently she is the education specialist for Biofilms: The Hypertextbook, an NSF/Montana State University initiative, and an evaluator on a five-year NSF/STEM CoSMiC Scholars grant at TU. She has served as a consultant for agencies such as the American Society for Microbiology, U.S. Peace Corps, Maryland Writing Project, Quality Undergraduate Education project, Appalachian College Association, United Arab Emirates, Mellon Foundation, and extensively over the past five years for the Middle States Commission on Higher Education.

Effective Grading

Chapter 1

Introduction

WE WROTE THIS BOOK because, as teachers of English and biology, we have struggled across our careers to make our grading fair, time efficient, and conducive to student learning and to figure out how the grading process can be part of departmental and general education assessment. When Walvoord, as director of four teaching-learning centers, would ask faculty for suggestions about workshop topics, grading was always at the top. And in the hundreds of workshops for faculty that we have led, we have found that workshops on teaching always have to address grading issues. Workshops on assessment in departments or general education always raise questions about the role of grades.

Grading infuses everything that happens in the classroom. It needs to be acknowledged and managed from the first moment that an instructor begins planning a class. Trying to keep students from caring about grades is futile. Trying to pretend that grades are not important is unrealistic. Trying to establish an institutional assessment program unconnected to the grading process is wasteful. Grades are the elephant in the classroom. Instead of ignoring the elephant, we want to use its power for student learning.

Grading as a Complex Process

By *"grading,"* we mean not only bestowing an "A" or a "C" on a piece of student work. We also mean the process by which a teacher assesses student learning through classroom tests and assignments, the context in which good teachers establish that process, and the dialogue that surrounds grades and defines their meaning to various audiences. Grading encompasses tailoring the test or assignment to the learning goals of the course, establishing criteria and standards, helping students acquire the skills and knowledge they need, assessing student learning over time, shaping student motivation, planning course content and teaching methods, using in-class and out-of-class time, offering feedback so students can develop as thinkers and writers, communicating about students' learning to appropriate audiences, and using results to plan improvements in the classroom, department, and institution. When we talk about grading, we have student learning most in mind.

For example, a biologist teaching a capstone course for undergraduate majors asks the students to complete scientific experiments and write them up in scientific report form. She chooses this assignment because it will teach and test her learning goals for the course—goals that she carefully discusses with her students and for which she asks the students to be responsible. She sets clear criteria and standards, and she communicates these to her students. Across the semester, she helps students learn the requisite knowledge and skills. She responds to drafts and final reports in ways that help students learn from their experiences. And after grading the set of scientific reports, she thinks, *Well, the students did better than last year on experimental design, but they still didn't do very well on graphing data. I wonder if that would improve if I. . . .* and she plans a new teaching strategy. After turning in her final course grades, she analyzes the strengths and weaknesses of her students as a group, considering how their prior training in the department prepared them for the culminating research project in her course. With her report, she goes to the final faculty meeting of the semester and talks with her colleagues about how skills such as graphing might be more effectively developed earlier in the curriculum. At this point, her classroom assessment becomes departmental assessment.

In short, we view grading as a complex context-dependent process that serves multiple roles:

- *Evaluation.* The grading process should produce a valid, fair, and trustworthy judgment about the quality of each student's work.
- *Communication.* The grade itself is a communication to the student, as well as to employers, graduate schools, and others. The grading process also spurs communication between faculty and students, among faculty colleagues, and between institutions and their constituents.
- *Motivation.* Grading affects how students study, what they focus on, how much time they spend, and how involved they become in the course. Thus, it is a powerful part of the motivational structure of the course.
- *Organization.* A grade on a test or assignment helps to mark transitions, bring closure, and focus effort for both students and teachers.
- *Faculty and student reflection.* The grading process can yield rich information about what students are learning collectively and can serve as the first step in systematic assessment and information-driven teaching.

This book is divided into two parts: one for classroom grading and one for wider purposes of assessment.

Part One: Grading in the Classroom

Faculty in our workshops have posed the questions that shape Part One of this book:

- What are the principles of good practice in managing the grading process?
- How can I construct good assignments?
- How can I foster healthy motivation around grades? How should I respond to the student who asks, "What do I need to do to get an 'A' [or a 'C']?"
- How can I establish criteria and standards for student work? Should effort and improvement count? Should I grade on the curve? How should I handle grammar and punctuation? How can I fairly grade students who enter with a wide range of skills and preparation?
- How can I guide students' learning process in the most effective way?
- How should I calculate course grades?
- How can I communicate effectively with students about their grades? Which kinds of comments and feedback are most useful? How can I help my students without doing their work for them?
- How can I handle the workload and make grading time efficient?
- How can I analyze the factors that are influencing learning in my classroom? How can I tell which teaching strategies work well for my students? How can what I learn through the grading process help me improve my teaching?

Part Two: How Grading Serves Broader Assessment Purposes

As faculty members assess student learning in their own classes, it makes sense for them to work collaboratively to evaluate students' learning in broader settings: a grant-funded program, an undergraduate major, a graduate degree, a certificate program, or a general education curriculum.

In the context of requirements by accreditors and others, "assessment" is commonly defined as the systematic collection of information about student learning, or programs of student learning, for the purpose of improving that learning. Assessment has three main components:

1. Articulate the goals for student learning.

2. Gather information about how well students are achieving the goals.

3. Use the information for improvement.

In the chapters in Part Two, we argue that students' classroom work, evaluated by faculty, can be a rich and fruitful component for assessment of student learning in wider settings. Departments and institutions need not, and should not, rely solely on standardized tests or on surveys of students and alumni.

We have shaped the second part of the book around questions that faculty and administrators ask in the assessment workshops we have led at colleges and universities. The chapters in this part address questions such as:

- Are grades themselves acceptable for assessment? If we give fair grades, what else do we need to do? What is the relationship between assessment and grades?
- How can we use students' classroom work to evaluate learning in an entire degree program or in general education?
- What is the relationship between students' classroom work and other assessment measures, such as surveys and standardized tests?
- How do we assess the highest kinds of learning, such as originality, global perspective, or ethical decision making? Will assessment force us to "dumb down" what we teach?
- Does assessment have to be "objective"?
- What about portfolios?
- How do we handle the workload of assessment?

Using This Book Individually or in Faculty Workshops

Part One of this book follows a course planning sequence that is as appropriate in planning a course for the first time as rethinking the course after twenty times. At the end of each chapter are suggested activities to help readers apply the suggestions presented in the chapter to their own course planning. Readers can complete the activities by working individually, but the activities are also designed for use in a workshop setting. A group of faculty might read each chapter in turn, complete the activities, and then discuss their ideas with each other before moving on to the next chapter.

Part One
Grading in the Classroom

Chapter 2

Clarifying Goals, Constructing Assignments

THE WAY TO SAVE TIME, make every moment count, and integrate grading, learning, and motivation is to plan your grading from the moment you begin planning the course. To do otherwise—to regard grading as an afterthought—is to create wasted time, dead-end efforts, and post hoc rationalizations as students question their grades.

Beginning with this chapter, we follow a course planning process, referred to as assignment centered or learner centered, that has long been recommended by experts familiar with research on learning and teaching (Fink, 2003; Weimer, 2002). In a review of the research on critical thinking, Kurfiss (1988) recommended that rather than begin with, "I must cover . . . ," the instructor begins with, "I want my students to learn to. . . . " Students will still be expected to master facts, concepts, and procedures, but in course planning, the faculty member keeps her eye on the ball: What do I want my students to learn, and how will I structure the course so as to maximize their learning? This chapter leads you through the first steps of the assignment-centered approach to course planning.

Establish Learning Goals

Effective grading practices begin when the teacher says to herself, *By the end of the course, I want my students to be able to. . . .* Concrete verbs such as *define, argue, solve,* and *create* are more helpful for course planning than vague verbs such as *know* or *understand* or passive verbs such as *be exposed to*. If you write, "I want students to think like economists," elaborate on what that means. How does an economist think? Which aspects of that thinking do you want to cultivate in students? We refer to these statements as *learning goals*, but other possible terms are *learning objectives* or *learning outcomes*.

It may be helpful to think of goals in categories, as in these examples:

Identifying or Describing Content, Vocabulary, and Concepts

- Identify key economic terms.
- Describe important concepts, principles, and theories of psychology.
- Be able to state physics concepts in students' own words, and discuss what the students do not know.

Conduct Research or Solve Problems in the Discipline

- Analyze the feasibility of marketing a consumer item in a foreign country.
- Synthesize information from various sources to arrive at intervention tactics for a client.

Make Ethical Choices

- Follow the ethical practices of the discipline in human and animal research, use of sources, and collaboration.
- Identify ethical issues, and use ethical reasoning to address them.

Expand Worldview; Consider Big Questions

- Exit with a sense of wonder [for a physics course].
- Clarify the student's own values and convictions.
- Develop creativity by making unusual connections, looking at something in a fresh way, noticing unusual relationships or aspects of the topic, pushing beyond surface observations, challenging what others take for granted, or taking a risk with a rhetorical technique, an unpopular idea, or a difficult topic.

Develop Qualities and Habits of Mind

- Form habits of lifelong reading in the field.
- Habitually question statistical data for their reliability and validity.
- Develop appreciation for unfamiliar works of art.
- Appreciate the pig. (Really! This one appeared in a swine management course in the agriculture college of a large state university.)

You may not be able to measure or grade everything that you care about, but at this early planning stage, we urge you to include your most precious goals. The Internet is a wonderful place to find goals: search "learning goals" or "student learning outcomes." Also helpful is Bloom's *Taxonomy of Education Objectives* (1956) and a revision of Bloom's categories in L. Anderson and others (2001).

Construct Major Assignments and Tests

Because grading is perhaps one of the most labor-intensive things faculty do, why spend the time grading student work that doesn't address your most important goals? Try to ensure that any assignments, tests, and exams that you give and grade will facilitate the acquisition of the knowledge, skills, and attitudes that you most want students to learn and retain. Resource 2.1 offers further help on assignments and test construction (see References for full bibliographic information).

Resource 2.1. Sources About Assignment and Test Construction

Achacoso and Svinicki (2004). Provocative essays on how traditional testing methods may be adapted to new emphases on active learning, problem solving, student engagement, new technologies, and students' collaborative work.

Adelman (1989). Oriented to natural science and technology.

Anderson, Bauer, and Speck (2002). Assessment for online classes.

Anderson and Speck (1998). Assessment for learning-centered paradigms.

Bloom, Hastings, and Madaus (1971). On assessing the learning outcomes defined in Bloom (1956).

Boud, Dunn, and Hegarty-Hazel (1986). On laboratory skills.

Carey (1994). General textbook on measurement and evaluation with sections on designing and using multiple-choice, essay, and other types of assessment.

Cashin (1987). Short summary on improving essay tests.

Clegg and Cashin (1986). Short summary on improving multiple-choice tests.

Comeaux (2005). New modes and new technologies for assessing online learning.

Facione (1990). Assessing and teaching critical thinking.

Feinberg (1990). Strengths and weaknesses of multiple-choice tests.

Fenwick and Parsons (2000). Basics of evaluation and test design.

Haladyna (1994). On developing and validating multiple-choice tests.

Huba and Freed (2000). Learner-centered assessment.

Jacobs and Chase (1992). Handbook for faculty on test construction, validity, and reliability; advice for various types of tests. Includes a section on computer-assisted testing.

Linn (1993). Standard reference. Covers theories and principles; construction, administration, and scoring; and applications.

Lowman (1996, 2000). General overview of testing and assignment making, with special attention to motivation.

Mezeske and Mezeske (2007). Creative ideas for unusual kinds of assessment.

Nilson (2003). Pages 191–206 overview basics of constructing assignments and tests.

Rock (1991). How to test higher-order cognitive skills.

Tobias (1994, 1996). Based on previous studies of science departments, science teaching, and science students, recommends new practices for in-class exams in college-level science.

Wiggins (1998). Argues for authentic assessment; critiques traditional testing methods.

Yelon and Duley (1978). Assessing students' field experiences.

Zubizarreta (2009). Using portfolios for learning and assessment.

Construct Assignments That Fit Your Learning Goals

Research indicates that faculty may not achieve a good fit between the learning they say they want and the tests and assignments they actually give:

> *Faculty often state that they are seeking to develop students' abilities to analyze, synthesize, and think critically. However, research indicates that faculty do not follow their good intentions when they develop their courses. A formal review and analysis of course syllabi and exams revealed that college faculty do not in reality focus on these advanced skills but instead are far more concerned with students' abilities to acquire knowledge, comprehend basic concepts or ideas and terms, and apply this basic knowledge [National Center for Education Statistics, 1995, p. 167].*

A combination of careful forethought, knowledge of your students, and analysis of your students' work are the keys here. For example, a mathematician realized his existing testing and grading system was putting too much emphasis on merely getting the right answers. Instead, he wanted his students to solve problems and explain the process, so he added a requirement to some of his assignments and exams: students had to draw a vertical line down the center of a page, dividing it into two columns. In one column they solved the problem. In the opposite column, they wrote in sentences, for each step, what they did and why they did it.

A psychologist with whom we worked wanted students to think critically. She was very proud of herself for giving essay tests—not just multiple-choice tests—in an introductory psychology course with a class of ninety and no teaching assistants. But when, in a workshop, she looked carefully at her grading processes and criteria, she saw that she was primarily grading on mastery of facts, vocabulary, and basic concepts. She promptly instituted a multiple-choice test for that elementary knowledge and refocused her valuable grading and responding time on a take-home essay that elicited synthesis and evaluation from the learners.

Pay attention to what you name your assignments and tests and what those names mean to your students. A sociologist was asking for a "term paper" from his students and getting encyclopedia-based reports that did not meet his goals for the assignment. In a workshop, when asked to define what he really wanted, he realized he wanted a review of the literature, so he began to call it that. Two positive results ensued. First, students no longer imported notions of the term paper as an encyclopedia-based pastiche of paraphrased material on a topic; they had never written a review of the literature before, so they knew they had to listen very carefully to his instructions about the assignment. Second, he was forced to clarify for them and for himself what he meant and to teach them how to write a review of the literature.

Pay attention also to how polished or finished an assignment must be in order to fulfill your goals. A political scientist has his students construct a set of questions for a major term paper, compile an annotated bibliography, and then write the introduction—but he does not have students complete the whole paper because by the time they have done the annotated bibliography and the introduction, they have learned what he most wanted them to learn.

Make Assignments Interesting to Students

The kinds of assignments and tests you give will influence students' motivation (Svinicki, 2004, 2005). Consider creative kinds of assignments without being carried away by something cute that does not meet your needs. For example, an American historian asked students to write diary entries for a hypothetical Nebraska farm woman in the 1890s. He liked this assignment because it required that students know about economics, social class, transportation, gender roles, technology, family relations, religion, diet, and so on, and it also gave them a chance to use their imaginations. He found that when he was explicit about his desire for them to use the diary to display the breadth of their historical knowledge, the assignment achieved his learning goals in a way that the students enjoyed.

Consider Peer Collaboration

Do not automatically think that every test or assignment must be completed by the individual student in isolation. Consider activities, tests, and assignments that students complete in groups. Cooperation among students is listed by Chickering and Gamson (1987) as one of their classic, research-based "Seven Principles of Good Practice for Undergraduate Education," a finding reaffirmed by recent research (Kuh and others, 2007; Pascarella and Terenzini, 2005). As Astin (1996). puts it, summarizing his comprehensive study of factors that influence college students' learning, "The strongest single source of influence on cognitive and affective development [in college] is the student's peer group. . . . The study strongly suggests that the peer group is powerful because it has the capacity to involve the student more intensely in the educational experience" (p. 126).

Assignments that get students involved with one another and with their teacher may draw on this powerful force. Resource 2.2 contains helpful resources on designing and managing student cooperation and collaboration.

Resource 2.2. Collaborative and Cooperative Learning

Barkley, Cross, and Major (2005). Clear and helpful.

Michaelsen, Knight, and Fink (2004). Creative ideas about how to use student teams in transformative ways.

Millis (2002). Short online summary of ideas for collaborative learning, from a well-known expert.

Millis and Cottell (1998). A standard resource with many good ideas.

Nilson (2003). A fine, clear book on teaching, with a helpful ten-page treatment of student learning in groups.

Speck (2002). Explores issues and recommendations for students' collaborative writing, including both short in-class collaborations and longer projects.

Stein and Hurd (2000). Thoughtful and practical treatment of using student groups.

Weimer (2008). A one-page list of design problems that contribute to students' frustration with group assignments.

The literature suggests these principles for designing assignments that students will complete with peers:

- *Design a task that groups can do better than individuals.* There has to be a compelling reason that the people in the group need one another; otherwise, some of them will rightly think, *I could do this better by myself.* For example, a professor of international marketing designed, for his senior students, a research project in which they had to interview a number of people, consult multiple sources, and develop a number of different aspects of a complex project. The task was simply too long, complex, and time-consuming for one person. In contrast, a professor of a capstone course in business management asked students to conduct a final project that required several different areas of expertise, including technical expertise in financial instruments and statistics. In forming the groups, he polled his students about their previous expertise—courses they had taken or business experience they had acquired. Then he made sure that each team contained at least one person who had the special skills that would be needed.

- *Design a task that is hard to divide into silos.* A business instructor assigned students to write a report with several sections. In some of the groups, the students simply divided up the sections and then never met again. Their final reports were collections of unconnected individual writings, not a coherent and logical development of the issues.

Thereafter, the professor expressly forbade the students to divide the task in this way, suggested several better ways of dividing the work, and asked each team, early on, to report to him their plan for each person's part of the job.

- *Design a task that includes individual responsibility.* Students may feel fear and frustration if their entire grade is dependent on other people's work. Some faculty believe that in their disciplines, students must learn to work in settings where the team as a whole is held responsible for its work. These faculty tell students, "You're learning important skills. I'll help you learn, but in the end, the team's grade is everyone's grade, just as it is in professional life." However, some faculty members want to allow room in their assignments for individual responsibility. A history professor assigned his ten seminar students to use primary sources from the college's archives to produce a volume of short, researched essays on their town's history, with chapters on the town's origins, religion, commerce, politics, and other topics. Each person was individually responsible for one chapter, but each person also sat on an "editorial board" that responded to emerging chapter drafts and established common characteristics for all the chapters. Part of each person's grade was based on the quality of each individual chapter; part was based on how well the students contributed to the quality of the volume as a whole.

Fit Tests to Learning Goals

It's easy to construct multiple-choice and short-answer tests by the content you want to cover. But think also about the learning goals you want to achieve. For example, you might have as a goal that after completing Soil Science 101, students should be able to read and interpret graphic information. The process of linking tests to learning goals has been termed *test blueprinting* (Middle States Commission on Higher Education, 2007; Suskie, 2009).

To "read and interpret graphic information" is an example of a deep learning task as described by Entwistle (2001). Students must succeed at four skills: reading graphic information, processing graphic information quantitatively, interpreting graphic information, and making connections between graphic information and scientific issues (concepts or ethical concerns). Table 2.1 shows how short-answer questions could be matched to aspects of the deep learning goal. The table uses data from a graphic on banana and mango exports (not shown).

We will return to this process of test blueprinting to show how objective test results might be mapped to a rubric (Chapter Four), inform teaching

TABLE 2.1

Learning Goals and Short-Answer Test Question Indicators

Goals: Students Will:	Test Questions
Read graphic information	For what years does this graph show export data?
Process graphic information quantitatively	True or false: Total banana and mango exports have increased over the past twenty years.
	What additional scientific data would you need to know to determine whether Fiji exports more mangoes than bananas?
Interpret graphic information	True or false: If the current trend continues, mango exports will increase.
Make connections between graphic information and scientific issues (concepts or ethical concerns, or both)	What are two questions you would like to ask about the soil composition in Fiji as related to information we have discussed in class?
	If mangoes have a higher nitrogen content than bananas, what ethical concerns might islanders have about these data?

(Chapter Ten), and contribute to departmental and general education assessment (Chapters Eleven and Twelve). The point here is that a test or an assignment is a valid measurement only if it elicits from students the kinds of learning you want to measure.

Construct a Course Skeleton

Once you have effective tests and assignments in mind, the next step is to plan how they will be placed across the semester. We suggest a course skeleton that shows just the bare bones of the course—the goals and the major assignments. This skeleton shows the course in a unique light for planning, more useful than simply a list of the topics to be covered. The skeleton helps the instructor move from a topic- or coverage-centered approach to an assignment-centered approach. But remember that content is not given up. It gets integrated later in the planning process, after the faculty member has clarified the student learning and the assignments that will teach and test that learning. Content is part of what the students need if they are to reach the goals and do well on the assignment.

To see how the course skeleton works, we follow two history professors, each planning a Western civilization course that is a general education requirement for first-year students.

Our first example is a hypothetical professor who begins to think about the course when her department head says, "Jane, will you teach Western

Civ this fall?" She next checks the catalogue description, which tells the content of the course: Western civilization from 1500 to the end of the Cold War, emphasizing such-and-such themes. Now she plans her fifteen weeks of coverage, saying to herself, *Let's see. I'd like to use Burke and Paine, Marx, Lafore, and* Heart of Darkness *in addition to the textbook. I'll cover 1500 to 1800 in six weeks and get through the French Revolution by midterm. Then in the second half of the course, I'll cover 1800 to the present.* Her outline of the course might look like this:

Week	Topic
1	Renaissance and Reformation
2	Seventeenth-Century Crisis
3	Absolutism
4	Age of Reason
5	French Revolution
6	Burke, *Reflections*, and Paine, *Rights of Man*
7	MIDTERM
8	Industrial Revolution
9	Marx, *Communist Manifesto*
10	Imperialism
11	Conrad, *Heart of Darkness*
12	World War I
13	Lafore, *Long Fuse*
14	World War I, World War II, and the Cold War
15	FINAL

Note that in her conversation with herself, the subject of her sentences is *I*. The most common verb is *cover*. This teacher is already well launched on the topic- and coverage-centered model. Next, she will compose her syllabus. It will go something like this:

Tues., Sept. 5: Social and religious background of the Renaissance and Reformation. Read chaps. 1 and 2 in textbook.

Thurs., Sept. 7: Economic and political background of the Renaissance and Reformation. Read chap. 3 in textbook; Machiavelli handout.

When students first see this syllabus, they are likely to assume that in class, the teacher will tell them about the topics. They might also assume that they need not necessarily read the chapter before they come to class because the teacher will lecture. Thus, the traditional course planning process and the syllabus that results from it can trap both the faculty member and the students into the coverage-centered model.

Assessment in this coverage-centered scheme is also problematic. Once the teacher has filled in the topics she has to cover, she is likely to say to herself, *I'll use essay tests at midterm and final, with questions on lecture, textbook, and supplementary readings. The midterm will cover 1500 to 1800. I'll have a comprehensive final, covering all the course material, but I'll weight it in favor of 1-800 to the present. And I'll assign a term paper due near the end of the course. Students can choose which of the supplementary readings they'll cover in their term papers.*

In this coverage-centered planning process, the tests and papers are added at the end, and their implied role is to test coverage. When asked what she wants students to achieve at the end of the course, this faculty member is likely to say that she wants students to describe events and also to analyze and construct arguments about historical issues. However, her exams and term paper are not likely to elicit coherent arguments with full evidence and answers to counterarguments. Essay exams may be merely what one teacher calls "fact dumps."

Research indicates that many students experience school reading as a collection of discrete facts to be memorized and regurgitated on tests (Geisler, 1994). Furthermore, some students have taken essay exams that were graded in this way: the teacher went through the student's answer, placing a check mark next to every fact or idea that "counted," and the student's score was the total of the check marks. The savvy student's way of taking such a test is to dump as much information as possible as quickly as possible. Moreover, if the students see the exam question for the first time when they walk into the class and then have twenty minutes or fifty minutes to write a cogent argument, are they likely to produce a cogent, tightly argued, thoroughly logical essay?

There might also be problems in this class with the term paper. Students might submit cut-and-paste pastiches of library or online sources, following the term paper models they learned in other settings. Pioneering writing-across-the-curriculum researchers Schwegler and Shamoon (1982) found that students they surveyed often described the term paper or research paper as a collection and combination of sources, not as an exploration, an analysis, or an argument. The term *term paper* may imply undesirable meanings for your students.

The true failure of the coverage-centered course is the set of assumptions it may foster about what school means:

- Sitting in lecture and taking down what teachers say
- Studying lecture notes and the textbook the night before the test
- Regurgitating the right answers on the test

As part of a research project by Walvoord, McCarthy, and others (1990), a student described to the interviewer her expectations on the first day of a Western civilization course: "I remember going in there thinking, O.K., this is just a basic history course, you know. It's not going to be a lot of work; you know what I mean. It's just going to be basically all lecture, and then I'm going to have to restate what he told me on an exam" (p. 99). Another student said, "I haven't done things like this before. In high school we took the answers straight from the book. I am not in the habit of developing arguments" (p. 102). The coverage-centered course may affirm these students' notions of the educational process.

To see what an assignment-centered course might look like, let's examine an actual Western civilization course whose faculty member collaborated with Walvoord to document students' learning in the class (Walvoord and Breihan, 1990). History professor John Breihan begins by identifying what he wants students to be able to do at the end of the course:

1. I want my students to describe historical events and people

2. Most of all, I want my students to be able to use historical data to develop the elements of an argument:

   - Taking a position

   - Backing the position with evidence

   - Answering counterarguments

As Breihan concentrated on eliciting the kinds of thinking and learning he wanted students to achieve, he decided to assign three argumentative essays, one for each major area of course content. He fashioned questions that would require students to synthesize what they had studied, not simply parrot it. He then turned to the strategic timing of these three assignments in his fifteen-week course skeleton:

Week 1: Emphasizing and modeling argument and counterargument, building foundational knowledge

Week 6: Argumentative essay on Age of Reason, French Revolution

Week 10: Same format on Industrial Revolution and imperialism

Week 15: Same format on World War I, World War II, and Cold War [this was given as the final exam]

First, notice that the course has no term paper or final essay exam. Instead, Breihan concentrated on three argumentative essays, the last of which became the final exam. He fashioned questions that would require students to synthesize what they had studied and make an argument.

He decided to give students the essay questions ahead of time so they could prepare rather than write hastily to answer a question they had not seen before. For the first essay, to help students achieve independence from merely copying their sources, he asked students to draft their essays in class without notes. Then he responded to the drafts, and students revised their essays out of class and resubmitted them.

Using the assignment-centered approach and focusing first on the essential course skeleton, Breihan selected the type of assignment that he believed had the best chance of eliciting from his students the careful arguments he most valued. He kept the paper load manageable. He structured the writing experiences so that students had the time and conditions necessary to produce coherent arguments. (The skeleton does not include minor assignments such as response to reading, map quizzes, and the like.)

We suggest that you begin course planning in this same way. Your discipline may be quite different from history; you may have labs or clinics in addition to class, for example. But the same principle applies: state what you want your students to learn; then list the major assignments and tests that will both teach and test that learning. Think carefully about the basic types of the classroom assessments you might choose and perhaps a few of their most salient characteristics. For example, if you are planning multiple-choice exams, problem-solving exams, or short-answer exams, include a summary of the skills and knowledge that the exam will test. Even if you have only one assignment (for example, a senior seminar course with one presentation or an art capstone with a single portfolio), do not list the smaller classroom tasks at this time. Stay focused on how each major assignment will enable each student to engage in and excel at the learning that you want him or her to achieve.

Check Assignments and Tests for Fit and Feasibility

As you examine your assignment-centered course skeleton, ask yourself two questions:

1. Do my tests and assignments fit the kind of learning I most want?

2. Is the workload I am planning for myself and my students feasible: reasonable, strategically placed, and sustainable?

Exhibit 2.1 presents two course skeletons: one constructed by a sociology professor and one by a business professor. As a mini-case study in fit and feasibility, examine each of these, and identify what you see as the major potential problem in each.

EXHIBIT 2.1

Problematic Course Skeletons

Week of the Semester Schedule	Sociology General Education Course, Nonmajors, 100 Level: "I want my students to be able to apply sociological analysis to what they see around them."	Business Management Senior Capstone: "I want my students to make business decisions, using the tools we have been studying."
1 (week)		
2		Written case analysis
3		
4		Written case analysis
5		
6		Written case analysis
7		
8	Essay and objective test (midterm)	Written case analysis
9		
10		Written case analysis
11		
12		Written case analysis
13		
14	Term paper	Written case analysis
15	Essay and objective exam (final)	Written case analysis as final exam

Laying out his course major course assessments in this skeletal way, the sociology professor realized that his tests and exams did not fit well with the learning he most wanted. Students were likely to study all night before the exams, using their texts and class notes, a procedure not likely to elicit thoughtful application of sociological perspectives to what they saw around them. The term paper was also likely to appear to students as a rather detached, meaningless academic exercise.

The professor decided to change his assignments to fit more closely with what he wanted students to learn. He abandoned the term paper and the exams and instead asked his students, every other week, to write a journal in which they applied sociological analysis to something they had observed. However, the word *journal*, as he discovered the next semester, was a mistake: students interpreted the term *journal* too loosely and did not give him the rigorous sociological analysis he wanted. So he renamed the assignment *sociological analysis*. He explained that he wanted students to analyze some event or situation they observed in light of the sociological viewpoints they had been studying.

For example, suppose students had been studying the writings of French sociologist Émile Durkheim. A student attended his cousin's bar mitzvah. For his analysis that week, the student might ask himself, *What would Durkheim make of this?* The professor stated three criteria for the analysis: (1) the student had to summarize accurately the sociological perspective—in this case, Durkheim's views; (2) the student had to include the kinds of specific details that sociologists observe (it did not suffice to say "the food was great"); and (3) the student had to link the theories and the observations in a reasonable and thoughtful way, applying Durkheim's perspective to the bar mitzvah. These changes helped the sociology professor not only fit his assignments and tests to student learning but also spread the workload across the semester.

Now let's focus on the second problematic course skeleton in Exhibit 2.1. When asked about fit, the business management professor affirmed his choice of the case method, saying, "I know there is some controversy in my field about whether the case method really does teach decision making, but it works as well as anything else I know." Although he was happy with the fit, his class size had risen from fifteen to forty in the past few years. His former plan was no longer feasible. He would never get a handle on the paper load.

Colleagues in a workshop asked him, "Can the students write fewer cases?" He answered, "No, there are eight units in the course. I can't drop a unit because students need all of them, and they are all mandated by our business accrediting agency. And if they don't write on each unit, they don't learn it." Then colleagues asked, "Do students need to do a full five- to eight-page case study each time?" That question was the solution to the workload problem.

The business professor began to ponder whether, for some of the full case studies, especially early in the course, he could design shorter assignments that would help students learn what they needed. He had long recognized that there was a cohort of students in his class who wrote one mediocre case study after another. But the papers were coming at him so fast, and there were so many of them, that he didn't have time to give these students the guidance they needed to improve, so they kept repeating their mistakes.

In particular, he noted that weaker students tended to stay too close to the chronological order of the case materials. Students were given sales figures, a history of the firm, interviews with employees and managers, descriptions of the firm's branches, copies of relevant legislation that governed the firm's operations, and so on, all in deliberately random order. Some students read through this case material, making suggestions along the way but never fully transcending its sequence.

A second but related problem was that students tended to recommend low-level solutions. They would say, "This person and that person need to talk to one another more often," or "The company should put more resources into its aluminum business," but they would not see the deeper underlying structural problems.

What could this professor do, in a one-page assignment in week 2, to help students transcend these problems? The professor tried having students write down the most important problem they saw in that week's case and then list three pieces of evidence from the case out of chronological order. However, he found that students could not yet identify the underlying problem so early in the semester. So instead he focused the first assignments on building-block skills. In the first assignment, in week 2, he asked students to analyze the life stage of the business, a topic they had covered in the textbook. Was the business in question an infant business? A mature business? They had studied the kinds of problems typically associated with these life stages, so he asked them to place the business in its appropriate stage and then discern whether it exhibited problems typical for that stage. In so doing, he propelled them out of a read-and-suggest mode and gave them a larger conceptual framework. He also facilitated their use of the language by which business professionals describe the basic underlying problems of businesses. In the fourth week, he asked them for another short but more complex assignment, and he proceeded this way until the eighth week, when they wrote their first full case analysis. The teacher reported that the cases were now better than before.

A biologist used the same principle in a different form. Weekly lab reports were killing him with the workload, yet like the business teacher, he was reluctant to give up having his students write for each lab. He realized that some of his students were writing twelve mediocre lab reports; they never seemed to get the reports right, and he had to read and grade all those repetitively mediocre works. He finally asked himself, *What do I want?* and answered, *I want students to learn to produce a good lab report—not twelve mediocre lab reports.* So he decided to teach lab report writing more thoroughly and to use short, well-sequenced assignments to build students' skills. Instead of asking for a full report on each lab, he would require, on the first two labs, that students write just the first section, the Introduction. He would concentrate on helping them do that section well. For the next two labs, he would ask for the Introduction and the Methods and Materials sections, and so on through the parts of the scientific report. He not only cut his paper load that way but was able to give more focused instruction to help his students master one section at a time. By the end

Chapter 3

Fostering Healthy Student Motivation

NOW THAT YOU HAVE A SET OF LEARNING GOALS, major assignments, and a course skeleton, it is time to flesh out the skeleton by determining the day-to-day activities that can help students learn what they need to know. While making those plans, it is important to consider the issue of student motivation. As teachers, we can facilitate learning, but we cannot make it happen alone. Students must take an active role in shaping their own learning. Grades are sometimes blamed for creating a "grade-grubbing" value system in the classroom that replaces or upstages students' motivation to learn for learning's sake. Motivation is much more complicated, however. This chapter explores how grades might be a force for positive motivation in the classroom. In the course planning process, before you begin to flesh out your course skeleton and outline your day-to-day course activities, consider the factors that influence student motivation and engagement.

Student Motivation

It's tempting for a teacher to complain about the "unmotivated student" or the student who says, "What do I need to do to get an A [or a C]?" It's tempting to feel powerless in the face of students' apathy or their focus on grades. Looking at closed, wary faces on the first day of class can be daunting. Certainly the values, goals, and expectations that students bring to a situation will affect their learning (Ginsberg and Wlodkowski, 2009; Wlodkowski, 2008). However, we do not have to accept the "unmotivated" student as a fixed and hopeless lump in the classroom. Research strongly suggests that motivation is changeable; what we do in the classroom can affect students' motivation for learning (Covington, 2007a). Our responsibility as teachers is to create an environment that encourages student motivation for learning.

Several important principles can guide us in creating such an environment.

Principle 1: Grades Do Not Necessarily Decrease Students' Intrinsic Motivation

It's easy to ascribe to an oversimplified view of extrinsic and intrinsic motivation. We may fear that extrinsic rewards such as grades will diminish students' intrinsic sense of satisfaction and their motivation to learn for learning's sake. But the actual situation is more complex. An important finding is that rewards do not necessarily decrease intrinsic motivation if:

The rewards convey information about the person's competence.

The feedback is informative and constructive.

Feedback conveys positive recognition of a person's work [Baer and Kaufman, 2006, p. 18].

The lesson, then, is that the grading process must inform the student about the strengths and weaknesses of her work, offer constructive criticism, and convey recognition of what the student has achieved. Later chapters discuss how to accomplish those ends without perishing under the workload.

Principle 2: Motivation Affects Behavior, But Behavior Also Affects Motivation

A well-known psychological principle is that while beliefs shape action, the opposite is also true: action shapes belief. In other words, if we can help our students act like highly motivated learners, they may begin to be more highly motivated. The lesson here is that we can use pedagogical strategies, as well as the grading process itself, to encourage and reward the behaviors of a well-motivated student: coming to class well prepared, asking thoughtful questions, seeking engagement with faculty and fellow students, and spending time on assignments. The following chapters demonstrate how to encourage such behaviors.

Principle 3: Motivation Can Be Influenced by the Qualities of a Course

Many authors have written about the qualities that enhance student motivation in a course. Some are listed in Resource 3.1 (see References for full bibliographic information).

The research suggests that a course may increase student motivation for learning when it has:

- Learning goals and assignments that are clear, challenging, relevant, and important to the student
- Criteria, standards, and expectations for student performance that are clear, challenging, and fairly applied to everyone

---

Resource 3.1. Student Motivation, Engagement, and Learning

Bransford, Brown, and Cocking (1999). Explores research on learning and its implications for schooling.

Covington (2007a, 2007b). Emphasizes motivational factors and self-worth perceptions in student motivation.

Fife (1994). Practical three-page list of qualities that enhance student motivation.

Ginsberg and Wlodkowski (2009). Explores how instructors can consistently support student motivation across diverse student groups.

Halpern and Hakel (2002). Collection of essays on how the research on learning can be used for instruction.

Innes (2004). Course design with emphasis on learning and motivation.

Perry, Menec, and Struthers (1996). Short, helpful chapter that summarizes theories of motivation and the research that suggests best teaching practices for student motivation.

Petrosino, Martin, and Svihla (2007). Collection of essays on developing student expertise and community.

Pintrich and Schunk (2002). Research, theories, and practices for student motivation.

Svinicki (2004, 2005). The 2004 work is a book that summarizes theories and makes practical teaching suggestions. Especially see the appendix, which contains a chart summarizing various motivational theories. The 2005 work is a brief summary. In both, Svinicki focuses on the strong role of goals in motivation and the importance of the teacher as a model of good motivation.

Theall (1999). Collection of ideas for enhancing motivation.

Wlodkowski (2008). Focuses especially on motivation in adult students.

Zull (2002). Emphasizes the role of emotion in changing the brain.

- Pedagogical strategies that encourage students to engage actively with the subject, their peers, and their teacher, in a safe and supportive environment where failure is viewed as an opportunity for learning
- Feedback that is frequent, informative, and constructive; recognizes students' achievement; and encourages students to attribute success and failure to their own effort

This chapter takes up the first of these items: learning goals and assignments. The next chapters will take up the other items.

And One More Thing

Perhaps the most important ingredient is the teacher's own attitude or (dare we say it?) the teacher's motivation. A sociologist embodied what we are talking about when he said in an interview about his general education students at an open-admissions two-year college: "You always get the students who are interested right from the start, but the ones I really like, the ones that get my adrenalin going, are the ones who are slouching in the back, thinking, 'What a jerky course this is.' Then you show them what sociologists do, and how much fun it is, and sometimes, wow. They *get* it."

Students' Goals: A Key to Motivation

In the previous chapter, we discussed the learning goals you establish before you meet any of your students. But once you walk into the classroom on the first day, there is another powerful set of goals in your classroom: your students' goals. If you don't know what those goals are and if you don't help students to shape appropriate goals, it's like trying to steer a boat with your rudder while someone else is steering in a different direction with a different rudder: the boat will likely go in circles.

Instructors in every discipline can learn from a group of teachers who have big-time goal issues in their classrooms—teachers of religious studies in public and private colleges and universities. Walvoord (2008) studied 533 introductory religion courses with titles such as "World Religions," "The Nature of Religion," or various approaches to the Christian Bible or sacred texts from other religions. All of the courses were general education. In public institutions, such courses are typically an option for fulfilling a humanities requirement; in religiously affiliated institutions, a religion course is usually required. When asked to state their learning goals for the course, virtually all the faculty members, in all types of institutions, even religiously affiliated ones, chose some aspect of critical thinking as highly important. They wanted a scholarly, evidence-based approach appropriate to the academic environment. They wanted students to consider the cultural and literary contexts of sacred texts, analyze religious practices using scholarly tools, and achieve a certain analytical distance from students' own backgrounds and beliefs. Students' goals, in contrast, were all over the map. Writing anonymously at the beginning of the course, some students said their goal was just to get a good grade. Some wanted to learn about different religions. Some wanted to increase their own spirituality, get closer to God, become a better Christian, or "forgive God for taking my mother." Whew.

Religion courses are not the only ones where student and faculty goals diverge. A recent study asked students and faculty outside of religion courses to prioritize a list of eight learning goals: critical thinking, basic academic skills, career preparation, scientific reasoning, personal development, mastery of discipline content, citizenship and values, and art and cultural appreciation. Faculty and students "differed statistically and practically on six of the eight learning goals" (Myers, 2008, p. 56). The differences were especially prominent around critical thinking, to which faculty gave a much higher priority than students did.

So you need to address goals in your classroom. Here are some helpful strategies that arose from our faculty colleagues in workshops we have led and also from sixty-six religion faculty who were described by their department chairs as "highly effective" teachers (Walvoord, 2008).

Students' In-Class Writing About Goals

At the beginning of the course, you can ask students to write anonymously, in class, on a half-sheet of paper, what their goals are for learning. If you have to read sixty-five responses that begin, "I want to get a good grade," you may never recover. So tell your students, "Do NOT say you want to get a good grade or get the requirement out of the way. I know those things exist. Instead, tell me what you want to learn." Some faculty ask additional questions such as, "What are your greatest concerns about this course," or "Define sociology [or religion or engineering]," or "What is the best English class [or chemistry or history] you've had so far, why was it so good, and what did you learn there?"

Responding to Students' In-Class Writing

The conversation should not stop with the students' writing. You can read their short papers at home and present a summary for discussion in class the next day. Or you can use the writings as the basis for a discussion of goals right then in the class. Several techniques are possible. For example, have students share what they have written in small groups so that everyone gets a sense of what others have written. Or you can redistribute the sheets by asking each student to pass a sheet to someone else. Do this five times, so everyone loses track of whose sheet is whose. Or have students ball up their sheets and toss them to a different part of the room. Then each student has to scramble to pick up a ball, unfold the sheet, and be ready to read it to the full class. Some faculty like the scrambling and laughter that accompany this mode of distribution. Call on at least seven to ten students so that everyone gets a sense of the range of goals in the class.

All of these modes can be used even in very large classes. If you have a smaller class and think that students are comfortable enough to be candid in a full-class discussion, you may want to simply ask students to talk from their own sheets about their goals.

Once your students have articulated their goals and everyone has gotten a sense of the range of goals students bring to the class, then you can discuss how the class will or will not address those goals. Now might be a good moment to hand out the syllabus and go over the course learning goals that you have stated there, relating those goals to what the students have written.

Students Revise Their Goals

You can ask students to rewrite their own goals if needed, based on what they have just learned about what the course actually will do. You can ask the student to keep these goals for their own reference, or collect these writings and again make a summary. Some instructors schedule a five- to ten-minute individual conference with each student at this point to go over course goals and get acquainted. That strategy is time-consuming, but faculty who use it report that it pays off enormously in terms of student motivation and engagement. Some faculty members hold an open discussion hour in a coffee shop or lounge on campus, inviting any students who want to engage in more informal exchange about the course or the issues it will address.

Students Revisit Their Goals

Later in the term, you can ask students to revisit their goals. Ask them to reference the goals they wrote earlier. Which goals are they achieving? What problems have arisen in reaching their goals? You can let the students keep these writings for their own reference, share them in the whole class or in small groups, or collect the sheets and make a summary for class discussion.

From Goals to Plans

Some faculty ask students, after stating their learning goals, to write their plans for achieving these goals. You can leave the instructions open-ended or structure them. You might, for example, ask students to discuss how they will try to meet their learning goals by the actions they intend to take in each of these areas: preparation for class, class attendance, contributions in class, contacts with the professor, outside-class study groups if relevant, work on assignments, preparation for tests, and handling problems that might come up. At midterm, you can ask students to review these plans, indicate how well they are fulfilling them, and establish new goals for the rest of the course. A case study of a faculty member who uses such a planning process with her students, drawing on techniques applicable to any discipline, can be found in Walvoord (2008, pp. 160–179).

Feedback on Teaching Methods

Some faculty include, in their questions about goals, room for students to reflect on the teaching strategies being used in the course, as this faculty member did in the seventh week of the semester: "Review your goals for learning in this class. What actions by the instructor have been most useful to your learning? What actions by your classmates? What actions that you yourself have taken? What changes by the teacher, peers, or you yourself would make the course more helpful to your learning?" Notice that the question is not, "What do you like?" but rather, "What is useful to your learning?"

End-of-term student evaluations often contain an umbrella item such as, "Overall the quality of instruction in this course was excellent/good/ etc." Or "I would recommend this course to someone else: strongly agree, agree, etc." The evaluation form also asks students to evaluate the teacher's qualities, such as being well organized, clear, helpful, or fair, qualities that research has linked to teaching and learning.

However, what we are suggesting here is a conversation with your students that focuses on goals for learning and on the actions by teachers, peers, and self that can help achieve those goals. You can institute such a conversation in your classroom, whether or not you are using a standard evaluation form. Note that many standard evaluation forms allow room at the end for the instructor's additional multiple-choice questions or for instructor questions to which students give open-ended comments. You could use the extra multiple-choice blanks for items such as "I fully achieved my learning goals for this course: strongly agree, agree, etc.," and "The instructor's actions were very helpful to my learning: strongly agree, agree, etc." Use the open-ended space for questions such as those suggested earlier about how actions by the student, peers, or instructor helped or could better have helped the responder in achieving her learning goals.

Our point is that goals matter—both your goals and your students' goals. Goals help to shape motivation and action. Focusing on learning goals can change the atmosphere in your class from dutiful (or not so dutiful) citizens going through the teacher-directed exercises to learners who are focused on achieving their learning goals.

Communicating About Assignments

Goals are one important factor in student motivation. Clear expectations are another. The previous chapter addressed your own planning process as you decided on the key assignments. You checked your assignments for fit and feasibility. You tried your best to construct assignments that were challenging but not impossible for your students' abilities, were potentially relevant and interesting to your students, addressed the course's learning goals, and were feasible in terms of workload.

But all that work will be wasted unless the assignment is clear to students. Students will complete the assignment they think you made, not the assignment you actually made. With sketchy or ambiguous instructions, you risk having students draw on previous learning that may not be relevant or desirable in your situation. Students' diversity in interpreting assignments was documented in an investigation in which Flower and her colleagues (Flower, 1990) gave first-year students a deliberately vague assignment to write a paper. They found that different students reading this vague assignment came up with quite different definitions of what their task was supposed to be. Some thought they should simply summarize the texts they had been assigned to read; some thought they should synthesize ideas around a controlling concept; others imagined something altogether different (see also Kantz, 1989; Walvoord and Sherman, 1990). How can we measure the learning we want to measure when students define the task so differently? With a careful and thorough assignment sheet, you can be more confident that an assignment will measure the knowledge and skills you want it to.

First, write down the instructions for the assignment. Put on that sheet or Web page everything you think students will need to know, because when they are working on the assignment, that sheet is the one they will turn to and the one they will most likely be able to find. Additional assignment instructions you gave orally in class or using the online discussion board are surely out there somewhere, but can your student find them when she needs them?

Anderson, teaching a biology capstone course, developed an assignment that asked students to conduct original biological research and report their findings in a scientific research report. She developed this assignment influenced by two conditions: her course did not have lab time or space allotted to it, and she wanted a valid, authentic writing assignment because many of her students would, at graduation, be hired by laboratories in commercial firms and would test various characteristics of commercial products.

Anderson used the acronym AMPS—Audience, Main point and purpose, Pattern and procedures, and Standards and criteria—to help her remember what needed to be included in an assignment sheet if students were to have the information they needed for successful writing decisions (Exhibit 3.1).

EXHIBIT 3.1

Anderson's Assignment for a Biology Capstone Course

In this assignment you will compare two commercially available products on the basis of at least four criteria to determine which is the "better" product as operationally defined. You will conduct original science research and compose a twelve-hundred- to fifteen-hundred-word original scientific research report.

• • •

Audience: Write for your peers as junior colleagues in the scientific community.

Main point and purpose: For you to learn and demonstrate use of the scientific method for original scientific research. The skills you will develop in this project are those used by many Towson University graduates in their jobs at companies such as Noxell [a local firm that hires Towson graduates].

Pattern and procedures: Please follow a scientific report form. Your final copy should be word-processed and should contain the following components:

- Title (twenty-five words or fewer, with appropriate descriptors)
- Abstract
- Introduction
- Methods and materials section
- Results section
- Conclusions and implications section
- Reference section (only if needed; not required)
- Minimum of three graphics with self-contained labels
- Preference tests (if used) with an n (sample size) of 20+
- Statistics appropriate to your expertise

[Anderson explains how to conduct the pilot, the experiment, and write the report. She includes deadlines for early proposal and draft.]

Standards and criteria: In completing this assignment, demonstrate that you can conduct scientific inquiry. Your written report should demonstrate that you have formulated a hypothesis, designed a good experiment, controlled variables, operationally defined terms, and interpreted data appropriately. In addition, you should demonstrate that you understand the scope and sequence of the scientific report format and the importance of quantification to scientific writing. [This section would also include a rubric or other specific statement of standards and criteria. The rubric for this assignment is in example 1 in Appendix A.]

Activity

If you followed our suggested course planning process, you now have a course skeleton that begins with what you want your students to learn and includes a sequence of major assignments that teach and test those goals. This chapter has discussed how to enhance student motivation and has explored two of the motivational principles: clarify goals with your students and make assignment instructions clear. We invite you now to do the following:

- Plan how you will find out about your students' goals, discuss course goals with them, help them to appropriately reshape their goals if necessary, reference their goals throughout the course, and construct plans to meet their goals.

- Share best goal-shaping strategies with your colleagues. Then revise your own strategies based on what you learned.
- Draft instructions for one of the major tests or assignments on your course skeleton. Use the AMPS acronym to help you.
- Ask a colleague outside your discipline to read your assignment draft. Ask the colleague to put himself or herself in the place of the student and discuss where the assignment seems fuzzy or lacks needed information.
- Work with your colleagues collaboratively to improve your assignment. Share strategies for collaborating with students that have worked for you.

Chapter 4

Establishing Criteria and Standards for Grading

MUCH OF WHAT WE DO and say in our classrooms—face-to-face or online—plays a role in letting the students get the message of what we expect of them. However, this chapter focuses on the written set of criteria and standards that a teacher presents to the students before they begin the assignment or exam and that the teacher, a department, or a general education program may use to assess student learning (departmental and general education assessment are discussed in Chapters Eleven and Twelve). We illustrate three common forms for such documents:

- *Grade descriptions*—what constitutes an A grade, a B, and so on
- *Check sheet*—lists of what the student (or peer responders) should check for and what the teacher will look for
- *Rubric*—a format in which each trait of the student's work (such as evidence, organization, use of graphs) is described using a scale from high to low

The forms may blend or overlap. Each has its advantages and disadvantages.

Descriptions of Grades

One way to clarify criteria and standards for students is to describe the requirements for each grade. An example is Dorothy Solé's description of the work required to earn points in student journals for introductory Spanish at Raymond Walters College of the University of Cincinnati (Exhibit 4.1).

Solé's scale directly addresses students' question, *What do I need to do to get each level of points?* It makes clear that merely producing correct language is not enough for full points; for the highest level, Solé values risk taking and stretching to the edge of one's capability. Such a description can prevent students from coming to Solé to complain that they got only three points even though they made no errors.

> **EXHIBIT 4.1**
>
> ## Description of Point Levels for Journals in Introductory Spanish
>
> 4   The content of the journal is comprehensible. Although there are errors, verb tenses, sentence structure, and vocabulary are correctly used. The author has taken some chances, employing sentence structures or expressing thoughts that are on the edge of what we have been studying. The entries are varied in subject and form.
>
> 3   There is some use of appropriate verb tenses and correct Spanish structure and vocabulary, but incorrect usage or vocabulary interferes with the reader's comprehension.
>
> 2   The reader finds many of the entries difficult to understand or many entries are simplistic or repetitious.
>
> 1   The majority of the entries are incomprehensible.

A grade-based scale like this lumps together various factors that could explain why a student got a certain number of points. If a student got three points instead of four, did the problems lie with verb tenses, Spanish structure, usage, vocabulary, or risk taking? An aggregated grade-based scale like this must rely on the teacher's comments to identify specific successes and problems.

Another example is a grade description that John Breihan, the history faculty member we have been following, distributes to students before they begin their argumentative essays about, for example, whether Louis XIV was a "good" king (Exhibit 4.2).

Breihan constructed the scale by examining actual student papers, and his eleven statements describe the kinds of papers he typically receives. He indicates approximate grade equivalents along the left-hand side of his sheet. When he responds to a student's draft or finished essay, he circles one of the eleven statements that most nearly describes that students' paper. He also makes marginal comments designed to illustrate and expand on the information offered by the statement.

Solé's and Breihan's grading descriptions are assignment specific. It is also possible to construct more broadly stated descriptions that can apply to more than one assignment, provided the assignments have common elements. For example, Facione and Facione (2004) offer a scoring sheet for critical thinking that describes each of four levels of critical thinking. For level 4 (the top score), the student's performance "consistently does

EXHIBIT 4.2

Breihan's Grading Scale for Argumentative Essays in Western Civilization Course

This scale describes the common types of paper but may not exactly describe yours; my mark on the scale denotes roughly where your essay falls. More precise information can be derived from comments and conferences with the instructor.

Grade

F
1. The paper is dishonest.
2. The paper completely ignores the questions set.
3. The paper is incomprehensible due to errors in language or usage.
4. The paper contains very serious factual errors.

D
5. The paper simply lists, narrates, or describes historical data and includes several factual errors.
6. The paper correctly lists, narrates, or describes historical data but makes little or no attempt to frame an argument or thesis.
7. The paper states an argument or thesis, but the argument or thesis does not address the question set.

C
8. The paper states an argument or thesis, but supporting subtheses and factual evidence are:
Missing
Incorrect or anachronistic
Irrelevant
Not sufficiently specific
All or partly obscured by errors in language or usage
9. The paper states an argument on the appropriate topic, clearly supported by relevant subtheses and specific factual evidence, but counterarguments and counterexamples are not mentioned or answered.

B
10. The paper contains an argument, relevant subtheses, and specific evidence; counterarguments and counterexamples are mentioned but not adequately answered:
Factual evidence is incorrect, missing, or not specific.
Linking subtheses are either unclear or missing.
Counterarguments and counterexamples not clearly stated; employs "straw man" argument.

A
11. The paper adequately states and defends an argument and answers all counterarguments and counterexamples suggested by:
Lectures
Reading assignments (specific arguments and authors are mentioned by name)
Common sense

all or most of the following." The rubric then lists a number of factors that various assignments might require, including students' management of evidence, argument, alternative points of view, conclusions, results, and procedures. Next, the authors describe a level 3 performance, including descriptions of the same factors, but at a lower level of competence.

This choice of factors allows the rubric to be applied to a variety of assignments. This broader use may be important as a department or a general education program attempts to score student work from multiple classes (see Chapters Eleven and Twelve).

Checklists

Another way to convey criteria and standards is by constructing a list of items that the teacher will use in grading the paper and that the student or peers can self-check beforehand. Checklists may simply name categories ("I will base the grade on the quality of your argument, your ability to engage your audience . . . ") or describe the highest type of work the teacher expects ("Does your essay contain a clear thesis? Does it support the thesis with evidence from the texts?"). Checklists ask the student or peers to attend to items without requiring a scale or graded description. Exhibit 4.3 is a checklist that Walvoord uses for students who are submitting analyses of editorials for a course in political writing.

EXHIBIT 4.3

Checklist for Analysis of Newspaper Editorials

— I have chosen an editorial that takes a position on a debatable issue of public policy at the local, state, or national level.
— I have attached a copy of the editorial to this paper.
— I have summarized the editorial's main point in a few sentences. The summary is less than 10 percent of the length of my analysis.
— I have NOT focused on whether I agree or disagree with the author's position; instead, I have analyzed the editorial.
— I have analyzed the editorial in the ways we have been learning in class, including:
   — how the writer explains the background and sets the stage
   — what audience the writer appears to be addressing
   — how the writer states what she or he wants the audience to do or believe
   — how the writer tries to convince or change the audience
   — the type and quality of evidence the writer uses
   — the accuracy and integrity of any statistics or data the writer uses
   — unstated assumptions behind the writer's position
   — writer's bias or use of loaded terms
— I have evaluated the strengths and weaknesses of the editorial in terms of its effectiveness for its audience.
— I have included an evaluation of the integrity of the writer in avoiding bias, prejudice, distortion of facts, or unsupported claims.

Walvoord asks the students to put a written check mark next to each item to show they have done it to the best of their ability. Students submit the checklist with their assignment. Walvoord does not accept the assignment unless the checklist is attached. Can a student check something she has not done? Can she believe she has done something that she in fact has not done? Sure. But the checklist brings the criteria and standards strongly into mind, and it reinforces the importance of students' self-assessing their work. Students do report that they have revised their work again after using the checklist. Such a list could also be used for peer checking.

Rubrics

The term *rubric* is widely used to refer to a format in which the traits of the student's work are separately named, and each trait is evaluated according to a scale from high to low. You can find many rubrics online with search terms such as *rubric* and the name of the discipline. (See Stevens and Levi, 2005.)

Rubrics vary in their level of detail. The most minimal rubric simply names a trait with a noun or noun phrase and lists the numbers or letters of the scale. Exhibit 4.4 is an example of a minimal rubric for senior history seminar papers.

A minimal rubric is probably better than nothing. It helps faculty to articulate, and students to understand, the qualities faculty are looking for in a senior seminar paper. However, because the individual numbers are not described, a minimal rubric provides little guidance. If an individual teacher uses such a rubric, many students are still likely to ask why they got a 4 in organization. If multiple faculty use the rubric for assessing the quality of students' senior papers as a whole, the department is likely to discover that a single paper will be rated differently by different faculty

EXHIBIT 4.4

Minimal Rubric for Senior History Seminar Papers

	5	4	3	2	1
Title					
Thesis					
Argumentation					
Historical significance of project					
Organization					

EXHIBIT 4.5

Rubric for a Business Management Case Analysis: Analysis of the Firm's Goals

	5	4	3	2	1
The statement about goals is consistent with the materials in the case.					
The writer presents sufficient and clearly organized evidence for the summary of the firm's goals.					
The writer has chosen the most important or primary goals.					

members. A minimal rubric works as a starting place, but most faculty want to move toward greater specificity.

Somewhat greater detail is provided by a rubric that describes the highest performance and then lists the scoring levels. Exhibit 4.5 shows a rubric used for students' case analyses in a senior-level business course (the complete rubric is example 12 in Appendix A). This rubric provides more guidance than a minimal rubric because it describes what students should aim for. Nevertheless, it still leaves some questions—for example, what is the difference between a 2 and a 3 for "sufficient and clearly organized evidence"?

The most complete type of rubric describes the qualities of student work at each level of the scale. Anderson's rubric for students' original scientific experiment names each trait she wants to measure: for example, methods and materials, experimental design, and interpretation of results. Then she describes each level of performance. (The partial rubric is in Exhibit 4.6. The assignment sheet is in Exhibit 3.1. The full rubric is example 1 in Appendix A.)

Fully articulated rubrics such as Anderson's require thought and hard work to construct, but they represent the most complete description of criteria and standards. They offer the best chance at interrater reliability—that is, the probability that several faculty raters will score a particular student's work in the same way. Full rubrics force the faculty member to clarify in great detail what she is looking for. Thus, full rubrics provide explicit guidance for teaching and for students' peer review and self-checking. (The term *primary trait analysis* is sometimes used to refer to full rubrics.

EXHIBIT 4.6

Rubric with Full Descriptions of Each Scoring Level

Assignment: Design and conduct an original scientific experiment and write a report using scientific format.

Trait: Title

Level 5 — Is appropriate in tone and structure to a science journal; contains all necessary descriptors for placement in a scientific database; contains necessary brand names; identifies functions of experimentation; allows reader to anticipate design.

Level 4 — Is appropriate in tone and structure to science journal; contains most descriptors; identifies function and brand names; suggests aspects of design.

Level 3 — Identifies function and brand name but does not allow reader to anticipate design.

Level 2 — Identifies function or brand name, but not both; lacks design information or is misleading.

Level 1 — Is patterned after another discipline or missing.

Trait: Methods and Materials Section

Level 5 — Contains appropriate, quantifiable, concisely organized information that allows the experiment to be replicated. All information in the report can be related back to this section. Identifies sources of data. Sequences information appropriately. No wordiness.

Level 4 — As above, but contains unnecessary information or wordiness.

Level 3 — Experiment could be replicated from the information given. All information in the report can be related back to this section. However, fails to identify some data sources or has problematic sequencing.

Level 2 — Marginally replicable. Parts of basic design must be inferred. Procedures not quantitatively described. Some information in Results or Conclusions sections cannot be anticipated by reading this section.

Level 1 — Describes experiment so poorly it cannot be replicated.

See Lloyd-Jones, 1977.) The rest of this chapter discusses how to construct and use full rubrics.

How to Construct a Rubric

Exhibit 4.7 summarizes the steps for constructing a scoring rubric. If possible, work from examples of past student performances, grading checklists,

---

EXHIBIT 4.7

Steps for Constructing a Rubric

1. Choose a test or assignment that tests what you want to evaluate. Make clear your objectives for the assignment—what you want students to learn and do.
2. Identify the criteria, or "traits," that will count in the evaluation. These are nouns or noun phrases, such as "thesis," "eye contact with client," "use of color," or "control of variables."
3. For each trait, construct a two- to five-point scale. These are descriptive statements. For example, the trait may be "thesis." The scale for "thesis" will have several levels, each with a description of the performance for that level. For example, a thesis that scores a 5 does X, Y, and Z. A thesis that scores a 4 does X and Y. And so on.
4. Try out the scale with a sample of student work or review with colleagues and revise.

---

descriptions of criteria, comments on assignments or tests—and anything else that has helped you in the past to articulate criteria for student performance. The last part of this chapter addresses common questions that arise in constructing rubrics.

Using the Rubric for Scoring

Once you have a rubric, the next topic is how to score student work with it. For a quick and easy example, use Anderson's "title" trait, set out in Exhibit 4.6, to rate each of following titles, written by Anderson's students before she developed her rubric:

U   A Comparison of Prell and Suave Shampoo
V   The Battle of the Suds: Budweiser and Weiderman Beer
W   Would You Eat Machine-Made or Homemade Cookies?
X   A Comparison of Arizona and Snapple Ice Tea for pH, Residue, Light Absorbency, and Taste
Y   Research to Determine the Better Paper Towel
Z   A Comparison of Amway Laundry Detergent and Tide Laundry Detergent for Characteristics of Stain Removal, Fading, Freshness, and Cloth Strength

All titles contain fewer than twenty-five words, as the assignment sheet stated. When you try your hand at scoring these, use whole scores, not halves. To see how you did, look at Exhibit 4.8, which contains the scores Anderson gave.

EXHIBIT 4.8

Anderson's Scores for Title of a Scientific Report

Title	Score	Reason
U	3	Prell and Suave identify the brand names. The word *comparison* vaguely hints at design and function but without specificity.
V	2	Only the brand names are explicit, and the title is almost misleading.
W	1	Perhaps it is modeled after a Speech l0l title that worked, but it doesn't fit this upper-level biology assignment.
X	5	The design is clearly specified, and the writer includes all the key words that will accurately classify this report in permuterm indexes or electronic databases.
Y	2	As perfunctory as "Book Report on *Silas Marner*."
Z	4	Very good, but wordy.

After trying this scoring, you might recommend changes to the scale. Perhaps, after trying to score title Z, you would recommend that the words "is concise" be added to level 5 and "meets all criteria for 5 but may be wordy" be added to level 4. After trying to score title W, you may suggest that the scale specify whether modeling after another discipline forces a score of 1 regardless of whether the writer identifies brand names or includes other features.

Rubrics tend to be revised as you use them, and they should be. The benefit of constructing a scoring rubric lies as much in the hard thinking it requires, and in the influences it exerts on teaching and learning, as in the final score that emerges.

Why Take the Time to Do a Rubric?

How much time does it take to do a rubric? That depends on how many traits, whether you have previous grading criteria to work from, and whether you're wired to think in this way. Faculty members working from previous grading checklists have produced a draft of a four-trait or even an eight-trait rubric in under an hour. Some faculty may need up to ten hours, spread over time.

Why should you spend the time? When Anderson was constructing her scale, she was teaching a twelve-hour load, working for her doctorate at an institution fifty miles from her home, and was a single mother with two teenagers and a baby. She did it because she wanted to:

- Make grading more consistent and fair.
- Save time in the grading process. Once she was very clear about what she was looking for and had a scoring rubric, she could move quickly through students' work.
- Diagnose her students' strengths and weaknesses very specifically in order to teach more effectively.
- Track changes in her students' performance over several semesters so she could see how changes in her teaching affected student performance (see Anderson and Walvoord, 1990).

Here are some reasons that other faculty in our experience have found it worthwhile to do rubrics:

- To help teaching assistants (TAs) grade papers consistently.
- To reach agreement with colleagues on criteria for common exams, multiple sections, or sequenced courses.
- To introduce greater distinctions into one's grading. For example, a psychologist had written a set of loosely stated criteria, but she found herself giving A's to papers she felt did not deserve an A. Somehow she had not captured in her loose list the full range of criteria she wanted to use to make distinctions. A full rubric, with its greater specificity, helped her tease out for herself what those criteria were and then to distinguish the truly excellent papers from the others.
- As data for departmental and general education assessment (see Chapters Eleven and Twelve).

Using Rubrics for Grading

Rubric scoring and grading are not the same thing, though grades can be derived from rubrics. Anderson had several reasons for using rubrics, not all of them linked to grading. For example, she could track whether her students improved from one semester to the next on a trait such as "experimental design." A paper might get a low grade but score high on that trait. In this case, the teacher's attention would be focused on the design score, not the grade.

Nonetheless, rubrics can lead directly to a grade if the teacher wishes. There are several ways to do this. First, constructing a rubric may act as a clarifying exercise to inform grading in a general way, making the teacher clearer about criteria. In this case, the teacher can continue using a grade description or a checklist and let her own private construction of the rubric inform those two types of documents.

A second strategy is to share the rubric with students but not translate it into a grading instrument. Students use the rubric to guide their work, and the teacher uses the rubric to guide her grading in a general way, but the actual grading is done holistically, without assigning specific points to items in the rubric. The rubric thus works for both students and teacher as a guide, not as a calculator.

A third approach is to translate the rubric scores into a grade. For example, Anderson's rubric awards a separate score on each of the ten traits for a scientific report. To reach a single grade for the entire student's work, the traits have to be weighted. The maximum number of points students can gain on each item will be different, depending on the importance the teacher attaches to the item. The total points for all the items combined can then be translated directly into a grade. For example, in grading students' scientific reports, Anderson used the five "sciencing" sections of the rubric as worth a potential maximum of 20 points each. She multiplied the rubric score by 4, so a rubric score of 5 yielded 20 points; a rubric score of 1 yielded 4 points. She counted the writing skills sections of the rubric as worth a potential of 10 points (she multiplied the actual rubric score by 2). Now she had a total number. She took two-thirds of the total as the project grade.

Some faculty construct a regular rubric, but instead of a scale ranging from 5 to 1 on every item, the rubric assigns points. For example, in rating a speech, the trait of organization might have a scale of 20 points down to 1; eye contact with audience might have a scale of 5 down to 1. After scoring each item, the teacher counts the total number of points. Other faculty designate a percentage for each rubric item. That is, statement of the thesis counts 10 percent of the final grade, quality of evidence 20 percent, and so on.

Frequent Questions in Developing Rubrics

In working with faculty as they construct rubrics, we have found some common questions.

At What Level of Generality Should I State the Traits?

Everyone we have known who composed a rubric has struggled with this issue. Let's take Anderson's biology scale as an example (Exhibit 4.6). Her "materials and methods" trait incorporates other traits: how replicable and quantifiable the data are, whether information is properly sequenced, and so on. Some of those might become separate traits, but there is no absolute rule about this; you can state traits at whatever level meets your needs. As your scale develops, you may not only disaggregate traits but also combine them.

Typically traits continue to be revised over time. For example, when Anderson composed her scale, she chose "nonexperimental information" and "control of variables" as separate traits. Subsequent experience showed her that as her students became more proficient at controlling variables (the more inclusive skill), their ability to recognize nonexperimental information also improved. She might, if it were worthwhile to take the time, now fold the two together.

Which Forms of Language Should I Use?

We examined a type of rubric that describes the highest level of performance and then simply lists, but does not describe, the levels of performance (Exhibit 4.5). In a full rubric, however, the traits are stated as nouns or noun phrases. This keeps the naming of the trait separate from descriptions of the levels of performance. We think this rule should be broken only if you have thought carefully about it and made a conscious decision to change it for good reasons. Here are traits taken from two faculty members' drafts of rubrics. They are not stated as nouns:

Trait from an English course: "Make inferences that are supported by specific information presented in the paper."

Trait from a statistics course: "Obtain an appropriate random sample of members of the population."

If you use verb phrases such as these instead of noun phrases, the traits in essence become a command or a description of actions or of levels of performance. The character of the scale changes, and confusion may result. We suggest changing the traits just mentioned to nouns:

English revision: "Inferences"

Statistics revision: "Random sample [or sampling]"

In a full rubric, the traits are nouns, but the scales within each trait are descriptions of student work. Scoring is done by matching student work to the description within various levels. For example, in a draft scale for a computer spreadsheet project under the trait "spreadsheet accuracy," the teacher took over some of the language from the assignment sheet: "Spreadsheet must provide . . . " It is better for the teacher to leave out "must" because she is describing rather than giving orders. A revision would read, "[A top-level] spreadsheet provides . . . "

Be careful about ascribing things you cannot know. A draft of a scale for essays in French reads, "Student has made an attempt to follow correct French verb forms and syntax." It would be better to just describe the verbs and syntax that will appear in the paper because no professor can know whether the student made an attempt.

How Many Levels Should the Scale Contain?

You may have any number of traits, such as "title" or "materials and methods." Under each trait, the number of levels depends on your purpose. You could have a two-level scale, which is a pass-fail scale. We have illustrated five levels, but three or four or six are certainly possible. How many distinctions do you need to make? How many can you make, given your insight and the language you can find to describe what you want? Teachers often begin with two or three distinctions and then gradually find ways to distinguish additional levels. For rubrics to be used by multiple scorers, as in departmental or general education assessment, one school of thought holds that four levels are better than five because with five levels, a large percentage of scorers may settle on the middle score of 3.

What Are the Relations Among Levels in a Scale?

The most common strategy for describing performance in a rubric is to begin with the optimum performance as the top value and describe the lower levels of performance as less than, or lacking, the qualities of the top performance. Anderson's title rubric was modeled in that way. Another is to fully describe the baseline performance and then identify value-added features for the scale. For example, the lowest level contains valuable information about the topic. The next level does that and also contains a thesis or main idea. The third level does those things and also uses the information in a logical way to support the thesis. And so on.

A second approach is for the levels to represent different qualities. Here is a draft from sociologist Grace Auyang of Raymond Walters College of the University of Cincinnati for an assignment where students must respond to sociological articles:

Trait: Approach to the Problem Described in the Article

5   Student synthesizes the problem.
4   Student analyzes the problem.
3   Student explains the problem.
2   Student describes the problem.
1   Student merely identifies the problem or does not address the problem.

Auyang provides further descriptions of what she means by the terms *identify, synthesize,* and so on, but our point here is to show in skeletal form that the scale is not quantitative; each level represents a different skill.

How Should I Handle Concepts such as "Adequate" and "Appropriate"?

You can use such terms as long as they are specific enough for your needs. If you want to explain your criteria to students, ask yourself (and them) whether they know what "appropriate" means or whether you need to be specific. If you are preparing the rubric scale for use by an outsider, ask whether that person is sufficiently familiar with your discipline to know what you mean.

Let us look at the use of *appropriate, correct,* and similar terms in an example. Here is the draft of Bill Marsh's rubric scale for a statistics assignment at Raymond Walters College of the University of Cincinnati. In this study, students construct a null hypothesis, select a random sample, collect data, and draw conclusions. Here is a portion of his rubric (his full rubric is example 9 in Appendix A). Note his use of words such as *correct* and *appropriate.*

Trait: Methodology

5   Correct statement of problem with accompanying null and alternative hypothesis. Well-defined population with appropriate random sample. Data collection is free of bias or contamination.

In this discipline, statistics, the words *correct, appropriate,* and so on refer to commonly accepted procedures on which professionals generally agree. It would take pages of a statistics textbook to explain what an "appropriate" random sample would be for each of the projects students might choose. Marsh will spend the semester teaching his students the meaning of *correct* and *appropriate* in these settings. Whether and to what extent the teacher would enlarge the rubric to explain these terms would depend on the audience and purpose.

A different slant on words such as *correct* and *appropriate* is presented by a historian, Jim Cebula of Raymond Walters College, who in this rubric draft is trying to describe what he calls the elegance of argument for history essays:

Trait: Elegance of Argument

5   Original and clearly stated thesis; persuasive, well-organized, imaginative use of source material

4   Clearly stated thesis, good use of sources, well organized

3   Facts straight with a reasonable explanation of the subject under consideration

2   Poorly stated thesis, inadequate survey of available sources, poor organization

1   No awareness of argument or complexity

This rubric contains words of quality such as *good, well,* and *poor*. Depending on audience and purpose, the faculty member might want to define these. There are also words that describe characteristics, such as *original, persuasive,* and *imaginative*. Again, depending on audience and purpose, the teacher may want to try to pin down at least some of the characteristics by which she or he decides that a student's work is original or imaginative.

When teachers are trying to construct rubrics, words such as those we have examined here crop up regularly. Decisions about such terms must be based on use. Is this teacher simply trying to articulate her criteria for herself and her students? If so, whatever level of specificity is needed for her own and her students' understanding will be enough. If these rubrics are being used for departmental or institutional assessment, some terms may need further definition, depending on how much agreement there is among the external readers about what *correct* in statistics or *original* in history means.

When dealing with such issues, do not forget the power of examples. Here is part of a primary trait scale draft by Ruth Benander of Raymond Walters College for a first-year composition course. Her assignment calls for students to read several essays on a single topic and then write an essay that synthesizes the readings. Here is her scale for the trait "Synthesis of Ideas":

Trait: Synthesis of Ideas

4   Presents a perspective that synthesizes the main ideas of several readings. This perspective creates an informative way to view the several main ideas of the readings in a way that gives more meaning to the readings as a whole rather than if the main ideas were presented individually.
Example: "Urban and rural violence may differ in frequency but not in the intensity with which they affect the lives of the people involved."

3   Presents a perspective that synthesizes the main ideas of several readings. This perspective may be very general.
Example: Violence is everywhere and affects us all.
At least two different readings are presented, though they may not be clearly related to each other under the umbrella of the synthesizing idea. The two different readings chosen may demonstrate similar rather than different views of the perspective that synthesizes them.

2   The main idea of one reading is presented as the dominant perspective of the paper.
Example: "The article 'Gangster Wake-Up Call' deals with gang violence."
The main points of the reading are used to support the main ideas of the reading. (The paper will look more like a summary of the article than a synthesis of ideas.) No alternative views are presented.

1   There is no clear main idea to the paper.
A reading may be discussed, but the main idea is not related to any other ideas.

Such examples are one way to clarify broad or vague concepts within a rubric. Another way is to focus on describing those physical, observable, or even, if possible, quantifiable aspects that led you to decide what is creative or appropriate to the conventions of the discipline. For example, an education department was struggling with how to reach consensus on evaluating students' senior portfolios. The portfolios contained three kinds of material: lesson plans, observations of individual students or of classrooms, and essays in which the seniors considered theoretical or practical issues in teaching and learning.

One element that all of the professors valued as a trait for the portfolios is what they called *reflective practice*. It means that the student teacher habitually reflects on and theorizes about his or her teaching experience rather than merely following unexamined practices or recording events.

To try to describe reflective practice more concretely, they took some portfolios they all agreed were outstanding in reflective practice and some they agreed were poor in that quality. Then they said, "There must have been some physical, observable characteristics in these written artifacts that led us to conclude that this portfolio shows a reflective practitioner and this one does not. What were they?" Carefully examining the students' texts, the faculty saw that the students who scored high on reflective practice shared these characteristics:

- They routinely stated why they themselves, or students with whom they were working, exhibited certain behaviors.
- They explained reasons and outcomes in terms of theoretical statements or hypotheses about teaching, usually expressed in the present tense.
- They routinely recorded questions and dilemmas.
- They recorded and described patterns in their own or in others' behavior.
- They reported having done reflective thinking. ("All that week, I thought about why Randy's behavior had surprised me so much.")
- They exhibited a musing, questioning tone.
- They noted missing information needed to draw conclusions from data or experience.
- They hypothesized as to causes, connections, or outcomes.

Detailed descriptions of the physical characteristics of the student's work can help you be specific about qualities that are indicators for abstract terms such as *reflective practice*.

What Kinds of Student Performances Can Be Scored by Rubrics?

Almost any type of student performance—oral, clinical, artistic—involving higher-order thinking, creativity, or integration of skills can be examined effectively with a rubric. For example, Judith Bloomer of the Department of Occupational Therapy and Evelyn Lutz of the Department of Nursing at Xavier College in Cincinnati assessed these traits in evaluating their students in Work-Related Interactions with Others: Collaboration, Participation, Attitude, Independence, Communication, and Responsiveness. (See the full scale in example 2 in Appendix A.)

Team performances can also be examined effectively with rubrics. Lawrence Fredendall, at Clemson University, developed a twenty-four-trait rubric to help members of local businesses evaluate teams of student interns. The rubric includes criteria for group behaviors such as team punctuality, courtesy, appearance, communications, and enthusiasm. (See example 7 in Appendix A.)

What If the Scale Leads Me to a Score That Does Not Feel Right?

Suppose that you find yourself giving high scores to student work you find competent but somehow lacking in the originality, creativity, or risk taking you want for A work. Often the problem is that you have not included in the scale all the traits you are using. Look again at the student work that makes you uneasy. Compare it with samples that score above and below it. Ask yourself these questions: *What is missing in my scale? What is most important?* Try to capture that in the scale. Use the best language you can. It is fine to say, as one faculty member did, "This paper shows a curious mind at work." If you don't want to give an A to any work that does not have originality, then weight your scale accordingly.

How About Involving Students in Constructing Standards and Criteria?

We know faculty who like to involve their students in establishing criteria for student work. For example, a physicist whose students give oral reports on a physics project asks the students to brainstorm a list of the qualities that make an effective oral presentation from their point of view. Students typically offer items such as "speaker talks clearly and can be heard by everyone," "has good eye contact," "uses charts and graphs that are clear and correctly labeled," "explains the experiment in a well-organized way," and so on.

The instructor can then incorporate these when building the rubric scale. For example, some traits suggested by these sample student comments might include "delivery," "charts and graphs," and "organization." In composing the scale under "delivery," the students' comments suggest that a high score might include speaking clearly, being heard by everyone, and maintaining consistent eye contact with all areas of the room.

Can Rubrics Be Used with TAs as Graders?

Yes, very effectively. Gisela Escoe, Philip Way, and their graduate assistant, Jack Julian, teaching economics at the University of Cincinnati, used rubrics to help TA graders in large introductory economics classes. They held an introductory session in which the TAs went over the rubrics and scored sample papers. During the semester, the TAs graded all the papers. They were encouraged to bring to the faculty any papers about which they are unsure.

When TAs are new or inexperienced or when TA populations turn over frequently, a common practice is for a single faculty member or small number of key personnel to construct the rubric. Faculty then hold a TA training session on using rubrics. However, in a team-taught course, multisection courses, or a situation where TAs participate as colleagues in establishing criteria and standards, the goal is to establish a collaborative way of arriving at rubrics. In order to maximize participation while not wasting time, we suggest following a procedure.

In step 1, your group establishes course goals, key assignments, and, the criteria and standards by which the most important assignments and exams will be evaluated and by which students will receive ongoing feedback on their progress.

Working from the basic outlines established in those discussions, the group next meets to establish the rubric traits and scale to be used for each major assignment and test.

If you have sample papers, you might begin by talking about which grade you would give them and why. This discussion will reveal traits. For example, suppose someone says, "I'd give this paper a B because it has a clear problem statement and it analyzes the problem well, but the solutions do not take into account all of the important factors." At least three traits are embedded in that statement: (1) the problem statement, (2) analysis of the problem, and (3) solution. Someone should be listing these traits on a board or newsprint pad. Do not try to assign weights to the traits at this point (though you might want to jot down information that emerges about the relative importance of traits for later use). If the group disagrees, try to pinpoint the traits that are at issue and to reach consensus.

You will have traits stated at various levels of generality. For example, in this situation, the "solution" might be a trait embodying several considerations including the factors, but "factors considered in the solution" might also be a separate trait with its own scale. At this stage, jot down people's insights about which traits are overlapping or subordinate, but do not try to make decisions about aggregating or separating traits in the large group because it will take too long and lead to confusion.

As the discussion proceeds, it may emerge that the assignment or even the entire course plan needs to be changed or explained more clearly. If you have time, let that happen. One of the most useful outcomes of discussions about standards and criteria is the opportunity to rethink course goals, course structure, and the nature of tests and assignments.

In step 3, the group should decide how many levels the rubric needs at the start. We suggest three to six levels.

Now, in step 4, we suggest that one or two people be tasked with drafting a rubric using this brainstormed list. When they prepare and distribute the draft, the entire group offers suggestions for changes in it, which the writers then incorporate. Repeat this cycle until everyone is comfortable with the scale (or until everyone is too tired to object). If you cannot reach consensus on all the traits, consider the possibility that common traits on which people do agree may be used by everyone and give individuals the freedom to construct their own scales around other traits.

As soon as you have sample student papers, step 5 is to let the group score papers using the scale. Have individuals score papers independently at first, meet to compare scores, discuss discrepancies, and change the scales as needed.

In the final, and ongoing, step, you will hold periodic discussions in which sample papers are scored, discrepancies discussed, and the scale and assignments changed as needed.

This procedure assumes everyone's participation. If there are too many people for this approach, a committee may do this work. A useful description of how composition faculty from six different institutions together constructed a rubric for student work can be found in Pagano and others (2008).

Can Rubrics Be Used for Portfolios?

Yes. We define a portfolio as a collection of work by the same student completed over time. Your department or assessment committee can follow the same basic process we have just outlined. The reason for using a portfolio rather than a single piece of work from each student is to evaluate attributes that can be assessed only by multiple works—for example, the consistency of a particular student performance in multiple situations, a broad range of student skills, the flexibility with which the student applies principles to varying situations, or the growth of the student's skills or knowledge over time. (Chapter Eleven provides a discussion of using portfolios as part of departmental or general education assessment.)

Can Rubrics Be Used for Multiple-Choice and Short-Answer Tests?

Yes. Rubrics are particularly useful for these tests because they force the teacher to state explicitly what skills and knowledge she expects and to provide students with direct feedback about how well they are achieving course goals. A process that has been called test blueprinting shows how to connect course goals, test questions, and rubrics (Middle States Commission on Higher Education, 2007; Suskie, 2009). For example, Table 2.1 shows how a teacher might generate test questions linked to rubric traits such as "reading graphic information" or "making connections between graphic information and scientific issues." Table 4.1 shows how you might go further, filling out the full rubric, including descriptions of the levels of performance, and then matching students' test answers to levels of the rubric. Table 4.1 contains one trait; the full rubric is in example 14 in Appendix A.

When you draw test items from a test bank, perhaps provided by the textbook publisher, you may need to consider not only what type of reasoning the test item calls for, but whether it asks merely for recall of textbook material or requires students to reason on their own. For example, Patricia Schlecht, of the Nursing Department at Raymond Walters College of the University of Cincinnati, categorized the multiple-choice questions

TABLE 4.1

Students' Test Answers Mapped to Rubric Levels

Trait: Reading Graphic Information	Percentage of Students Answering at This Level on Relevant Sets of Multiple-Choice, True-False, and Short-Answer Questions
Level 4. Accurately describes the function of the graph; identifies points and ranges	33 percent
Level 3. Partially identifies the functions of the graphic; identifies points and ranges	55
Level 2. Identifies points OR ranges only	12
Level 1. Lacks competency	0

that she gave students on tests by deciding whether the question required a high level of thinking, using Bloom's *Taxonomy of Educational Objectives* (1956), and whether the textbook or her lectures had given students the answer directly. She pointed out that although a multiple-choice question may appear, by Bloom's taxonomy, to require critical thinking, it may in fact only ask the student to repeat material given in the textbook or in lecture. She developed these categories:

- *Higher critical thinking*. Questions would fall in the analysis, synthesis, or evaluation levels of Bloom's taxonomy. Course materials give needed background to answer the questions. There is no directly visible connection between the course material and the test question.
- *Lower critical thinking*. Questions would fall in the application level of Bloom's taxonomy. Course materials give needed background to answer the questions. There is a directly visible connection between course material and the test questions.
- *Knowledge and comprehension levels of Bloom's taxonomy*. Material is directly from the course presentation, with some changes in wording and phraseology.

Using such well-defined levels to categorize critical thinking, faculty can group multiple-choice items into critical thinking sets. Exhibit 4.9 is a hypothetical rubric.

More important, this classroom assessment strategy has the potential to collect aggregated student data that can inform and improve the whole nursing program (see Chapters Eleven and Twelve for more examples of how to use rubrics and test blueprinting to collect valuable data from multiple-choice and short-answer questions).

EXHIBIT 4.9

Rubric for Critical Thinking Performance on a Twenty-Five-Item Multiple-Choice Test

4	Answers correctly all or all but one of questions 4, 7, 12, 13, 20, 21, and 24 (designated higher critical thinking questions on a given test)
3	Answers correctly 4 or 5 of the higher critical thinking questions. Total test score is 70 percent or above.
2	Limited evidence of critical thinking (only 1 to 3 questions correct within the critical thinking set); however, score for total test score is 70 percent or above.
1	Lacks evidence of critical thinking and/or score for total test is 68 percent or below.

Selecting a format—a grade description, a checklist, or a rubric—to express your standards and criteria is an important cornerstone for your teaching. When well constructed, such instruments show you what to teach and help students learn the standards for good work in their field.

Criteria Outside the Rubric

Rubric scores can be used to establish only a portion of the grade. Anderson reserved a small portion of the grade to evaluate whether the student had followed the word limit, met deadlines for rough draft submission, and conducted the required peer editing conference. Dorothy Solé's scale (Exhibit 4.1) determines only a portion of the grade given to student journals in a beginning Spanish class. The other portion is based on length and number of entries.

Gateway Criteria

The instructor can establish what we call gateway criteria in which students are asked to comply with certain requirements before the paper is even subjected to rubric scoring. In other words, students must meet certain requirements even to get into the ballpark where the rubric score will be used. Work that does not meet the gateway criteria is returned to the student with a failing grade or instructions to revise and resubmit. So if a student turns in a final scientific report that does not meet the teacher's announced standard for word processing, labeling of graphs, grammar, punctuation, or other aspects, the teacher responds by handing it back with either an F grade or instructions to revise and resubmit for grading. Such a report does not make it into the ballpark, so it does not even get to the point of applying a rubric.

Criteria for Grammar and Punctuation

Issues of grammar and punctuation can be integrated into the grading scheme in several ways.

Grammar and Punctuation as Gateway Criteria

One strategy is to establish a certain level of grammar and punctuation as a gateway requirement. The philosophy behind this approach is that if a student later submits a proposal to her boss or a letter to a client that does not adhere to standard English grammar and punctuation, the boss or client may simply dismiss the writing. The truth is that societies do use language as a sorting device, making judgments about writers based on their command of the standard language.

We suggest that you not only explain to students your policy about use of standard English, but that you also establish a research-based understanding of language in your classroom. Exhibit 4.10 is a sheet that

---

EXHIBIT 4.10

Handout Used to Explain Walvoord's Gateway Criteria

Policy for Use of Edited Standard Written English

Suppose a group of people were living on an island, all using the same language, until one day the island broke in two, separated by impassable water. In one hundred years, with no contact, would the people on both halves still use the same language forms? No. Human language is always changing. Language on each half of the island would evolve with different forms and rules. Neither would be better in any absolute sense—just different. Similarly, in the United States, language variations have developed among people separated by culture, socioeconomic status, ethnic background, or geography.

Nevertheless, the language of the ruling class commonly comes to be regarded as standard. In the United States, the "standard" is the language of the white middle and upper classes. Forms of English developed by people of color and by people who have been poor or geographically isolated (as in Appalachia) are sometimes said to be "bad" or "incorrect" English, but such forms are only different, not bad. Each form of English has its own rules. People who say "she working" are not speaking "bad" English; they are using a different set of rules for forming the present tense.

One of the tasks of a good education is to make students aware of these facts about language. Another task of education, however, is to prepare students to function effectively in the world where readers generally expect writers to use edited standard written English (ESWE). Thus, in this class, you must use ESWE. Here is the standard I will apply.

On finished, final, formal papers (not on drafts, in-class writings, or writing that I specifically label as informal), you must have no more than an average of two departures from ESWE per page, in any combination of the following areas:

- End-of-sentence punctuation (avoid run-on sentences, comma splices, fragments, or misuse of semi-colon). Occasionally you may use a fragment or comma splice for a special effect. Label it in the margin.

- Verb forms (use ESWE rules for adding -ed and -s, for using helping verbs, and so on).

- Verb tense (avoid confusing shifts in verb tenses).

- Agreement of subject and verb.

- Pronoun form (use ESWE rules to choose between I and me, she and her, who and whom, and so on).

- Agreement of pronoun with antecedent (the antecedent is the word the pronoun refers to).

- Use of apostrophe s and the -es.

- Use of quotation marks for all quoted words.

- Spelling (a typo counts as a misspelling).

- Proper sentence sense (no words omitted, scrambled, or incomprehensible).

Walvoord used to explain to her students a gateway policy of grammar, punctuation, and spelling and a research-based concept of how standard and nonstandard languages function in a society. Note that Walvoord did not apply this policy to drafts, in-class writing, or informal writing, only to finished, formal work.

Walvoord reminded her students that the writing center would help them with these criteria, and she gave students a list of the writing center's Web page, hours, and location. She reminded her students about her gateway policy frequently, both orally and in writing, and let her department head know that she was implementing this policy. She offered students an opportunity to bring her, or send electronically, a typed draft of the paper at least twenty-four hours before the paper was due. She did not edit these papers by finding all the departures from edited standard written English for the students (finding their departures from standard English was their job), but she made a judgment about whether the paper met the gateway criteria. If it did not, she offered suggestions about writing center help and about the most common problems she saw, so students could look up those items in a composition handbook or online. In other words, she tried to integrate the real-world criteria that students must meet with the support and help appropriate to a learning environment.

The result of this gateway policy is that virtually all the final papers Walvoord receives make it through the gate. Walvoord has used the policy with first-year students in a selective private college and at a state research university.

You may want to set the criteria at different levels for different groups of students. You will also want to consider the effect of this policy on students who speak English as a nonnative language. You can hold nonnative speakers to the same standard, asking them to get help at the writing center or the English language center, or you can establish separate levels for them that stretch them beyond where they are but do not present them with an impossible task. The idea is not to hand out a lot of F grades but to teach students that to function in the outside world, they will have to master ESWE or their work will be dismissed before the reader has even dealt with the writer's ideas.

Integrating Grammar and Punctuation into the Grading Scale

Instead of a gateway policy, some faculty integrate grammar and punctuation into the grading scheme. For example, Breihan, the historian whose grade-based sheet appears in Exhibit 4.2, integrates grammar and punctuation into the sheet. One factor in the description of a failing essay is to be "incomprehensible due to errors in language or usage." One factor in a C paper is that meaning is "all or partly obscured by errors in language or usage." The advantage of this mode is that, as in real life, the management of grammar and punctuation is closely intertwined with other aspects of the student's writing, and it combines with those aspects to make an impression on its reader.

Other faculty members integrate grammar and punctuation into their check sheets. For example, a check sheet may ask students to check off that, before submitting the paper, they have used spellcheck, have reread the paper at least twice for grammar and punctuation, and have asked one other person to read the paper to check for grammar and punctuation.

Many faculty construct a separate item in the rubric for grammar and punctuation—for example:

5   No departures from ESWE.
4   Occasional departures from ESWE, but not in the critical areas listed in Exhibit 4.10.
3   No more than two departures from ESWE in the critical areas.
2   More than two departures in critical areas, but writing is still readable.
1   Departures from ESWE are very frequent, interfering with smooth reading.

A developmental approach is to have each student keep a written record of his or her most common problems with grammar and punctuation. For example, Amy, based on her earlier papers or her own self-knowledge, might list use of the apostrophe as one of her common problems. The check sheet then asks students to assert that they have checked the paper especially carefully for their own issues. You can ask each student to establish a "never again" list. With each paper, the student adds to the list one area of ESWE that she vows "never again." This sheet is handed in with the final paper, and the writer is held responsible for the "never again" list, but not for other aspects of ESWE. This approach can be very helpful for nonnative speakers of English. An instructor can work with a writing center or English language instructional program to define the course of a student's progress and the ESWE issues for which that student will be held responsible.

Activity

If you have been following our course planning procedures, you now have a course skeleton, a draft of at least one assignment, and a big-picture view of linking criteria and grading.

Now we invite you to do the following:

- Construct a list of traits for one of your assignments or tests. You may simply choose two or three traits that seem most important, or you may try to construct a list of all the traits you want to use for grading. Remember that some aspects, such as editing for edited standard written English or avoiding numerical errors, may be handled as gateway characteristics separate from the rubric scale.

- Construct a grade-based guide, a check sheet, or a rubric for your traits. For the rubric, you may use a two-, three-, four-, or five-level scale, depending on how many levels you can or want to construct.

- Score or grade one or several assignments or tests with your instrument, and revise it as needed.

- Revise your draft of assignment instructions to students to reflect clearly your criteria and standards. Remember that you may include a grading description, a check sheet, a rubric, or other language that makes criteria and standards clear.

Chapter 5

Linking Teaching, Learning, and Grading

BONES BUT NO FLESH is what you have now: a set of goals, a course skeleton containing major assignments, and some ideas for fostering healthy motivation and establishing criteria and standards for student work. This is not yet a full plan for the daily instructional activities that will help students reach the learning goals.

The most important principle is this: grading should be integrated with everything else that happens in the classroom. The grade is not an isolated artifact slapped on at the end; it is part of a system that includes shaping goals and assignments, communicating with students, helping them learn what they need, responding to them, and evaluating the quality of their work. *Integrating* means teaching what you are grading and grading what you are teaching. This chapter contains examples of both principles. It leads to the next chapter, which discusses how to manage in-class and out-of-class time or, if you are teaching online, how to manage the various synchronous and asynchronous modes.

These two chapters only hint at the wealth of ideas that can help an instructor construct learning activities: when to use lecture, when to use discussion, how to structure online discussion boards, how to integrate small-group work, how to make sure students are reading and preparing for class, how to keep them practicing necessary skills and learning necessary content without yourself perishing under the paper load, and how to put it all together into a coherent whole.

Resource 5.1 lists some of our favorite books on course design—books that follow or are consonant with our assignment-centered approach and are full of ideas for active student learning. For further resources on large classes, scientific and technical disciplines, and online or hybrid courses, see Resource 6.1.

Teach What You Are Grading

We faculty sometimes pride ourselves on not teaching to the test. But if the test or assignment is right—if it really tests the central learning goals of

---

Resource 5.1. Books on Teaching That Emphasize Course Design

Bean (1996). Rich with specific, creative ideas to engage students in learning, focused especially on critical thinking and writing.

Davis (2009). Second edition of a popular and useful book on teaching.

Fink (2003). Thorough, step-by-step treatment of course design for "significant learning."

Garrison and Vaughan (2008). How to design a course that blends classroom and online learning.

Kalman (2007). Practical suggestions about how science and engineering classes can encourage students' preclass preparation and critical thinking skills. Emphasis on use of reflective writing to increase conceptual understanding. Includes sections on student groups.

Nilson (2003). A fine book on teaching with many practical suggestions.

Novak, Patterson, Gavrin, and Christian (1999). Explains "just-in-time teaching," in which students' preclass preparatory writings serve as the basis for in-class lecture, exercise, and discussion. Aimed at science and engineering but applicable to any discipline.

Weimer, M. (2002). Discusses five reasonable and sustainable changes faculty can implement to make their courses more learner centered.

Wulff, D. H. (2005). Based on research about student learning and effective teaching; illustrates how to align key components: student learning, content, students, professors, and context.

---

the course—then we should teach to it. In fact, it seems criminal not to. Why would we test and grade students on skills and subject matter we have not taught them? At the same time, we do not want to teach to the test too narrowly. Faculty developer and author Deborah De Zure put it nicely in a conversation with Walvoord: "Teach not to the test but to the criteria by which you will evaluate the test."

The sociologist we met in a previous chapter changed his class assignment from a term paper to a review of the literature. His students often produced merely an annotated bibliography in prose form: "this author said this," "this author found this," and so on in the "beads on a string" plan for organization. Instead, the sociologist wanted students to construct an interpretive frame for the review, analyzing and evaluating how the research and theory had progressed and what its shape was. He began to plan how he would teach his students to provide such a frame. When asking himself which frames are common, he came up with three:

- "Stand on my shoulders": The writer sees the field as a steady progression in which each person's work builds on previous work.

- "Major shift": The writer sees the field as having gone in one direction until a major new discovery, theory, or paradigm shift sent the field in a different direction.
- "Warring camps": The writer sees the field as characterized by warring camps adhering to diverse theories or modes of research.

Next, the sociologist asked himself, *How does the writer of a review decide which frame is most appropriate?* Examining his own writing processes, he realized he looked in the literature for certain indicators: Did the researcher view his or her work as contradictory to others? As an extension? Did the researcher refer to shifts in the field? The sociologist also realized that he used certain techniques, such as listing the findings of each researcher in sequence and examining the list to see which pattern or combination of patterns applied.

Now that he had the frames, along with clues about how he chose an appropriate frame, the sociologist could teach these frames to his students. He could have them:

- Read reviews of the literature and, individually or in groups, identify the frames the review author had constructed
- Read research articles and underline information that would suggest an interpretive frame, then compare each other's underlined passages
- Read a preselected group of abstracts of articles and, in class or in small groups, identify which frame the group of articles suggested
- Draft their reviews, have peers identify and evaluate the interpretive frame the student writer had used, and then let the writer revise to make the frame more clear and appropriate

After using some combination of such strategies, the sociologist would collect and grade his students' reviews of the literature, and his grades would demonstrate whether students had learned what he taught: a process and a set of skills for analyzing the literature in the field and writing a review of the literature. At the same time, he would have involved the students actively in learning, guided them, used the power of peer collaboration, and provided a structure that was likely to motivate students toward learning.

Here is how an art historian, Barbara Filo, was better able to teach what she was grading after a workshop Walvoord led at her college.

How I Taught What I Was Grading

Barbara Filo, Whitworth College

My syllabi for Art History I and II included an assignment requiring students to visit a gallery, observe the work displayed there, and write a two-page review of the art work. Accompanying each syllabus was a two-page list of vocabulary terms defining the visual elements and the principles of design. Those terms were further explained with a slide lecture. The actual assignment from an earlier syllabus asked students to "attend two on-campus art exhibits. Write a review of each, using visual art vocabulary, describing the exhibit and your reaction to it."

The purpose of this assignment was primarily to get students actually to visit an art gallery or museum twice during the term. For many students these visits were their first experience inside an art gallery or museum. Second, the review paper assignment was an attempt to inspire students' thoughtful reaction to the art works, in a written form.

But the entire experience, both the art gallery visit and the review papers, was a mixed bag. Some students had a positive experience both in their visual reaction and written response, but for most students the experience had little effect on their understanding or appreciation of art. Even with the vocabulary handout, unless I was present to guide the exhibit tour, the typical students seemed to lack the skill to really "see" what was before their eyes.

After participating in a faculty workshop, I was inspired to improve this particular assignment because I felt it was perhaps the most important assignment in Art History I and II. After all, long after students leave my class they continue to have the opportunity to view art. I wanted them to know how to intelligently interpret and critique what they see. I knew this type of assignment could make a long-lasting impression on the ways they view and think

about art if it could become a valid experience now, in the college classroom.

I searched and integrated many sources looking for ideas on how to view art and write critiques. *A Short Guide to Writing about Art* by Barnet (1989) [9th ed., 2008], *Writing About Art* by Sayre (1989) [6th ed., 2009], and *Living with Art* by Gilbert and McCarter (1988) [3rd ed., 1992] proved most helpful. Now, along with my review assignment, I guide the students' learning process by giving them this synthesized sheet on how to view works of art.

Handout to Students for Art Assignment

The goal of an artist is to create an interaction between the work and the observer. Fine art is created for the educated observer; therefore it is most important for the observer to become a critical thinker.

Here is a list you can use as a guide for the critical observation of works of art. It may also be used as a guide to writing reviews of art works.

- *Familiarity:* Is the work connected to other works you have seen, or is it something totally unlike anything you've ever seen?
- *Artist:* Who is the artist? Have you seen other works by the artist? What do you know about the artist? (Read artist's biography if possible.) Does knowledge of the artist's personal history influence your impressions of the work?
- *Style:* Does the work fall into a particular art history style? Can you recognize characteristics, whether in content or form, that show an influence of or a reaction to a particular style?
- *Historical context:* Note the original date and location of the art piece and the events—historical, political, social, scientific, geographical, cultural, and so on—taking place at the time of the creation.

- *Form:* Describe the appearance of the work and the materials and medium used.
- *Visual elements:* Look for the most emphasized elements: line, shape, color, value, light, space, texture, time and motion, and so on.
- *Composition:* Notice the principles of design used in the arrangement of the visual elements: unity, variety, balance, emphasis, proportion, rhythm.
- *Content:* Describe the iconography, subject matter, and symbolism. Is the subject matter recognizable?
- *Personal response:* How does the work make you feel—happy, sad, angry, excited, frightened, detached, inspired, depressed, uplifted, repulsed, disgusted, shocked? Are there any personal memories or associations evoked? What do you think the artist felt about the work during its creation? Do you feel any relationship with the artist?
- *Experience:* Would you buy this work so you could view it every day? Have you gained an appreciation for the work, whether or not you like it? [adapted from Gilbert and McCarter, 1988, and Gilbert, 1992].

The results of this guide, which I go over in class, have been most satisfying. Students now have in hand a personal guide for viewing art. Without exception, on the reviews, students write more than they did before. They are far more descriptive. The second review is typically better than the first. Many students are excited, responding that they never knew so much could be derived from a single piece of art.

At the start of each course, I always remind students that my intent is not to insist or expect they will "like" the art they see but that my hope is for them to become educated, intelligent viewers of art who can come to an appreciation for the art they see. This assignment seems to help me and the students reach that goal [adapted from Hunt, 1992].

Grade What You Are Teaching

Long before college classrooms had ceiling-mounted liquid crystal displays, wireless Internet, image projectors, and teleconferencing, faculty were broadcasting. We were (and still are) sending out intellectual "GPS" homing signals to students about what is really important in our disciplines. Speech 101 instructors tell students that listening skills are as important as speaking skills, chemists let first-year students know that lab success is the real measure of a scientist, and business professors advise seniors that they will be expected to work collaboratively within a corporate structure. Since many college and university students approach learning, at least initially, from a "will this be on the test?" perspective, it is imperative that we test and grade what we hold to be important. Let's look at two "grade what you are teaching" strategies in action.

The first is an instructional technology (IT) department that has three specific learning outcomes regarding e-mails in a 100-level course, Computers for Business Applications: the student should be able to (1) compose a literate, content-explicit e-mail to a business superior; (2) file, cc, send, and retrieve the e-mail; and (3) exhibit a willingness to value e-mail communication by exhibiting prompt and courteous response. Faculty developed and used a rubric to grade the content of the e-mails (see Trajkovski, 2006). However, the rubric addressed only the first of the three learning outcomes. Students were required to save all their work in a course file. One instructor hit on a way to grade what he really hoped that he was teaching: send out an e-mail asking the students to resubmit their messages to the instructor by e-mail. In this way, faculty could grade the task fairly by also scoring the other two expectations: managing storage and retrieval, as well as responding in a prompt and courteous manner.

The second example is a microbiology course. In this course, microbiology instructors teach students to "disinfect your work area thoroughly before beginning the lab." In the first weeks, students are intimidated by bacteria and follow the protocol zealously. As the semester progresses, however, they become more lax. Moreover, checking the disinfection procedures of eighteen to twenty-four students in the first five minutes of lab is impossible. One instructor found a strategy that worked. Since wax marking pencil marks are very soluble in Lysol (the disinfectant used), she placed a small, black marking-pencil X on each student's lab station countertop before class. As students began working on the lab, she walked around subtly looking for Xs. Finding some, she announced to all students to check for the Xs and to start the lab over if they had not disinfected the area. Then she explained that this lab "test" would be repeated at other times during the semester and any student failing to disinfect the lab area as evidenced by the X would receive an F for the lab. Success! (For this and other classroom assessment suggestions, see V. Anderson, 2001.)

Teaching and Grading Class Discussion

Discussion is perhaps the most valued and least graded skill in college classrooms. Faculty say they value class discussion; they wish students would discuss more, and more skillfully, but they do not know how to grade and respond to discussion. The problem exists in face-to-face classes: an instructor who cannot get good discussion going is tempted to fall back on lecture. The problem takes a different form in online courses, where lectures and course material are delivered electronically: the discussion board is the mainstay of student discussion, but if the instructor requires only a certain number of posts, the quality of discussion is likely to be disappointing.

If we instead use the motto, "Grade what you teach, and teach what you grade," we can align our teaching and grading more fully with the goal of enhancing students' discussion skills and helping them learn through discussion.

Example: Grading Class Participation

Grading class participation effectively for learning requires a system that:

- Does not suffocate the freedom of discussion or make students overly nervous about being judged for every word out of their mouths
- Does not take too much time
- Establishes clear criteria for participation, so everyone knows what is expected
- Systematically documents students' participation rather than relying on an instructor's impression

Attempting to find a system that accomplishes these ends, Walvoord asks her students to self-report at the end of each discussion class using the set of criteria in Exhibit 5.1.

As soon as possible after the class is over, while she still remembers the class interaction, Walvoord records whether the students did or did not meet the criteria. She has found that self-reports are almost always accurate, and she rarely makes changes to a student's record. If the class is large, small-group work can give every student a fair chance to contribute at least once within the small group. Thus, this self-report technique can be used with both large and small classes.

The final course grade can incorporate these reports simply by counting the number of discussion class sessions for which the student met all the criteria. For example, if the student meets the participation criteria for 90 percent or more of the total number of classes devoted to discussion, then that part of the grade is an A. If the student meets the criteria for 80 percent of the class sessions, that part of the grade is B, and so on. Or you could use points: a student who meets the criteria for participation in discussion for each class period earns five points.

Example: Grading Small-Group Discussions

In another class, Walvoord became even more deliberate and explicit about teaching and grading discussion. In a general education literature class for forty-five students, she decided to focus deliberately on the university's general education goal of oral communication. First, she constructed a graded assignment that would focus on students' ability to participate in

EXHIBIT 5.1

Student Self-Report on Class Discussion

Name _____

Date _____

To receive credit for this class session, you must honestly be able to check all of the following:

_____ 1. I made every effort to come to class on time. (Lateness that was not your fault is excused: for example, the previous professor held the class overtime. Oversleeping is NOT excused.)

_____ 2. I had read all the assigned works carefully before I came.

_____ 3. I brought to class my written notes on the works we read.

_____ 4. I had prepared for class by being well rested, well nourished, alert, and mentally ready.

_____ 5. I contributed at least once to class discussion today.

_____ 6. I did not too heavily dominate the class, but gave others a chance to contribute.

_____ 7. I listened actively to others at all times, and I showed by my face and body posture that I was listening.

_____ 8. My goal was to contribute effectively to the high quality of the groups discussion and learning rather than just to demonstrate my own excellence. As in team sports, I played for the well-being of the team.

_____ 9. My contributions tended to do the following:

- Start the group on a rich, productive track by posing a question or position that is not too obvious, but richly debatable, dealing with a significant question or aspect of the work.
- Respond to others' contributions by:
  - Asking for clarification or evidence
  - Helping to support the point by contributing evidence and examples
  - Linking the point creatively to other readings or issues
  - Pointing out unspoken assumptions behind the other person's point
  - Raising a problem or complication for the other person's point
  - Synthesizing or pulling together the discussion so far in order to help the group see where they are
  - Stating a different point of view and backing it up
  - Talking about how this literature has helped to develop my own appreciation of self, society, and nature, and my understanding of the diversity of human experience

_____10. When I had a genuine question that seemed stupid or simple, I asked it anyway.

The following questions do not count for credit, but they help me to assess how well the discussions are going and how we can improve:

_____11. I thought the discussion today went:

_____ Extremely well   _____ Very well   _____ Quite well   _____ Not at all well

Why did you answer as you did?

_____12. What could the professor have done to make the discussion more successful?

_____13. What could I, the student, have done to make the discussion more successful?

a small-group discussion. In groups of seven, students were to conduct a thirty-minute discussion of a work of literature without any teacher intervention. They would be graded on several criteria:

- Whether contributions were spread fairly evenly among all seven people
- Whether the seven people helped and encouraged each other and worked together to create a fruitful discussion rather than grandstanding or dominating
- Whether students demonstrated a thorough knowledge of the work of literature
- Whether students used the literary-critical strategies they were learning as they analyzed the work of literature
- Whether students built on one another's contributions

Students were divided into six groups of seven or eight people each. The groups were assigned to a fifty-minute time slot during the tenth week, when the assignment was due (for example, the Wednesday 9:00 A.M. group, the Thursday 5:00 P.M. group). Walvoord worked with the registrar to find small meeting rooms for these six time slots. During the fifty-minute time slot, the group of seven would conduct a thirty-minute discussion of a short story that had not yet been discussed in class. Walvoord sat outside the circle, observing but not saying anything. The final twenty minutes were for the group to debrief its own experience and for Walvoord to give feedback. Walvoord then e-mailed the students their grade. Typically everyone in the group got the same grade, though Walvoord reserved the right to lower the grade of an individual who was problematic in the group or raise the grade of someone who did a masterful job of functioning within a problematic group.

But before Walvoord could grade these discussions, she had to teach what she graded. She did this in several ways:

- Giving students a written guide about how to run a good discussion of literature (Exhibit 5.2).
- Conducting a fishbowl discussion by seven invited graduate students who discussed a work of literature for thirty minutes while the class observed, guided by a set of questions about the dynamics of the discussion. Then the class and graduate students analyzed the discussion process.
- In the next six class sessions, conducting a ten-minute fishbowl discussion by one group of seven students, followed by ten minutes of feedback to the group from Walvoord and the rest of the class, and

then a full-class discussion of the literature, building on the fishbowl discussion.

- On one class day, arranging for each group of seven students to meet simultaneously in a place of their choosing, conduct a thirty-minute discussion, and write analyses of their discussion, which Walvoord collected and read but did not grade.
- Conducting D-Day. During one week, regular classes were replaced by six fifty-minute sessions, some held during the class hour and some in other time slots. In each time slot, one group of seven students met with Walvoord. They conducted a graded thirty-minute discussion of a new piece of literature, with Walvoord silent as the observer-grader. At the end, they critiqued their own discussion. Walvoord gave feedback and later sent them their grades.

EXHIBIT 5.2

A Student's Guide to Effective Discussion

What Is the Goal of Discussion Groups?

A major aspect of this course is for you to learn more about participating in effective discussions. The learning goals are:

- To increase your skills of analytical reading and critical thinking
- To increase your skills of effectively contributing to a successful group discussion

How Does the Group Function in Interpreting Literature?

In interpreting literature, there is no one "right" answer. But not all interpretations are equally acceptable. In this classroom, we will place high value on those interpretations that are supported by evidence from the literary work. We will constantly be asking you, "Where in the literary work do you find evidence for your statement?"

Of course, a passage of the work may be read as evidence for different points of view, or a reader may place more or less emphasis on that passage in relation to other aspects of the work. So there are always legitimately different interpretations of a story, play, or poem. That's what makes literature challenging and interesting.

In a successful discussion, the group helps each individual to expand, deepen, and challenge his or her individual interpretations of the work. I myself, even though I'm the teacher, expect to deepen and change my own interpretations as I discuss the literature with you.

What Are the Characteristics of a Good Discussion Group?

A successful discussion group about literature differs markedly from some other kinds of discussions we all engage in. It's a specific kind of group interaction with its own ground rules and ways of interacting. It is not a debate. The purpose of a debate is to convince other people of the rightness of your own positions.

A group discussion is not a bull session either. A bull session may be a friendly contest in which one person tells a story and another person seeks to top it with still another.

A group discussion of literature is an exploration. Group members pool their questions, insights, and ponderings to build insights that help each person extend his or her understanding of the literature.

What Happens in a Discussion Group?

Discussion begins with someone's observation or question. It should be a question that opens up the work of literature in some provoking or interesting way. Express what you do not understand or what you find intriguing. Statements often begin, "I noticed that …" or "I was intrigued by …" or "I didn't understand why …" or "I wonder …"

If the observation is rich in possibilities, group members stay with it for a number of contributions. To keep the conversation going, members use the analytical strategies we have been learning. It is not the goal to have everyone adhere to one "right" way of looking at the text, but to have everyone expand and check his or her insights by group interaction and by grounding discussion in the text. It is expected that people will refer specifically to the text to support their points.

In response to one member's contribution, the next person may:

- Ask for clarification: "What did you mean by …?"
- Ask for further support: "Where in the story do you find evidence for that?"
- Suggest further evidence to support the position: "Yes, and that's also supported by …"
- Give examples to support and extend the position: "An example I can think of is …"
- Add further related ideas: "This connects to what Kerry said earlier …" or "Our reading from Brown's book would suggest that …"
- Raise complications or disagreements: "The problem with that interpretation is …" or "What about …" or "I don't see it that way. I think that … because …"
- Note contrasts and similarities: "Yes, and it's similar to …" or "this is handled very differently in the story we discussed last time …"
- Apply a statement to a new situation: "What if we took that same analysis and applied it to …"

By staying with the topic, group members push beyond the superficial and obvious. When the topic has been explored for a while, the group may pick up on something that suggests a new line of inquiry, or someone may offer another observation or question, and the discussion moves forward.

Group Dynamics

- Everyone should contribute about the same number of times. If someone is not contributing, slow the group down, look at the person, let there be a pause, or directly ask, "Kim, what do you think?" If you are contributing significantly more than others, keep quiet for a while.
- Listen and build. Group discussion is a team inquiry, not a chance for one person to dominate the group or display his or her own brilliant ideas. Connect your contribution to what others have said.
- Don't be afraid to attack the hardest aspects of the literature. Don't play too safe. Don't spend time merely agreeing with the obvious. Disagree, challenge, or push a difficult point. Be tough-minded. As long as disagreements are expressed firmly but courteously, the group will thrive by bringing up different points of view or wrestling with difficult issues.
- At the same time, be ready to listen and entertain other people's ideas. Don't judge an idea prematurely. It's not about right or wrong; it's about exploring together.

EXHIBIT 5.2 (*Continued*)

How Can I Prepare for a Group Discussion?

Successful group discussions don't just happen. They are the product of careful preparation and committed action on the part of each person in the group. Before the group meeting, each person should:

- Read the work of literature carefully and thoughtfully, at least twice.
- Think about how you would address the inquiry questions we have been using.
- Write out three provocative questions that you think would be good openers for group discussion.

This handout was loosely based on one written by Craig Nelson of the Department of Biology at Indiana University. He, in turn, adapted and in part copied verbatim a handout written by Judith Hansen of Indiana University's Anthropology Department. Both versions rely heavily on ideas from Hill (1982).

The steps Walvoord took to prepare her students for the graded discussion illustrate the full sense of "teach what you grade." Walvoord not only tells her students what constitutes effective discussion and grades them on the quality of their discussion; she also structures opportunities for them to practice and get feedback on their discussion skills. Simultaneously, the class is moving through the same body of literature that Walvoord would cover if she were devoting more time to lecture. Her decision to run the class by discussion is dictated not by devaluing the literature or the literary analytical skills she wants her students to master, but by her knowledge of the research on learning, which clearly says that students will learn the analytical techniques most effectively if they practice discussing and get feedback. You can't learn to ride a bike except by riding it. You can't learn to discuss literature except by opening your mouth.

Online Discussions

Online discussion boards may serve as informal venues for students to write freely from their own impressions and for students to get to know one another. However, if the teacher's goal is for students to think critically and engage in evidence-based discussion that builds on one another's contributions, then more structure must be provided. Elaine Bennington and Laurie Kirkner, instructional technologists at Ivy Tech Community College of Indiana, note, "Meaningful online discussions that promote learning and build community usually do not happen spontaneously. They require planning, good use of questioning techniques, and incentives for student participation" ("A Plan for Effective Discussion Boards," 2007, p. 1). A study by John Thompson, associate professor in the computer information systems department at Buffalo State College, revealed that a large percentage of his students posted to the discussion board at the last moment, thus diminishing the ability of the discussion to build over time based on students' consistent contributions. "If left on their own, students [do] far too many postings [merely] to satisfy a grade," he concludes. "Simply mandating participation and making it a substantial part of the course grade does not guarantee the quality of participation that adds to the learning experience" (quoted in "A Plan for Effective Discussion Boards," 2007, p. 8).

It is important to grade what you teach and teach what you grade. Bennington and Kirkner recommend that students' participation in online discussion boards be graded by a rubric (for our example, see Exhibit 5.3). More detailed rubrics, as well as a fuller discussion of how to assess online learning, can be found in Comeaux (2005).

To teach the disciplinary skills and the discussion skills you are grading, consider some suggestions drawn from the practices of teachers with whom we have worked:

- Ask students to find, in the previous week's postings, an example of each of the types of critical thinking questions or contributions you want. For example, can they find an example where someone questioned assumptions? Probed evidence? Questioned viewpoints?
- Have students submit a self-report in which they analyze their own postings for the qualities you want.

EXHIBIT 5.3

Rubric for Online Discussion

1	Responder addresses the issue and includes at least one question.
2	Same as for 1, AND responder uses at least one of the critical thinking strategies we have been discussing: identifying assumptions, discussing multiple perspectives, raising and answering counterarguments, offering evidence, questioning evidence, drawing analogies, evaluating quality according to clear criteria, and exploring implications, causes, or consequences; OR the responder addresses other students' views in a way that goes beyond merely "I agree" or "I disagree."
3	Same as for 1, but the responder BOTH uses critical thinking strategies and refers to other students' views.
4	This one knocks my socks off. The response does everything for 3, AND the thinking is creative and exploratory. The writer recognizes the complexity of issues and raises provocative questions for further discussion. The writer may bring in material from outside readings in this or other classes. Response shows a highly creative, engaged, and curious mind at work.

Resource 5.2. Classroom Discussion

Brookfield and Preskill (2005). A rich, thoughtful book on this topic.

Laing (2007). Short summary of six ways to enhance discussion.

Neff and Weimer (2002). Short summary of strategies.

- Pair students into a buddy system, and have each person identify, in the postings of the buddy, examples of the qualities you want. Notice that you are not asking peers to evaluate or judge or grade their classmates' contributions, only to find postings that fit into certain categories: questioning assumptions, providing evidence, and the others.
- Provide your own analysis of posts in a message to the entire class. Choose some of the posts to analyze.
- Ask students periodically to take their three strongest posts and send them to you for a grade.
- Show a post on the screen, divide students into groups, and have each group compose a response to the post.
- Post one student's post and ask each individual student to post his or her most thoughtful and best response. Then ask students to comment on the differences and similarities, as well as the usefulness, of each other's responses.
- If your class is hybrid, with some class time as well as the discussion board, use some class time to discuss any of the exercises mentioned above or simply put a few sample posts on the screen and analyze them together as a class, talking about how they might be made more effective.

In other words, find ways to bring the discussion board front and center as a tool for learning. Bestow on it all the signals of value that communicate to students that you're not only assigning it; you're spending important time guiding and responding to it, and you're grading it by explicit criteria that focus not just on the frequency and length, but also on the quality of the students' thinking.

Resource 5.2 offers help for teaching and guiding class discussion.

Teaching and Grading Group Assignments

Group assignments are another area where faculty in our workshops raise many questions. When you assign several students to produce a major assignment together, you will have to consider not only the quality of the task they complete but also the effectiveness of their interaction. If one of your course objectives is that students will learn to work together with colleagues, then teach them how. The steps are the same as for teaching and grading discussion:

- Provide criteria and instructions.
- Provide opportunities for practice and feedback.

  Here are suggestions for guiding group processes:

- Begin with instructions and guidelines for group work. Address the ways in which groups could go astray.
- Construct a rubric by which the groups will be evaluated.
- Have groups compose and sign a written agreement, at the beginning of their work together, that details what all of them will be responsible for (for example, being on time for meetings, completing their share of the work by certain deadlines, communicating regularly with other group members) and what each will do (Mary will research this part; John will research this part; Ling-Chi will produce the first full draft; Jamal will edit the draft).
- Ask the group to appoint people to certain roles: record keeper, convener, and others.
- Ask the group for frequent feedback to you and to each other. At the end of each meeting, whether online or face-to-face, group members can write to one another what they thought was successful about the group meeting and what they thought needed improvement. Responses can be shared with you, and you can step in quickly if the group is struggling.
- Ask a recorder to post or submit to you a record of the group's activities. When did they get together? Who was present? What did each person do? What progress was made? What problems arose, and how did the group address them? What do they need from you, if anything?
- Schedule a face-to-face or synchronous online meeting with each group at intervals to check the group's progress and interaction. At these meetings, anyone who feels another group member is not doing her or his share should say so right there in the group so the issue can be discussed and you can facilitate.

We find in our workshops a number of faculty who want to grade students' contribution to the group as part of their grade for the project, but the faculty members don't know quite how to structure the grading. An obvious method is to ask students to report on, or even grade, other students' contributions. But think again whether this will supply the information you are looking for. Asking students to evaluate one another's contributions to the group can make you into the parent and the students into the tattling siblings. Group members may deliberately or subconsciously collude to cover up inequality of effort just to avoid conflict. Or the group may discount the contributions of women, historically underrepresented groups, or persons with disabilities—prejudices that turn up regularly in the research literature, so likely are present in your classroom as well. We suggest that you do not merely have students evaluate one another's group contributions at the end of the project. Spread the evaluation throughout the process, anchor it to behavior, be present as facilitator and listener, and help the group address any difficulties early on.

The guidance we have suggested helps you be the coach along the way, helps students raise workload and interaction issues while they can still be addressed, and results in ongoing, not just end point, information to you about how the groups are doing. (Resource 2.2 contains material that can help you manage collaborative and cooperative student work. Comeaux, 2005, addresses the assessment of online group work.)

What If They All Get A's?

Faculty members in workshops sometimes raise the possibility that if they teach what they are grading, more students will meet the highest criteria for student performance. You'd think this would be a good thing, but some faculty operate in environments where they fear they will be in trouble if they give too many A grades. We discuss grade inflation in general in Chapter Eight. In this special kind of case, where grades in your own class are rising because students are doing better work, you have two choices. The first is to raise the standards so that it takes more to get an A. Students are getting better teaching, so they should be performing at a higher level. A second option is to keep the standard the same, give an A to all students who reach the standard, and then, if you are questioned about it, be ready to show your department head or promotion tenure committee some samples of your assignments and tests, together with student work that earned an A and work that earned a B. You can begin a discussion on this topic in which you are open to the other person's ideas, and the other person has a chance to see what you are doing.

• • •

Grading what you teach and teaching what you grade are key principles that help to construct an integrated set of educational activities that lead students toward achieving the learning goals. You may have noticed that the suggestions in this chapter have implications for the use of in-class time, out-of-class time, and online time. Sometimes they are huge implications. So the next chapter takes up specifically the issue of planning the in-class, out-of-class, and online time, as well as the students' study time, and (that most precious of resources) your own time.

Activity

- Examine your course learning objectives. Make sure they include everything you want students to learn in your class. Now consider how you are teaching each of those objectives. Are there objectives that you want to grade as well as teach? Discuss your plans with colleagues.
- Make a list of the qualities of good discussion in your course. What would students do to create a good discussion? Plan ways to teach and encourage those actions. Do you want to grade student discussion? If so, plan how to both teach and grade. Discuss your plans with colleagues.
- If you are using student group work in your course, plan how you will guide and grade the groups. Share your plans with colleagues

Chapter 6

Managing Time for Teaching, Learning, and Responding

"YES BUT HOW WILL I have enough time?" "How will I cover the course material and also get students interacting?" "How will I find time to grade the assignments I know are beneficial?" Time is a faculty member's most precious resource. You cannot teach what you are grading, grade what you are teaching, or implement the principles of good practice unless you can solve the time problem. This chapter suggests that faculty members deliberately analyze their paradigms for using in-class and out-of-class time, online time, students' study time, and their own time. (Chapter Seven focuses more narrowly on how to manage that stack of papers on your desk or in your computer file.)

This chapter contains three parts:

- Three steps for planning the use of in-class time, out-of-class time, students' time, and the instructor's time. The steps are illustrated first with a detailed case study of how one faculty member, teaching a face-to-face history class of thirty students, radically reconsidered his use of time, with significant results for his own time and his students' learning.

- How the same steps can be applied to large classes, scientific and technical disciplines, and online courses or courses that combine significant online experience with some face-to-face time (often called hybrid or blended courses).

- Suggestions for managing the larger issues of faculty stress and burnout, written by Susan Robison, a psychology faculty member, former department chair, therapist, coach, and faculty workshop leader.

Three Steps for Managing Class Time: A Case History

To illustrate how a faculty member can reconsider the use of time, we return to the story of John Breihan, the historian we met in previous chapters, who wanted the students in his first-year general education Western civilization course to describe historical events and people, and, most important, to use that information to construct arguments about historical issues. Breihan chose the argumentative essay as the most effective format in which to assess students' skills of historical argumentation, and he constructed a course skeleton showing the three argumentative essays spaced across the semester.

He decided that the first essay he assigned, dealing with the years 1500 to 1800, would offer students several options, including an essay question in which students had to decide whether Edmond Burke and Thomas Paine would judge that Louis XIV of France was a "good" king for his time. He constructed a grading sheet for that assignment (Exhibit 4.2).

Now Breihan is ready to flesh out the course skeleton, arranging educational experiences both in class and out of class so as to help students learn to argue. He follows three steps that are widely applicable not only to his own situation, but to larger classes, scientific and technical disciplines, and online or hybrid courses.

Step 1: Analyze What Students Will Need to Learn

Step 1, analyzing what students will need to learn, begins as Breihan lists the knowledge and skills that his argumentative essays will require of students. His list includes reading accurately; realizing that published works have authors who are products of their own cultures and biases; perceiving and using standard analytical categories, such as political, social, economic, religious, and cultural factors often cited in explaining past events; perceiving historical theses; using written sources as evidence; stating and defending a historical thesis; and raising and answering counterarguments.

Such a list makes it harder for Breihan to assume that if he merely lectures the content, his students will automatically produce good arguments when they write their essays. Instead, Breihan has to proceed to the next step: how students will learn everything they need to do well on the assignments.

Step 2: Analyze How Students Will Learn What They Need

A good place to start with step 2 is the research literature. Exhibit 6.1 summarizes the teaching practices that research has shown to enhance students' learning of complex skills such as critical thinking.

The research literature and Breihan's experience tell him that students will learn to argue not only by taking lecture notes, but by engaging in argument, getting feedback, and trying again. This is how humans learn complicated processes.

Step 3: Reconsider the Use of Class Time

You may be thinking to yourself, *It's all fine and good to be interactive in class, but how can Breihan cover important events of 1500 through 1800 and also take time for in-class interaction? Students cannot frame cogent arguments if they don't know the basic facts, vocabulary, and concepts. Also, students often don't*

EXHIBIT 6.1

Best Teaching Practices: A Summary of the Research

- Have students write about and discuss what they are learning.
- Encourage faculty-student contact in and out of class.
- Get students working with one another on substantive tasks in and out of class.
- Give prompt and frequent feedback to students about their progress.
- Communicate high expectations.
- Make standards and grading criteria explicit.
- Help students meet those expectations and criteria.
- Respect diverse talents and ways of learning.
- Use problems, questions, or issues, not merely content coverage, as points of entry into the subject and as sources of motivation for sustained inquiry.
- Make courses assignment centered rather than merely text and lecture centered. Then focus on helping students successfully complete the assignments.

Sources: Bain (2004); Chickering and Gamson (1987); Kuh and others (2007); Kurfiss (1987); Pascarella and Terenzini (2005).

---

read the material ahead of time, or they don't read it carefully enough for intelligent discussion. If students haven't read Thomas Paine's work carefully, how can they discuss it? If they haven't grasped the basic principles, how can they be asked in class to show how the principles can be applied to arguments?

The answer to these dilemmas is that Breihan must think carefully about structuring coverage of basic facts, concepts, and vocabulary and about teaching argumentation skills. He must plan where students will encounter three aspects: *first exposure*, where they are first presented with new facts, concepts, and vocabulary; *process*, where students analyze, solve problems, and apply what they have learned; and *response*, in which students get feedback from their teacher, peers, or others. These three aspects of learning must be distributed among available times, which, in the face-to-face class, are the class time, the students' study time, and the teacher's own time.

If Breihan uses the class for first exposure, then process will necessarily be pushed into students' own time and response into his own time, resulting in a very heavy paper load every time he gives a test or assignment. If instead Breihan can make students responsible for first exposure in their own time, then he can use the class time for process and response. He'll reduce his paper load, be able to make many more assignments, and be able to put his own effort toward pushing students into higher levels of thinking by interacting with them in class. Table 6.1 shows these two choices about where to put first exposure.

The key to the alternative paradigm—using class time for processing and response—is to establish the first-exposure part: to get all or nearly all

TABLE 6.1

Choices About First Exposure

	In Class	Students' Own Time	Instructor's Own Time
Traditional model	First exposure	Process	Response to all assignments
Alternate model	Process; response to daily, short assignments and guidance for longer assignments	First exposure	Response to selected assignments

students to read the assignment in their own study time before class. Ask them to bring, send, or write in class some exercise that holds them responsible for having completed the first exposure. Then, in class, respond to and build on what they have done. Here is how Breihan did that:

- *Before class.* Each day, he asked students to bring to class a short (between a half-page and a full page) written response to study questions about the assigned texts. They brought two copies: one to give him at the beginning of the class and one to work on at their seats.

- *In class.* He used students' responses as the basis for discussion, argument, and response (Exhibit 6.2). During class, he asked them to revise and expand their own writing. They took this writing with them when they left; he did not see, check, or grade their revised writing. He had given them, in class, the response he otherwise would have had to write on their papers in his own time. This is the key to powerful teaching without killing yourself under the paper load.

- *After class.* He looked over the writings students had submitted prior to the class and simply gave each student credit for having come prepared, taking two or three seconds per paper. Getting credit for preparation counted heavily in the final course grade. Walvoord marks her students' class preparation work as pass or no credit. Anderson, in a class of 125, asks students to keep their daily writings in a portfolio and then, at midterm, to revise their two best writings and hand them in, along with the original versions of the other assignments and a tally of how many assignments are included. Anderson bases the portfolio grade on the quality of the two revisions and the presence of the other unrevised original writings.

At the end of the class, Breihan reminds students that a later class period will be a debate about Louis. Half the class will defend Louis as a good king for his era; half will argue Louis was not a good king. Breihan reminds students that they must bring written debate notes to class and be prepared to argue either side. He will assign them to sides at the beginning of that

EXHIBIT 6.2

Transcript of Breihan's Class

Students enter class with written answers to the following questions:

1. What is the issue at stake in the selections you read for today?
2. Bishop Bossuet: Who was he, and when did he write? How can his material be used as evidence on the issue?

     [For each of the other authors students read, the same questions are repeated as for question 2.]

     Students put a copy of their written work on the teacher's desk and take a copy of it to their seats to work with.

Teacher: Mr. Freiburg, do you have the issue at stake today?

Freiburg: Sorry, I was sick last night and didn't get the reading done. I'll be ready next time.

Teacher: Okay, hope you're feeling better. Ms. Washington, do you have it?

Washington: Yes.

Teacher: Would you put it on the board, please?

Washington [writes on the board]: The issue at stake is whether Louis XIV was a good king for his time.

Teacher: Everybody clear on the issue? Be sure to revise your own answer if you did not get this.

Class: [nods and murmurs in agreement]

Teacher: [reads the next question on the assignment] Bishop Bossuet: Who was he? When did he write? Mr. Ackerman?

Ackerman: He was a tutor in Louis's court.

Teacher: Right. So what is his position on the issue at stake? [silence; teacher waits]

Ruiz: Well, he thinks Louis was a good king. [Not a good answer.]

Breihan: Yes, but you've only summarized what he said. How can this material be used as evidence?

Ruiz: [silent]

Breihan: Anyone?

Robinson: He owed his job to Louis, so he probably had to say good things.

Breihan: So he may be biased. Excellent. But is the bishop's evidence totally useless?

Hammond: Well, he was there in the court, so it's eyewitness evidence.

Teacher: Yes! So his writings are good evidence in some ways and not so good in other ways. This is what I mean when I say that in your essays, you have to evaluate the historical material as evidence. Now let's ask what evidence the bishop himself uses to back up his position. [students reply]

Now let's take the next writer. Saint Simon. Who was he? When did he write? [continues in this vein; teacher eventually sets up a quasi-debate.] Ms. Lanahan, would you be Saint Simon? [Lanahan nods.] What did Saint Simon say about Louis improving the army?

[Lanahan explains.]

Teacher: Mr. Belanco, would you be the bishop? [Belanco nods.] How would the bishop have responded to Saint Simon?

[The two students answer one another; other students join in.]

     The transcript illustrates how, because students are prepared for class and have done first exposure on their own, Breihan can:

• Push the student who summarizes Bishop Bossuet instead of evaluating his writing as evidence.
• Help all the students toward revising and expanding their own preparatory writing.
• Get students to argue back and forth about issues, by giving them roles. ("Will you be the bishop?")
• Show students how the class session directly prepares them for their essay assignment, due shortly.

class. He reminds them that after the debate, there will be only ten more days until their argumentative essays are due, and the material on Louis will be needed for those essays. He refers them to the criteria for those essays, which are part of the assignment he has already given to them. He helps his students to see that he is teaching to the criteria. Thus, he helps to motivate their preparation and participation in class.

Breihan did not institute interactive strategies just for the sake of inter-activity. The exercises, the class session in the transcript, and the debate that followed it on the next class day were carefully sequenced as part of a plan to build necessary information, vocabulary, and skills sequentially across the semester. Exhibit 6.3 contains Breihan's plan for building knowl-edge and skills in the weeks before the first essay exam.

EXHIBIT 6.3

Breihan's Plan for Teaching Argumentation in a Western Civilization Course

Exercises	Skills
Stage 1: Showing How a Single Reading Can Be Used as Evidence	
Author's Purpose and Summary: Week 1	Recognize that history is written by people who reflect their cultural biases. Pay attention to author's subheads. Summarize.
What do you know about the textbook author? What can you guess? When was the text written? Published?	
List its subheadings, and summarize a chapter.	
Write a one-paragraph narrative of the English Civil War, incorporating eight terms provided by Breihan.	Summarize events accurately.
Analysis of Anarchic Episodes: Week 2	Become familiar with various analytical categories, and use them to categorize evidence.
From eyewitness accounts of seventeenth-century riots, find evidence of the following fac-tors: economic, political, social, religious, and so on.	
Primary Sources on Louis XIV: Week 3	Understand how primary source material can be used as evidence by stating connection between eyewitness material and opinions on the historical issue.
What is the issue at stake in this collection of documents?	
Who was the author of each document? When did the author live? How can the author's mate-rial be used as evidence on the position at stake?	
[Questions are repeated for each source.]	

Exercises	Skills
Secondary Sources on Louis XIV: Week 4	Understand what a secondary source is.
What is the issue at stake?	Use secondary sources as models for shaping historical arguments. Understand how arguments are backed by evidence.
Who is the author? When did the author write?	
What is the author's position on the issue?	
How does he or she back it up?	

Stage 2: Contributing to an Argument on an Assigned Historical Opinion

Louis XIV Debate: Week 5	Understand that history is argument about the past.
Louis XIV debate worksheet: Prepare notes in support of your assigned position on whether Louis was a good king for his era, plus arguments for the opposing opinion.	Collect evidence for a position.
	Take notes that allow easy access to evidence during debate.
Second chance on Louis XIV debate: (1) Write two points that were not discussed in the class debate. (2) For extra credit, say why you did not say them in the debate.	Learn skills and points not used in the debate.

Stage 3: Choosing One's Own Position on a Historical Issue and Briefly Defending It with Evidence

Best Solution to Anarchy Essay: Week 6	Choose one's own position.
In a one-paragraph essay, state which solution to the problem of seventeenth-century anarchy—French or English—you personally find more realistic and attractive. Try to explain why you feel the way you do, and back your feelings with evidence.	Address the relevant issue.
	Support the position with evidence.

Stage 4: Choosing One's Own Position and Defending It in a Full Essay, Including Counterarguments and Answers to Counterarguments

Essay 1: Week 7	Use several techniques for historical argument: analyzing the problem, stating your position, supporting your position with evidence, and answering counterarguments.
Select from among three essay topics:	
1. For a hypothetical country (whose characteristics are described) suggest an optimal style of government, based on governments studied in class.	
2. Whose theories about the French Revolution—Burke's or Paine's—were more "valid"?	
3. From class readings by Burke and Paine, infer their views, pro and con, of Louis XIV's reign.	

By using class time for process and response, Breihan was able to assign writing as often as every class day while keeping his at-home paper-grading load manageable. He helped his students learn the argumentative skills, the vocabulary, and the factual knowledge they would need to write high-quality argumentative essays that met his criteria and standards for their learning. He helped them not by lecturing over their passive heads but by getting them involved in judging evidence, constructing arguments, and answering counterarguments. When process takes place in the class-room, students can learn from peer interaction and teacher guidance in this, the hardest part of the learning process. When response takes place in the classroom, rather than entirely in the teacher's own time, the teacher can generate many assignments—one of the most powerful tools for learning—and still not pay a heavy price in terms of grading time.

Teachers sometimes fear that if they teach interactively, they will not be able to keep the class on task. For that reason, we have highlighted Breihan's class, where the interactive discussion is highly structured. The students are given roles to play. The teacher guides the class by carefully planned activities with specific goals linked to learning and to assessment. In some contexts, the teacher may want a more loosely structured discus-sion, but this example illustrates that interaction in the classroom can be highly structured and focused and that it can demand sophisticated kinds of reasoning and inquiry.

Further help for making class time interactive can be found in Resources 5.1 and 5.2. Hobson (2004) presents ideas about encouraging student class preparation.

Managing Time in Other Types of Teaching Situations

The three planning steps Breihan followed can be applied to any teaching situation:

- Analyze what students need to learn.
- Consider how they will best learn it.
- Construct a sequence of educational experiences that will most effec-tively help students learn what they need to achieve the course goals and be successful on assignments and tests. As you do so, make intelli-gent choices about where to put first exposure, process, and response.

The general books on good teaching listed in Resource 5.1 present fur-ther ideas for all types of teaching situations. Resource 6.1 focuses spe-cifically on large classes, scientific and technical disciplines, and online or hybrid courses.

Resource 6.1 Using Time Effectively in Large Classes, Scientific and Technical Disciplines, or Online and Hybrid Courses

Bates and Poole (2003). Presents a decision-making model to help instructors consider uses of time and technology for online courses.

Conrad and Donaldson (2004). Focuses on a tool for planning student engagement, whether the course is entirely online or hybrid. Examples from many situations nationwide.

Dabbagh and Bannan-Ritland (2005). Integrates theory and practice for designing online courses.

Erikson, Peter, and Strommer (2006). Includes discussion of large classes.

Garrison and Vaughan (2008). Teaching blended classes that combine face-to-face and online educational experiences. A thoughtful, well-researched treatment.

Golub (2005). Contains a wealth of practical ideas adaptable to many disciplines and teaching situations. Aimed at high school and college English teachers.

McManus (2005). An oceanographer's detailed, candid account of how he changed from lecture to collaborative learning and project evaluation for a class of twenty-two students.

National Center for Academic Transformation. Web site with examples of institutions that redesigned large courses to enhance learning and make more efficient use of faculty and teaching assistant time. www.theNCAT.org.

Novak, Patterson, Gavrin, and Christian (1999). Explains just-in-time teaching, in which students complete preparatory exercises prior to class and the instructor uses those writings as the basis for classroom activities. Focuses on physics but applicable to many disciplines.

Online Classroom: Ideas for Effective Online Instruction. A monthly newsletter full of practice ideas from faculty around the country, as well as articles that summarize best practices or research findings. www.magnapubs.com.

Palloff and Pratt (2001). Highly practical book about online teaching and course design.

Simonson, Smaldino, Albright, and Zvacek (2009). Standard guide to online learning, now in its fourth edition. Contains research and theory, as well as practical guides to planning and teaching in various distance environments.

Thiell, Peterman, and Brown (2008). Redesign of a college algebra class leads to greater student success. See also "A Course Redesign That Contributed to Student Success" (2009).

Tobias (1994). Reports how a chemistry professor improved students' pass rate in large classes.

Walvoord and Williams (1995). Video for faculty shows how five faculty from various disciplines make their large classes interactive.

See also Resource 5.1

The following short cases illustrate some possible applications of the three basic steps for a class that is larger than thirty or forty students, has labs or clinics or recitation sections attached, is conducted wholly or partly online, or is in a scientific or technical discipline.

Lecture Moved to Students' Time; Homework Done in Class

A physics faculty member teaching a large introductory physics class, with teaching assistants (TAs) to help, decided to place first exposure outside class by having students view his videotaped lectures in their own study time. In class, he had students form small groups to do their physics homework, while he and the TAs moved around the classroom helping as needed or stopping to explain, in an on-the-spot mini-lecture, some concept that many students were finding difficult. Group members helped and taught each other, and when they all got stuck, a group could raise their hands and get help immediately from the teacher or TAs. When they had all the problems completed, they raised their hands, and the teacher or TA came over to check whether they had correctly completed the problems and whether any random member of the group could answer a question posed by the teacher or TA about the problem: "Randy, can you tell me why the group took this step here?" If the group met the two criteria, they could leave.

What this teacher did was turn the course on its head: first exposure was moved from class to students' study time. Process (homework problems) was moved to the class time. Response was moved from the teacher's or TAs' private time spent correcting homework to the class time.

Students Submit Writing Ahead of Time; Class Lecture and Interaction Based on Student Writing
Mary Beth Camp and Joan Middendorf*

The instructor of a large statistics class (Camp) asked students to read their text, complete a warm-up exercise before class, and send it to her online. She then used the students' responses to plan in-class lectures, exercises, and discussion that would directly address the misconceptions or problems that showed up in the preclass writings, a strategy referred to as "just-in-time teaching" (Novak, Patterson, Gavrin, and Christian, 1999).

To the instructor's surprise, a great deal of anger and frustration surfaced on student evaluations. To find out why, the authors inquired more fully into how the students were completing the warm-ups. They found that students' ways of completing the preclass exercises were not productive. Instead of reading the material carefully and then answering the multiple-choice warm-up questions, students were skimming through the reading looking for the answers to the questions and were not grasping the larger principles. As the semester progressed, these students began to get poor grades on their assignments and to get lost in class because they had not thoroughly read and grasped the earlier material. To address this problem,

---

*Adapted from Subiño Sullivan, Middendorf, and Camp (2008); Camp and Middendorf, forthcoming. Used by permission.

the instructor made the preclass exercises more open-ended to encourage students to base their answers on a fuller understanding of the reading. For example, instead of a multiple-choice question, a student might be asked, "What does a statistician mean when speaking of the 'dispersion' of a data set? How does the 'range' measure dispersion?" and, "What single concept or idea did you find most confusing or most difficult in the readings for this lesson? If nothing was confusing or difficult, what did you find of most interest?"

After implementing the change in warm-ups, the instructor administered student evaluations to the classes that had experienced the new warm-ups. In comparison to the previous semesters, students spent more time on the open-ended warm-ups: the number of students who spent less than ten minutes on the warm-ups fell from 80 percent to 43 percent; average time rose from 6.2 minutes to 14.4 minutes. The percentage of students who found the warm-ups moderately to extremely valuable increased from 33 percent to 47 percent. About 30 percent of the students commented, "I do wish I would have spent more time preparing because it would have saved me some time in the end when studying for the test," or "I wish I had taken them more seriously at the beginning." Students who did not find the warm-ups valuable noted, "None of the questions was on the test," or the questions in the warm-ups were not the same as those on the test.

In the future, the instructor plans to try to help more of the students take the warm-ups seriously at the beginning of the semester and to help students recognize that the same concepts appear on the tests as in the warm-ups, but in multiple-choice format, not open-ended.

Students Do First Exposure out of Class Using Multimedia; Class Becomes a Lab for Inquiry

In an introductory economics class at Miami University of Ohio, material traditionally covered in lecture was made available to students in multimedia forms, such as videotaped lectures and PowerPoint with sound. Students were required to use these materials in their own time. The class periods became a kind of "lab," devoted to problem solving, discussion, and economics experiments, all of which required students to apply what they had learned through the multimedia resources. Instructors documented student satisfaction with this method as compared to traditional lecture (Lage, Platt, and Treglia, 2000).

Lage and Platt (2000) explain in detail the importance and function of the class Web site, which was divided into four components: the classroom, where multimedia materials were available; the desk, which maintained students' problem sets, experiment debriefings, and personal grade information; the coffee shop for bulletin boards, e-mail, and chat; and the library for additional library and online resources and links.

Online Course: Interactive Discussion of Cases

Online courses present a quite different configuration because first exposure is perforce moved to students' time. The issue in online courses is to make the interaction of the class, whether synchronous or asynchronous, productive for student learning. How can the benefits of a highly productive, interactive, face-to-face class be captured for learning in an entirely online course? How can an instructor ensure that students come to online discussion prepared? How can the instructor's role be used to push students toward more sophisticated thought and analysis? We can only hint here at the wealth of advice and experience that faculty are bringing to these online challenges (see Resources 6.1).

One example is Dale Chisamore, teaching management courses at the University of Texas Dallas. For his face-to-face classes, Chisamore had been using the case method, widespread among business and other disciplines. When well used, the case method encourages student preparation, interaction, and learning through interactive class discussion.

When Chisamore began teaching management classes online, he had to adapt his methods for teaching cases. A recurring theme in the online teaching-practice literature is that online discussions must be carefully planned and structured. Chisamore structures the case discussion more tightly for his online class than for face-to-face classes. He has changed from having students work individually to having them work in groups of five to seven, because the groups make students more interactive. Online, he leads students through specific phases of case analysis. He monitors each group as it progresses through the stages to ensure the group is on track and to help resolve any group conflicts. In a face-to-face discussion, Chisamore allows wide latitude in terms of analytical methods the students may choose; the dynamics of face-to-face interaction help students abandon an unworkable approach. But online, Chisamore limits students' paths more tightly and intervenes to keep them from getting off-track ("Structuring the Case Method," 2004).

Time, Stress, and Burnout: What to Do If You Feel Overwhelmed

Beyond the strategies we described earlier in this chapter and the cases of faculty who found ways to enhance student learning by reorganizing in-class and out-of-class time, some readers may have turned to this section because they feel generally overwhelmed and stressed. We asked Susan Robison to insert some brief advice. Robison works with faculty as a coach and workshop leader for issues of peak performance, stress, and workload. She is a faculty member and former chair in psychology at the College of Notre Dame of Maryland. She has a long-time private practice in the Baltimore area and has received several awards for her work. Her own teaching is described in Walvoord and Robison (1990). Her newsletter, *Professor Destressor*, is available at no charge; contact her at Susan@ProfessorDestressor.com.

Time and Stress: The Bigger Picture
Susan Robison

If you are feeling overwhelmed, not just by grading but by the number of tasks related to your many roles, this section offers suggestions for achieving a sense of calm, peace, and purpose in your life. I have chosen to pack in many strategies; thus each can be only briefly explained. I trust you will use this section as a starting point to expand the strategies for your own purposes.

Strategy 1: Connect Your Tasks to a Deep Sense of Meaning and Purpose

Over the long haul of your lifetime, aim to do good while living well. Define those two for yourself, establish good work habits, and you will be on your way to a life of high productivity and high life satisfaction. Ask yourself:

- What does "doing good" mean specifically for you? If you were someday given a lifetime achievement award for your accomplishments, what would they be?
- What does "living well" mean specifically for you? If an award were given for a life well-lived, what would you have done to deserve it?

Draw a Life Line Try this life planning exercise to see how, rather than not having enough time, you have a whole lifetime to accomplish much. Draw a line horizontally across a piece of paper with hatch marks for five-year increments of your life from birth to death (must be later than age eighty). What elements of the above two goals—doing good and living well—would you like to do in each half-decade? As an academic, it is likely you will be productive well into your seventies and eighties if you have good health. All that you want to do does not need to be done by next Tuesday.

Construct a Pyramid of Power Here is a tool that has helped faculty and administrators in my workshops get specific about their sense of meaning. It is called the *pyramid of power*. This is a visual and verbal tool that acts as a reminder of the structure of meaning for all of your activities, professional as well as personal. On your bad days, it will power you up with energy to keep working on the tasks at hand, knowing that they are all connected into the big picture of your life.

The pyramid has four levels, like the floors of a house. The bottom is the rock-solid foundation of your purpose. Answering the question, "Why am I here?" you might write, "I am here to learn and develop as a human being," or "I am here to serve others," or "I am here to serve Allah/God." Carla is a physiology professor at a Research I university with a joint appointment in the biology department and the medical school. Here is what she wrote about her purpose: "I am here to share my wonder about creation especially about the human body."

The next level up is the mission statement, answering the question, "If _____ is my purpose, then what strengths can I draw on to bring my values to my contingencies? If_____ is my purpose, then what shall I do to live out that purpose?"

A formula would be: "My mission is to _____ (strength 1), _____ (strength 2), _____ (strength 3) for/to/with _____ (people 1) and _____ (people 2) who want _____ (value 1), _____ (value 2 and several other values up to six to eight values).

When Carla thought about what she was really good at, she knew it was teach, research, and create. She wanted to think about doing those things for her students, colleagues, and family. She had to struggle a bit to come up with her values, which turned out to be creation, fun, honesty, compassion, discovery, and wisdom.

Here is Carla's mission statement: "My mission is to create, research, and teach the wonder of creation to and with my colleagues, students, and family who want fun, honesty, compassion, discovery, and wisdom." She argued that her colleagues, students, or family might not want her values, but I pointed out that people get those values from her whether or not she ever speaks about them, because the values inform her work and life.

The next level up is the vision statement which answers the question, "If I live my purpose and do my mission, what will result for me and the world around me? What are the outcomes?"

Carla wanted results from her work: increased knowledge about the human body being shared with colleagues and students; fun, creative teaching methods that enlivened her classes and professional presentations; better care for the patients her medical students would treat when they became doctors; and several other aspects of her life consistent with her Purpose.

The last level at the pinnacle of the pyramid contains the goals anchored to the vision, anchored to the mission, and anchored to the purpose. Instead of being like many faculty with a set of goals floating around in the air with no anchor and little sense of why they are doing them, you will have your pyramid of power to remind you how the goals fit in with your larger big picture goal of living well while doing good.

Carla had goals for her parenting, her house, her hobbies, her retirement many years from now, and her professional development. She was feeling a little overwhelmed until we covered strategy 2.

Strategy 2: Generate Ideas Broadly, But Choose Wisely

Develop a system for allowing your creative brain to generate many ideas while your discerning brain decides which goals to invest in. Start generating all the goals that flow up from the base of your pyramid. Include goals related to your family and friends; teaching, research, and writing; and service to the academic and other communities.

Construct a Dream Book Here is the practical tip that will keep all of this from getting overwhelming: develop a system for parking all these goals so that they are out of your mind until you wish to work on them. I often work with faculty in my audiences to construct a dream book. About one-sixth of them prefer a dream wall, in which they park all of their goals in sight on a wall in their office; the other five-sixths don't like the visual clutter and also want to have something they can carry with them on retreat or vacation, or back and forth from home to work, as they keep track of progress. All of the following suggestions can be translated from books and walls into electronic forms.

The dream book will be a three-ring notebook with three or four pages of different-colored paper in each section. The sections represent areas of your life in your vision—for example, your home, your family, your research, or your teaching. As you generate goals, write them down on the smallest sized sticky notes and park them in the appropriate sections of your dream book.

It is very important that you write every goal down. Do not trust your goals to your memory. For one thing, George Miller's research (1994) suggests that the human memory capacity is only five to nine items. You will have more than five to nine goals in a lifetime, and you will forget them as soon as you think of them if you don't write them down. Second, holding things in your working memory without writing them down is a sure way to become overwhelmed. Third, as the work of Henrietta Klauser (2001) demonstrates, writing down a goal has a magical outcome of making it real, compelling, and inspiring. Opportunities will come into your life around your written goals that never appear with mental-only goals.

Put only one goal per sticky. Park them in the dream book on the front sides of the colored paper. When you complete a goal, move it to the back of the colored paper so that on a bad day, you can read your dream book from the back to the front and see all of your accomplishments. Also, when it comes time to write an annual report of your activities or revise your résumé, you will have an easy record of your professional accomplishments on the pages relevant to those areas.

Track Your Progress Toward Goals   Walt Disney is credited with devising a system for keeping track of all the illustrators working on the first feature length cartoon, *Snow White*. In the days before electronic graphics programs, cartoon illustrators drew many dozens of frames just to show one action by the character. Disney needed to know at a glance who was working on which scene with what progress. Exhibit 6.4 is how Carla and I replicated Disney's method on several of her current projects by using a table from a word processing program, a spreadsheet, or drawing by hand.

While common sense suggests writing the subgoals from left to right along the cells, I use authors Sher and Gottlieb's backward planning method (2003). In the last cell when the project is due for completion, write the final subgoals that need to be done. In Carla's example, it might be "run hard copies of the syllabus" or "post the syllabus on the electronic course Web site." Then Carla imagined what needed to be done by the halfway point and then filled in the rest of the cells from left to right and right to left with all the subtasks required for the completion of the syllabus. When she completed each subgoal, she marked it by drawing a line through it on paper or highlighting with a color on her electronic version. With all of

---

EXHIBIT 6.4

Tracking Progress Toward Goals

Goal	Jan. 8	Jan. 15	Jan. 22	Etc.
Syllabus for Physiology 301				
Article on ethics in medical research				
Prepare Kim's soccer team for tournament				

her current projects on the same tracking sheet, Carla could tell where she was in the progress of each. Furthermore, the vertical column formed her to-do list for each week.

All of the projects should be tied into your pyramid of power. Therefore you value each either for itself or because it is a means to an end of a bigger goal you wish to accomplish. You can have personal projects such as remodeling your kitchen on the tracking sheet, as well as your professional projects such as writing an article. That way, when someone asks you to do something, you can tell at a glance what projects and subtasks are slated for completion that week and whether you will have time to complete them. I often use a word processing table, which I run off and carry with me. Once a week on Friday night or Monday morning, I review all the projects I am working on; I cross off subgoals and move tasks around a bit. Eventually I use the cut-and-paste function to strip off the completed goals of a week and park them into a different document—another record of accomplishments for resumé revision time.

Strategy 3: Use Your Downtime to Truly Relax

The peak performance literature shows that rest is as important as hard work to achieve success. How do you recreate yourself so there is balance in your life? For example, faculty members who sit a lot need some physical outlets for their pent-up energy. The criterion for your recreational activities is whether they make you eager to get back to your work. If not, either they are not really recreating you, or you need a job change.

Don't underestimate the effect of having good health habits as a way to restore energy and increase effectiveness. That means adequate rest (most adults require eight hours of sleep), adequate nutrition (choose from all food groups, and stay away from the energy drainers), and regular exercise (aerobic, strength, and stretching) to achieve peak energy on a chemical, physical level.

Strategy 4: Use Stress Management Tools

Some examples follow.

Have to* Versus *Choose to This simple change in phraseology can make a big difference in your energy level. It is normative (Robertson, 2003) for faculty to earn prestige in the faculty lounge complaining about how hard they work, how much they have to do, and how beleaguered they are. What would it take for you to operate outside that norm by substituting the phrase, "I choose to" instead of, "I have to"? For example, instead of,

"I have to teach class, then I have to grade papers, then I have to fix dinner," substitute, "I choose to teach class, then I choose to grade papers, and then I choose to fix dinner." After all, you are choosing each task; they are derived from your pyramid of power and the job requirements at the college or university where you choose to work.

Fifteen-Minute Goals Break down every major goal into fifteen-minute subgoals. Even big goals like writing that book you have meaning to write can be broken down into small steps, such as "Define the audience for the proposal" or "Write the first section of the next chapter."

You may say, "Well it's going to take a long time to write a book that way." Yes, and it will take a long time to write a book any other way. But this way, it is guaranteed to get written. Although many faculty think a book should be written during a sabbatical binge, the data indicate that prolific writers write in small, regularly scheduled sessions (Gray, 2005; Boice, 2000; Johnson and Mullen, 2007).

Each subgoal should be on a sticky note so that you can move it from your dream book to your bathroom mirror, calendar, or computer screen and back again when you finish it. Now that you have all of the parts of book writing divided into fifteen-minute tasks, you can carry the equipment for some of those tasks with you so that idle time at your daughter's cross-country meet can be a good time to knock out one or two. When you are waiting for the dentist, have a contest with yourself to see how many fifteen-minute tasks you can complete before you are called in.

The Three Times Four Technique Here is a tool for getting a great to-do list ready for each day. Ask yourself these questions:

- What three things can I do tomorrow that advance my career mission with the most impact?
- What three things should I do tomorrow that if I don't do them I will be in trouble with the students, dean, chair, spouse, or someone else?
- What are three things I need to do to take care of myself, achieve balance, become a great person [or any other nonwork value or goal that you have]?
- What three things can I start on if I have leftover time that will be top priority goals for tomorrow?

There you go: three things for each category for a set of twelve, nine of which you have deemed absolutely necessary to call the day a great day, and three auxiliaries just in case it snows and class is cancelled.

These paragraphs have presented a brief overview of some strategies you can adapt to your own purposes. The central message is that you do not have to struggle with frequent feelings of stress and being overwhelmed. My coaching clients who use the strategies report significant reduction in feelings of stress. It is possible to do good while living well.

Activity

If you have been following our course planning process, you now have a course skeleton and the draft of instructions to students for your first major assignment. Now we invite you to complete the following steps:

- For the first assignment (or any other), list what your students will need to learn in order to be successful.
- List in-class, out-of-class, and online activities or small assignments that might help students learn those materials and skills.
- Consider one instance in your own teaching where you are doing first exposure in your classroom. Discuss with colleagues how you might move that first exposure to student study time and thus free class time for more interactive teaching.
- If you teach in a discipline that has labs, clinics, or similar scheduled sessions, ask yourself what the relationship is between the class and the lab or clinic. Is the class supposed to prepare students for the interaction of the lab or clinic? Does it do this effectively? Why or why not? How might I improve?
- Plan a schedule for one full course, following the three steps.
- Plan how to use one or more of the stress-reduction strategies Robison outlines. Discuss with colleagues.

Chapter 7

Making Grading More Time-Efficient

SO YOU'VE FOCUSED on your course goals, constructed the major assignments, guided the learning process, and used class time for response to short student work. But at some point, a stack of those finished, formal assignments or essay tests ends up on your desk, in draft or final version. This chapter offers strategies for keeping your grading time to a minimum and making that time effective for student learning. If you have turned to this chapter because you are generally overwhelmed and stressed, see Susan Robison's section at the end of Chapter Six.

Strategy 1: Find Out What the Student Knows

Why spend time writing comments about a paper's focus when the student, if asked, would respond, "Oh, I knew that paper wasn't well focused"? How can you tap this student information? One strategy is to ask students to submit a half-page evaluation of their own work (Exhibit 7.1).

If the performance is oral or technical rather than written (the student is making a speech, for example, or performing a clinical procedure), you

---

EXHIBIT 7.1

Student Check Sheet for a Literary Critical Essay

_____ I read the short story at least twice.

_____ I revised this essay at least once.

_____ I spent at least five hours on this essay.

_____ I started work on this essay at least three days ago.

_____ I have tried hard to do my best work on this essay.

_____ I have used the grading criteria in the assignment sheet to check and revise my work

_____ I proofread the essay at least twice for grammar and punctuation.

_____ I asked at least one other person to proofread the essay.

_____ I ran the essay through a spelling check.

_____ If I were to revise this paper again, I would ...

---

might take a few moments for the student to debrief—that is, tell you or the class what she or he thought about the presentation ("I thought I might have picked up the pace a little bit. Was it too slow?"). Then the class and teacher responses can build on those perceptions.

If you think the student's analysis and plans are on target, you may only need to say, "I agree." Or your comments may be able to amplify or correct the student's own estimation of what her work needs.

Strategy 2: Do Not Waste Time on Careless Student Work

If the check sheet or other evidence reveals that the student has not spent enough time on the paper or has not proofread it, get that paper off your desk very quickly. You can give it an F, or hand it back with instructions to revise and resubmit, perhaps with a grade cap or penalty for this second submission. But you need not spend time on careless student work. (See Chapter Four for a discussion of gateway criteria.)

Strategy 3: Do Not Extensively Mark Grammar and Punctuation

For drafts, informal work, or in-class writing, you may not want to count grammar and punctuation. But when you are grading a final, finished piece of work, we recommend that you require mastery of edited standard written English (ESWE), as we explained in Chapter Four. Papers with ESWE problems should not take you very long. First, when native-English-speaking students reach a college class without mastering ESWE, the effort and instruction required for them to do so is beyond what you can offer, by time or expertise. They need a consistent program of instruction by experts within a writing center, with a book, or online. Your goal should be to point them toward that kind of help. A great deal of research, over a long time, demonstrates that for you to mark every departure from ESWE simply does not work very well for student learning—certainly not well enough to merit the time you spend (Weaver, 1996, 82).

You can treat grammar and punctuation as a gateway issue, as described in Chapter Four. Or you might edit a paragraph or two as an example, show the student what needs to be done, or select one or two of the most egregious problems and circle a couple of examples ("You often misuse the apostrophe. I've circled a couple of examples. Please consult a handbook or the writing center to learn the rules"). For nonnative speakers of English, the same applies. You need not mark all of their departures from ESWE or from native sentence structure or idiom. They need to be working with a language center, tutor, or other resources. Point them in that direction.

That said, you can work with the tutor or center to help the student establish goals for attaining ESWE. For example, the center might suggest that John work on sentence boundary punctuation or Ling-Chi work on English pronouns. You can work with the center to establish grading and commenting practices that reinforce and contribute to the goals your student has established in the center. Some faculty ask the student to submit, with the paper, a list of the areas of ESWE or native idiom or usage they are working on, and you can simply put a check in the margin where you see problems in those areas.

Strategy 4: Address Fundamental Concerns First

So now you have winnowed down to only those pieces of student work that meet the checklist, have been constructed with reasonable care, and meet requirements for gateway criteria such as grammar and punctuation. Nevertheless, some of the students' work may quickly reveal substantial flaws. The principle here is not to spend the most time on the worst papers. Do not automatically assume you must comment on everything, offering both marginal and end comments. Nancy Sommers (1982), interviewing students after they had received back their papers with teacher comments, found that a number of things might go wrong when the teacher combines local-level suggestions about phrasing, paragraph structure, or grammar and punctuation with more global suggestions about overall focus, content, and organization. First, the student might be misled by a large number of local-level comments into spending disproportionate energy on those aspects and ignoring the larger issues of content and structure. Also, extensive local-level comments may encourage students in the view that it is the teacher's job to mark everything that is wrong and their job to change what the teacher wants changed. In this situation, the work is no longer theirs but the teacher's. Extensive comments may encourage a revision process by which a student merely goes through the paper line by line, fixing whatever the teacher has marked, without internalizing the principles that could guide revision in the student's future work. Finally, when revising the work their teacher has extensively marked, students may be reluctant to make any changes in unmarked text, thereby circumventing the growth and discovery that might otherwise take place in their thinking (see Walvoord and Breihan, 1990). So the time you spend marking local problems in the margins of the student's paper may backfire.

If the student's paper is flawed in its conception, evidence, structure, or line of reasoning, say only something to this effect: "I can't discern this paper's main point. Try writing in a single sentence, 'What I really want to say is . . . ' and then plan the paper to support that main point. If you need help, I'd be happy to discuss it with you." If you are responding to a draft, offer suggestions about how to amend the problem and offer further help. You may warn about lower-level problems to be addressed later ("Before you submit the final version, you'll need to work on your punctuation and grammar"), but you need not mark each error.

When commenting on global issues, use marginal comments or specific examples to illustrate what you mean—for example, "Your thesis is clear, but support for your claims is thin. I have marked a few examples in the margins. Your support is strongest in the third paragraph on page 3; my marginal comments try to show you why that paragraph is strong."

Strategy 5: Consider Comments Without Grades

Not every piece of student work needs both a grade and comments. For example, a draft, prospectus, or problem solution that is preliminary to a later work such as a full research project or an exam may need only comments.

Some faculty use a kind of portfolio system in which students turn in rough drafts of a number of pieces of work. The teacher selects some of these to discuss and critique in class. In a studio environment, everyone's work may be subjected to such a critique. Toward the end of the semester, the student chooses two of her strongest drafts and revises those for submission; the final grade is based on the presence of all the required pieces and the quality of the two revised ones. (For more on classroom portfolios, see Zubizarreta, 2009.)

In the examples we have given, students have not complained about not receiving grades for the informal writing. However, if your students do, you need to rethink what you are doing. We do not advocate doing anything that makes students feel their teacher has not paid appropriate attention to their work. One important action on your part is to explain fully and often why you are handling student work in the way you are, what you think grades are for, and why you are or are not giving grades or comments on a particular assignment. Relate ungraded work clearly to work that will be graded. Help students see how the ungraded work will be useful to them.

Even if a few students feel anxious about getting any paper back without a grade, you do not necessarily need to give grades to everyone.

You might offer to give unofficial grades to students who request them. Keep a record of what you told them so you can couch further communication in terms of the unofficial grade you gave.

Strategy 6: Use Comments Only for Teachable Moments

Ask yourself, *Have I chosen a teachable moment to make this comment?* Especially, you will want to question the usefulness of making extensive comments on students' finished, graded work when no further revision is possible. A true anecdote illustrates. Walvoord recently overheard a conversation between two students. One said to her friend, "What did you get on the paper?" The friend replied, "I only got a B. I was really disappointed." She went on to say, "He wrote all over the paper! He wrote a book! I didn't even read it." Imagine the faculty member, sitting there on a Sunday afternoon when he could have been out walking in the woods, earnestly writing comments all over the paper, trying to explain in great detail why this student got a B, perhaps knowing she'd be disappointed—and what happens? When she sees the B, which she cannot change, it's all over for her. This is an unteachable moment.

Often a teachable moment is when there is still something the student can do to improve the grade on an assignment. Comments on drafts or works in progress are likely to be more worthwhile than extensive comments on final work. It is usually wise to spend most of your time giving and guiding the assignment and very little on the final grading process—only enough to determine a fair grade and make a few encouraging comments the student can carry away.

Strategy 7: Spend More Time Guiding

To give yourself more time to guide the process while keeping your workload the same, move from a grading-heavy time schedule to a schedule that emphasizes giving the assignment and guiding it (Exhibit 7.2).

Strategy 8: Use Only as Many Grade Levels as You Need

The traditional grading system, with pluses and minuses, is a thirteen-level system. If you decide you should grade a particular assignment, ask yourself whether you need a thirteen-level system or whether fewer levels would accomplish the purpose. The fewer the levels, the faster you can grade.

EXHIBIT 7.2

Apportioning Time

Spending Most Time on Grading the Assignment		
Giving	Guiding	Grading

• • •

Spending Most Time on Giving and Guiding the Assignment		
Giving	Guiding	Grading

What can you use instead of a thirteen-level system?

- A six-level system (A through F) without pluses and minuses
- A four-level system: check, check-plus, check-minus, and no check
- A three-level system: outstanding, competent, and unacceptable
- A two-level system: pass-fail or credit–no credit

The basic rule is to use the lowest number of grading levels consonant with your purpose and with student learning. It is not necessary to assume that because at the end of the course you must assign grades in a thirteen-level system, every grade along the way must be calibrated on the same system. (See Chapter Eight for more detail on calculating course grades.)

Strategy 9: Limit the Basis for Grading

Not every assignment needs to be graded for every possible quality. When your tennis teacher wants to spend a lesson on your backhand stroke, she may comment only on that, leaving your wretched serve or your erratic net play for a later lesson. In a geography class of two hundred students, a professor gives students raw data on a chart and asks them to draw conclusions from it. In grading and responding to that assignment, he concerns himself only with the quality of their inferences from the data, and his comments address only that issue. If you limit the concerns you will address for a particular assignment, you need to inform students clearly and early, in class, online, and on the assignment sheet.

Strategy 10: Ask Students to Organize Their Work for Your Efficiency

Take a hint from your gas and electric company. They know that human beings cannot always think of all the little details. On the back flap of the envelope, they give the bill payer a checklist: "Did you write your account number on the check? Did you sign the check?" Podunk Gas and Electric has figured out how to prod the human mind, with its shortcomings, into actions that will save time for the company. You can do the same.

Ask yourself, *Where do I waste time in the physical or logistical aspects of grading?* For example:

- Do you hunt through students' papers to see whether all the parts are present? If so, how about requiring a contents page?
- [If papers are submitted in hard copy] Do you have to search for pages caught under someone else's paper clip? Ban paper clips.
- Do you want all students' papers to be readily identifiable in your computer files? Require file names with a common format.
- Have you graded a paper, made corrections and comments, only to find out that it was a rough draft? Require sequence and labeling.
- If you use a checklist such as the one in Figure 7.1, you can add efficiency items to it, or you can require a separate check sheet.

Here are some sample items for the student to check:

[If submitted in hard copy] This paper is stapled, not paper-clipped.

[If submitted online] This paper is submitted as an attachment in Word. The file is labeled with the name of the assignment and then the author's last name, for example, Essay 2 Jones.

I have included a Contents page.

The final copy comes first, with rough drafts behind it.

Strategy 11: Delegate the Work

In the old days, Anderson assigned a library position paper and then spent hours in the library or online checking students' sources for honesty and accuracy (probably because she recalled making up page numbers and author initials as an undergraduate). She asked herself whether someone else could do that checking. Aha! Now, early in the process of the library position paper, Anderson requires students to turn in a short "start" document and two primary source references correctly cited in American Psychological Association style. She has students put each reference on a separate index card with their name on the back. She distributes the cards to other class members, who must check the accuracy of the information and style of the references, and return a critique of the two references they checked. (You could also arrange this transfer of references online.) The exercise saves time for Anderson, shows the students the real purpose of references in academic work, and reinforces the importance of academic honesty.

Exhibit 7.3 is a peer checklist that anthropologist Mark Curchak of Arcadia University employed to guide students in responding to one another's

---

EXHIBIT 7.3

Curchak's Peer Checklist for First Draft of Term Papers in Sociology

Author of draft _____

Name of reviewer _____

Directions: By answering the following questions thoughtfully and clearly, be as helpful as possible to the author of this draft. Use complete sentences and specific examples to ensure clarity in your advice. You will be evaluated on the thoughtfulness and helpfulness of your responses.

• • •

1. *Overall situation:* How near to completion is this draft? What steps should the author take to complete this term paper? Be both specific and helpful in listing the three most important steps:

    A.

    B.

    C.

2. *Organization:* Is this draft organized in a standard pattern: an introductory section; the body of the paper, presenting the information in a reasonable sequence; and a summary and analysis of the situation? If there is an alternative organization, say what it is and whether it is effective.

3. *Introductory section:* The first few paragraphs should prepare the reader (another student in the course) for the research that has been done on the topic.

    A. Does the introduction explain the topic and why it is important? Briefly state why you think it is important.

    B. After reading the paper, say whether you think the introduction introduces what you've read. Does it? How?

4. *Body of the paper:* The major portion of the paper should present the collected information in an orderly and clear fashion.

    A. In the space below, outline in some detail the major points established in the body of the paper and the evidence used to support the points.

    B. Is the style of the writing appropriate to the intended audience: you and the others in the class?

    C. Compared with that of the textbook, is the style more or less formal? How?

D. Has the author thoroughly paraphrased the information from the references so that the writing style is consistent? Remember that inadequate paraphrasing is a common student problem and may even approach plagiarism.

E. Has the writer organized the information in the most effective way?

1. If not, suggest improvements.

2. How would you characterize the organization? Is it a list of equal points, an arrangement of topics and subtopics, a chronological sequence, an argument with two or more opposing viewpoints, or something else?

F. How has the writer handled citations?

1. Are they in an acceptable style, used consistently?

2. Is the number of citations adequate to the information taken from sources?

3. How has the information from sources been organized?

   a. One source per paragraph (give an example)

   b. Multiple sources for each paragraph (give an example)

G. Are the tables and figures used in the paper:

1. Clear and easy to understand?

2. Referred to in the text?

3. Labeled with a title or legend?

4. Cited (at the end of the title or legend)?

5. *Conclusions*: A conclusion can take several forms: a restatement of the overall argument of the paper, a summary of the key points, a combination of several points to make a final point, an analysis of the data, and so on.

A. What form has the writer used to conclude the paper?

B. Does the conclusion seem to be supported by the evidence? How or how not?

6. *Features of the writing*:

A. Are there any problems in the grammar, spelling, punctuation, paragraph structure, sentence structure, transition? Which one(s) in particular? Do these problems interfere with the meaning the writer is trying to express?

B. Has the writer acknowledged the help of others?

7. *General evaluation*: In the space remaining, give your general impression of the paper. Did you like it, and why? What did you learn from it? What else do you wish you had learned from it? Give any other ideas that you think might help the author.

Source: Reprinted from Walvoord (1986, pp. 47–49).

papers. Notice that the checklist is a reading guide for student peers. It leads them through the steps of a careful and helpful reading. Without this sort of guidance, students may focus too early on low-level problems such as comma errors, or they may miss some aspects their teacher knows are important, or they may believe they have to give a grade or a judgment on the paper.

The checklist guides them toward descriptive suggestions rather than outright judgments, which students find hard to express to their peers. The checklist also guides students in a sequence of questions; it is a guide to the reading-and-responding process. Armed with such a guide, students should be able to give good help to one another.

When you arrange for student peer response, it is important to consider what kind of response you want to elicit and at what point you want it to be given. A psychologist who was using peer response had organized the process so that students gave each other responses on the basic elements of their psychology papers; then they revised their papers based on those comments, received their teachers' comments, and revised again before the final grade. However, what happened in a number of cases is that student peers did not critique the papers deeply enough; they often did not catch the most fundamental problems of conceptualization, organization, and evidence. Moreover, students did not take seriously their peers' comments on these issues. Therefore, the first round of revisions, based on peer responses, tended to be too superficial. In the next round, when the teacher saw the papers, she made those fundamental criticisms and suggestions. By then, however, student writers had already invested a great deal of time in the papers, had revised them once, and were disinclined to make the fundamental changes their teacher suggested. The psychologist came to see that she might better have reversed the order of response, doing it herself on the first round, to get at the most fundamental conceptual problems, and letting peers respond to the smaller-scale problems that were likely to turn up in the further revisions. She also saw ways to improve the checklist she gave students as a guide for their responses.

How can you use an assistant other than peers? We described how to use teaching assistant graders in Chapter Four. In addition to using the suggestions in that chapter, see whether you can get unpaid "assistants" whom your students locate. We know a teacher who requires that all students find an "editor" somewhere in the outside world among their friends, children, parents, or spouse. The "editor" reads the paper and makes suggestions before the student hands it in. Students then write an acknowledgments page, just as their teacher does when publishing a book or article. The student might say, "I am indebted to my discussion group—John Anderson, Rafael Ruíz, Lawanda Washington, and Dawn O'Shaughnessy—for helping me work out the ideas for this paper, and to my friend Sandy Eckerd for proofreading it." You may have to give students an example or two of the language of an acknowledgment.

Strategy 12: Use Technology to Save Time and Enhance Results

Here are a few ideas about using technology to make your grading and commenting time more efficient:

- Use a course management system to simplify the processes of submitting, storing, and returning student work and allowing students to track their grades. It's often worth the time to learn the system.
- Instead of writing by hand on the student's paper, write the comments on your computer. When you find yourself writing the same thing over and over, create a boilerplate passage you can insert into your comments. You can simply insert your comments in bold or italics or in a certain color, or you can use the Comment function in word processing.
- Give students a handout, or make available to them on your course Web page your advice on various common problems—for example, your standard advice on a common math error. Then your comments can simply send them to the handout or Web page to read your explanation.
- Use a spreadsheet for grading. Find out whether your institution can send you a class list that you can download into a spreadsheet without rekeying all the student names.
- Record your spoken comments. In a recent workshop, faculty from multiple institutions reported a wide variety of technologies for recording their own voices and sending those words to the student in written or audio form. Check the technologies available in your own systems. The advantage of this method is that you can say more in five minutes than you can write in that time.
- Use e-mail or bulletin boards to help your students respond to each other's work.
- If possible, make yourself quickly accessible by e-mail, text message, discussion board, phone, or voice mail so students can quickly get answers to their questions as they work on their assignments. Answering a question as it comes up may save you later having to write a long explanation on the finished work.

Strategy 13: Keep a Grading Log

Since we are in the grading business, let's take some tips from the business sector. Begin with a "grading audit." Keep a time log in one course for a semester. Jot down what you graded and how much time you spent on it.

Be specific; make sure to record things that matter: one day's online discussion board entries given credit or no credit but no comments in thirty-five minutes, six hard copy journals given comments and a grade in fifty minutes, twenty-four objective tests graded in seventy-five minutes at home, forty-five minutes looking for the quizzes, or thirty-five minutes each way driving in to grade posters at school. Make sure to record the date for each entry.

Now you are ready for a time management analysis. Data (not feelings) reveal that you spent fourteen hours making, giving, and grading makeups. You evaluate journals extensively three times in the semester at weeks 6, 10, and 14 for your class of eighteen students. Your grading times were nine, seven, and eight hours, respectively, for a total of twenty-four hours.

The next business step is to do a cost-benefit study. You now realize you are spending forty hours on makeups and journals—in other words, an *entire* business workweek grading those two assignments! What can you do?

Let's start with makeups. Can you refuse to give makeups and instead take the average of the student's other work as the grade for the missing final? Or how about giving all the makeups for your course on a single time at the end of the semester? It would greatly reduce the time you spend in arranging, proctoring, and rescheduling your own work, and it does not hurt the deserving students because they are already learning for the long haul. If you teach a lab-oriented course with many different sections in your department, like anatomy, chemistry, or sign language, get together with your colleagues and work out a plan to handle all absentees by offering only one departmental makeup in that topic area. Rotate the job of giving the practical, and all of you will save valuable time.

Journals can be very meaningful to the students and rewarding to faculty to read. But, if you spend twenty-four hours of your valuable grading time on journals that count only 5 percent of the grade, the cost-benefit ratio is a little shaky. It's even shakier if you have not guided the journals effectively, so students are generating pages of superficial or careless writing, which you then must read. You could make the journals worth 15 percent and guide them more effectively. You could allow students to use their journals on quizzes, then use the quizzes as the grades and just read the journals, commenting but no longer needing to grade them. At what point in the semester do students profit most from your comments and grades on journals? Why spend ten hours on the last journal entries that get returned at the final, when your comments will probably never be read or used? Instead, you could ask students to select and circle their four best journal entries and write a final reflective statement at the end of week 12. You can read the four best entries and the final statement, check to see that other required journal entries are present, get the journals back to the students in week 13, and celebrate their accomplishments.

Activity

- Review this chapter, and list the suggestions you think you could use.
- Work out the details of one of your ideas.
- Discuss your ideas with peers and with students, and revise them as needed.
- Start your grading log.

Chapter 8
Calculating Course Grades

A MODEL FOR CALCULATING course grades is not just a mathematical formula; it is an expression of your values and goals, because different models express different relationships among types of student performance and have different effects on how students perceive the reward system in the course. Your model for weighting various components also communicates to your students what you think is most important and where you want them to put their effort.

Grading Models

It is worthwhile to consider the three models presented in this chapter and to choose thoughtfully among them. For each model, we present an example and a description. Models differ in their accommodation to students' development after a weak beginning and in whether they allow students to substitute high performance in one area for a low performance in another. At the end of the chapter, we discuss issues such as extra credit, contract learning, curving, grade distributions, and, most important, steps you can take to make grading go smoothly for you.

Imagine you are planning a 200-level course. You decide to give the following assignments:

- Three in-class essay tests on different topics, but the cognitive skills required are similar.
- A comprehensive final consisting of an essay calling for synthesis and fifteen key concept multiple-choice items.
- A field study project requiring that students pose a question, collect information, analyze it, apply course concepts, and design an action plan.
- Class participation (not just attendance) is required, and you want to reward it.

You are operating in a letter-grade-only system and your selected point range is A = 90 and above, B = 80 to 89, C = 70 to 79, D = 69 to 60, and F = below 60. Let's look at the options under our first two models.

Model 1: Weighted Letter Grades
Numerical Values

Tests—average letter grade = 40 percent of course grade

Field project letter grade = 30 percent of course grade

Final exam letter grade = 20 percent of course grade

Class participation grade = 10 percent of course grade

Characteristics

- The underlying pedagogical assumption is that several kinds of performances are distinct from one another and that they are differentially valued in calculating the final evaluation.
- Student performances in various categories are kept separate: for example, tests are separate from the field project. This separation tends to erase or minimize variances of performance within a single category. A student who has scored a high F average on tests has F as 40 percent of his or her grade; a student who has scored a low F average on tests also has F as 40 percent of his or her grade.
- Different kinds of excellence are differently valued. For example, if class participation counts as only 10 percent of the grade and a field research project counts as 30 percent, the very best class participator can only slightly influence his or her overall grade by stellar performance in class participation. However, the very best field project researcher can much more heavily influence his or her final grade.
- The teacher can assign various academic values and criteria in deciding how heavily to count each type of work.

Classroom Example

Tests: average letter grade (40 percent of course grade)	B
Field project letter grade (30 percent of course grade)	B
Final exam letter grade (20 percent of course grade)	C
Class participation grade (10 percent of course grade)	B
Student course grade	B

Model 2: Accumulated Points

Numerical Values

	Numeric Values
Tests	0–40 points
Field project	0–30 points
Final exam	0–20 points
Class participation	0–10 points

Characteristics

- The underlying pedagogical assumption is that to some extent at least, points are points. Poor performance in one area can be offset by good work in any of the other areas; the grade is simply determined by the sum of all points.
- This model is developmental in the sense that poor performance early in the course is not necessarily crippling if the student earns enough points over the course of the semester.
- This model allows students to decide to some extent where to put their effort. Just as students who make a poor start may be working very hard at the end, others may accumulate enough points for their desired grade in your course by the thirteenth week and then put their energy into other courses. This may affect class preparation or participation at the end of the course.

Let's look at grade calculations for two students using a grading scale of A = 90 and above, B = 80 to 89, C = 70 to 79, D = 69 to 60, F = below 60.

Classroom Example

	Student 1	Student 2
Tests (possible 40 points)	23 points	15 points
Field project (possible 30)	25 points	25 points
Final exam (possible 20)	15 points	15 points
Class participation (possible 10)	8 points	8 points
Total (100 points)	71 points	63 points
Grade	C	D

Both students did poorly on the tests. If points had been translated into letter grades, both would have received an F test grade. Both students did equally well on all the other categories. In the *weighted letter grades system*, they would have received the same course grade. However, in the *accumulated points system*, the fact that student 1 got more points on the tests than student 2 allowed student 1 to accumulate enough points to pass the course with a C, whereas student 2 made a D, which in many cases (such as teacher certification, credit for a course in the student's major, or certificate programs) will require that the student retake the entire course.

Model 3: Multiple Category System
Numerical Values

To get a particular course grade, the student must meet or exceed the standards for each category of work. Table 8.1 illustrates a course where there

TABLE 8.1

Multiple Category Grading Scheme for Graded Work and Pass-Fail Work

Course Grade	Graded Work	Pass-Fail Work
A	A average	Pass for 90 percent or more of assignments
B	B average	Pass for 83 percent or more of assignments
C	C average	Pass for 75 percent or more of assignments
D	D average	Pass for 65 percent or more of assignments

are two distinct categories of work: graded work and pass-fail work.

If a student gets an A average on graded work but earns a pass for only 65 percent of the pass-fail work, she receives a D for her course grade because D is the highest level at which she meets or exceeds the standards for both graded and pass-fail work.

Characteristics

- The underlying pedagogical assumption is that different categories of work are important, and the teacher does not want to allow one to compensate for the other in any way. For example, Walvoord uses this system in a literature class where students are required to bring to class, nearly every day, writing assignments based on their readings. She uses these writing assignments as the basis of class discussion, much as Breihan the historian does. Walvoord does not grade these assignments other than pass-fail. However, being prepared for class most of the time is a nonnegotiable and very important value to Walvoord. Thus, her definition of an A student is one who not only does well on tests and exams but also is prepared for class at least 90 percent of the time. If a student is habitually unprepared for class, no brilliance on tests and papers can raise that student to an A grade in Walvoord's system, because the student has not conformed to Walvoord's definition of an A student. But Walvoord also does not want to let students' class participation raise their grade beyond what they are able to achieve in their formal tests and papers.
- The multiple categories system is possible also when you give grades rather than pass-fail to every category.

For example, a science teacher may want to require that for an A grade in the course, the student score at least an A minus average on the tests and exams and at least B minus average on the lab reports:

Course grade	Tests and Exams	Lab Reports
A	A average	B average
B	B average	C average
C	C average	D average
D	D average	D average

- Again, there are two distinct categories of work, and the teacher values both. Performance in one is in no way a substitute for performance in another.
- A multicategory grading system must be carefully and thoroughly explained to students because it is not as common as the other models. Put your policy clearly in writing in the syllabus and on the assignment sheets, and explain it several times in class. Students will tend to assume that you will combine or average their grades in the various categories. It may appear to them that you are awarding them the grade determined by their lowest performance, and they may complain that they were knocked down to the lowest grade. Walvoord patiently explains, in answer, that they were not knocked down to their lowest grade; the system is not conceived that way. What they did was fail to meet her definition of the higher grade. A basketball player must both drop the ball into the basket and follow the dribbling and traveling rules. If any of these conditions is not met, the basket doesn't count.

Penalties and Extra Credit

The teacher may modify any of these grading systems with penalties or extra credit. A penalty occurs when, for example, the teacher lowers the grade a certain amount for infractions such as handing in late work or failing to edit carefully for grammar and punctuation. Extra credit refers to any work that is open to all students but not required of them, by which an instructor allows the student to influence a grade.

Characteristics

- Penalties place a premium on punishment for infractions. This calls the students' attention to the seriousness of the infraction. It is perhaps best used for matters about which the teacher feels strongly or which the teacher knows will carry a heavy penalty in the outside world.

- Being docked often inspires the pugilistic instincts of human beings, and students are likely to contest such penalties. Alternately, the penalties may be demoralizing to the students. Thus, a penalty system should be used with care. The teacher should make extra efforts to convey that although the work is being penalized, the teacher still respects the student, appreciates what she has achieved, and believes she can do better in the future.

- Additions such as extra credit are useful in situations where the teacher wants to let the students compensate for failures in one area by extra work in another one. In this sense, extra credit, used with any model, can enhance opportunities for the student to substitute work in one area for work in another.

Establishing Ceilings and Floors

In any of these systems, it is possible to establish ceilings or floors. For example, you can say that extra credit can raise the grade by only one letter, or in the multiple categories system, you can say that the student will be awarded only one grade below his or her test grades, no matter how little of the pass-fail work she or he has done. Such strategies help to blunt or extend some of the qualities of a grading system.

Developmental Versus Unit-Based Approaches

Within any of the systems mentioned earlier, you can work from a developmental or a unit-based approach. In the developmental approach, the student's work at the end of the course is assumed to demonstrate the stage she or he has reached and is counted much more heavily than earlier work, leaving lots of room for early failures and slow starts. In such a system, for example, a cumulative final exam or project may count very heavily or may even be the only official grade, with earlier work given unofficial grades or not graded at all.

The drawback to this system is that students may slack off in the earlier weeks, believing they can gain the golden ring at the end by a final spurt of energy. Another consideration is that some students will be uncomfortable or unhappy because so much weight is placed on final work. They want a more solid fix on how they are doing early in the course. Also, students may want credit for high-quality early work.

The unit-based approach considers that the course is composed of discrete units, each of which counts. Thus, the grade on the first unit test may be as heavily weighted or almost as heavily weighted as the grade on the final unit, because all units are important in and of themselves. This approach minimizes the developmental aspect—the notion that the student grows in ability and that early failures are less important than final achievement.

A middle ground is to count all tests and major assignments heavily but to allow the student to drop his or her lowest grade. However, be sure that students are responsible for all required knowledge. For example, if you are part of a faculty team that prepares nursing students for licensure exams, you can allow students to drop their lowest quiz grade, but the material should appear again on the final exam to ensure that the student has gone back and mastered it. Another middle ground is to count the final work somewhat more heavily than earlier work. Also, you can hold back a "fudge factor" of 10 percent or so that you can award students whose work shows major improvement over the semester. Or you may simply announce in the syllabus and orally to the class that you reserve the right to raise a grade when the student's work shows great improvement over the course of the semester.

Grading Drafts

Some faculty members do not grade drafts. The advantage of that system is that the draft is not intended to be judged as a final work. The problem with that system is getting students to put enough effort into a draft so responding to it is worth your time. For that reason, some faculty award grades or points to drafts, using one of several policies:

- Grade the draft, and count that grade separately from the grade on the revised version. Usually the draft grade weighs less or is worth fewer points in the course grade than the final version of the paper. This system allows the student to get as high a grade on the revision as possible, even if the draft earned a very low grade, but it also rewards the student for submitting a high-quality draft. The disadvantage is that the student may make a critical mistake in the draft, and then spend wasted time polishing it, in a case where a low-investment draft would have allowed the teacher to intervene before too much time and effort had gone down the drain.
- Grade the draft, and allow a revision to raise the grade by only one level, or average the draft grade and the revision grade. This system places even higher value on handing in a high-quality draft.

- Grade the draft, but allow a revision to completely replace the draft grade. This system shows students where their draft lies on the grading scale, which many students want to know, yet it offers complete opportunity to amend a weak draft without penalty.

- Require the draft to be handed in, but do not grade it. If the draft is not submitted on time, the student forfeits the right to submit the final paper, resulting in an F for the assignment. If the student does hand in the draft on time, it receives comments but no grade. This system emphasizes process: the student has to work through a draft stage in a timely way. The advantage of withholding a grade on drafts is that the student is forced to attend to the comments without calculating grades or points. Some students may be anxious if they do not get a grade, or they may deceive themselves about the seriousness of the draft's shortcomings.

- Respond to drafts of several assignments without grading them. At the end of the course, have students choose their two or three strongest papers, revise them, and submit them as a portfolio. The portfolio grade is based on the presence of all the required drafts and the quality of the revised papers. The advantage here is that the student, like many professionals, can abandon a fatally flawed draft or one that just does not gel and spend revision time on the most promising drafts. The disadvantage is that students may not put much work into ungraded drafts, and some students may be anxious that they do not know where they stand on a grade until the very end.

- If an assignment is submitted without meeting a gateway criterion such as meeting the standard for use of edited standard written English, you can hand it back to the student to be fixed and then accept the revision without further penalty for grading on its merits, or you can attach a penalty for having submitted work that does not meet the gateway. For example, the revised work cannot receive more than a C grade. The first of these options allows the student to recoup fully from a gateway failure; the second penalizes students for not meeting a gateway standard. Chapter Four discusses gateway criteria in more detail.

Contract Grading and Contract Learning

The term *contract grading* has now largely been replaced by *contract learning*—an expanded concept, differently framed. Contract learning is not so much a system for encouraging students to choose among various levels of teacher-determined work; rather, it is a way of negotiating with the students, of drawing them into the learning process (Knowles, 1986).

Characteristics of Contract Learning

- Contract learning attempts to maximize student choice and student responsibility.
- Contract learning allows tailoring of work to individual students' needs, learning styles, backgrounds, and goals. Students often have a voice in establishing learning goals and other aspects of the course.
- Contract learning makes explicit the contract-like aspects of any grading system, and it substantially extends and changes the traditional contract. In one sense, all grading systems are contracts. In the traditional system, the teacher establishes the learning goals and the categories of performance. The students assume that if they meet the criteria for a B, they will get a B. In contract learning, the student is invited to help establish the learning goals, standards, and criteria.
- The "contract" in contract learning may have a psychological effect of making the student feel more responsible for doing the work to which she or he aspired. Especially in systems where the teacher discusses with each student what she or he hopes to earn and what work will be done at what level, the personal nature of the contract may be a high motivator for the student.
- Contract learning may take more teacher time; it certainly will change the traditional dynamic of the classroom.

To Curve or Not to Curve

Grading on a curve means that a certain percentage of students receives each grade—for example, 10 percent get A's and so on. Grading on a curve, we believe, introduces dynamics that may be harmful to learning:

- The notion that grades, and the learning they supposedly represent, are a limited commodity dispensed by the teacher according to a statistical formula
- Competition among students for a limited number of high grades— competition that encourages students to keep the other person from learning, lest that other person take one of the precious and limited high grades
- The notion that learning is a demographic characteristic that will show a statistical distribution in a sample population
- The notion that each class is a sample population

- A teacher's role that focuses on awarding a limited number of grades by a formula rather than a role that includes rewarding all learning with the grade it deserves
- The possibility that standards for a grade will be lowered to enable a certain percentage of students to receive that grade

Instead of these dynamics, we recommend communicating to your class that learning often happens most richly from collaboration within a community of learners. You want learners to help each other (in legitimate ways), contribute their best ideas to class discussion, and work effectively in groups and teams, as they often will have to do in their future lives. You want them to believe that they and their classmates can be rewarded for outstanding effort and achievement. You want to be free to help and encourage all of them to their highest possible levels of achievement. Furthermore, we recommend setting standards for student work that represent your best judgment of what they need to know and of what they can achieve with their best effort and your best teaching.

Faculty sometimes tell us that they fear a political problem with the policy we recommend. When teachers teach well, coach students through the learning process, motivate them strongly, and facilitate learning in highly successful ways, students will learn more. So shouldn't they get higher grades? But if they get higher grades, will the professor's department head or dean or colleagues disapprove? Tough question. Unfortunately, we have no perfect answers.

One suggestion, though, is that before you assume that you cannot follow our recommendations about grading, you should find out exactly what the constraint on your grading is. Which forces motivate the person (department head, dean, colleagues) you think is imposing the constraint? Have a frank talk with that person. Ask if there is an expectation about the distribution of grades. If the person responds in the affirmative, probe politely but firmly to find out why the person wants your grades to fall within a certain distribution. Do not exaggerate the constraint. We have heard faculty talk as though they were being forced to grade on a curve, when in fact the only real constraint was that they not give too many A grades or too many F grades. Once you understand the worries that are influencing your department head or dean and the real constraints that are operating, perhaps you can work out a solution that both meets your and your department head's needs and enhances student learning and motivation.

Once you understand the constraints, you might consider one approach or a combination of several. One response to the criticism that your grades are too high is to raise your standards. You limit the number of A grades not by a statistical formula but rather by setting the standards sufficiently high that even with your brilliant teaching, getting an A takes special effort and talent. Raising the standards for an A may be all that is required. In many situations, it does not matter to the department head or dean how many B grades you give; after all, B is the national average grade. Teachers we know who follow this pattern save the A grade for truly outstanding work that, realistically, not many students can achieve, but the teacher's careful, interactive guidance and instruction create a setting in which many students who work hard get B grades.

If the constraint limits the number of D and F grades you can give, try working especially hard with students who are having difficulty. Try to understand what will motivate and help them rather than lower your standards.

A final way to meet criticism of your grade distribution is to offer to show the critic your assignments, tests, criteria, and standards for each grade and samples of student work at each level. If your critics are willing to look at your students' work, then you have initiated a dialogue about standards that may benefit both you and the department.

Grade Inflation

The meaning of a grade is socially determined. You have to teach and grade within the grading system as it is currently interpreted in the society that you and your students inhabit, and you have to teach and grade the students you have now, not the ones you wish you had, or the ones you had in 1985, or the ones you had when you were a teaching assistant at Berkeley. Check with colleagues who are teaching the same course as you are. Would the students who receive D or F in your class get higher grades in all of your colleagues' classes? If so, you are running a different currency system from the one in which you live. It's as if you tried to float Confederate dollars in Nebraska or tried to insist that a dollar has the same value now that it did in 1985. Grade inflation (whether an academic reality or artificially induced by the fact that D and F students can now drop courses in week 13) is a major national problem, but it can be addressed only on a national level, not by individuals working alone.

Like Coffee to Go, Shopping Carts, and Investment Portfolios

Everything seems to come with warnings these days: "Hot coffee is hot," "Do not leave child unattended in shopping cart," and "Stock values are subject to change." So let us offer this grading advice: Grading policies are different in different places. So please discuss your grading criteria, standards, and practices with your department head, especially in your first years at a new institution or when a new department head arrives. You need not ask his or her permission for decisions that should rightly be in your control, but you can talk with him or her in a spirit of consultation and information. Your department chair is the person first in line to listen and communicate with students if they complain about your grading practices. When those things happen, you want the department head to remember that you stopped in to discuss your syllabus, course plans, grading strategies, and commitment to meaningful student learning.

Activity

1. Jot down the most important things you want your course grading system to accomplish for you and for your students. You might use the following outline or devise one of your own:

   A. In this course, I want to allow good work in one area to compensate for poor work in another area.
   - Yes (consider the accumulated points model)
   - No (consider the definitional model)
   - To some extent (consider the weighted averages model)

   B. The work in this course is:
   Developmental: What the student has achieved by the end is far more important than early failures or slow starts (consider developmental approaches to your chosen model)
   Unit based: Each unit is important; units are not highly cumulative; there is no final exam or project that measures students' total achievement (consider unit-based approaches to your chosen model)

   C. My students are most powerfully motivated by a grading system that (you may check more than one):
   - Gives early, firm grades and rewards strong work no matter where it appears in the semester (consider the unit-based approach)
   - Allows early failure and slow starts (consider the developmental approach)
   - Allows a great deal of individual flexibility, student choice, and student participation in establishing expectations (consider the contract learning approach)

2. Construct a grading system for your course. Discuss it with colleagues and students. Modify as needed.

Chapter 9

Communicating with Students About Their Grades

CONVERSATIONS WITH STUDENTS about their grades can be difficult, time-consuming, or even contentious at times, but they are critical in shaping a healthy level of trust and motivation in your classroom. This chapter offers principles and guidelines for those conversations.

Principle 1: Make Grading Part of Learning

Grading should emerge as part of the learning process within a well-designed, assignment-centered course. Course goals are clear, tests and assignments help students reach those goals, student work is evaluated by clear criteria known ahead of time, teaching is interactive, and students receive ongoing feedback about their work. Following the strategies of Chapter Two, on establishing learning goals and major assignments, and Chapters Five and Six, on choosing meaningful learning experiences, will create a healthy context for your responses to student work.

Principle 2: Respect your Students

When communicating with students about their grades, avoid the assumption that they are all "grade-mongers." Listen carefully, appeal to their highest motivations, invite their input, and respect them as people who want to learn—perhaps in confused and limited ways, perhaps with mixed motivations, but nevertheless want to learn. This attitude of listening, dialogue, and respect undergirds all the suggestions in this chapter. Resource 9.1 lists works about establishing communication and trust in the classroom.

The following pages offer practical suggestions to guide communication with your students about their work and their grades and to help you establish a healthy level of trust and motivation in your classroom.

Resource 9.1 Sources for Establishing Good Student-Faculty Communication

Blumberg (2009). Chapter Seven, "Purposes and Processes of Assessment," discusses the role of grading in learner-centered teaching.

Boice (1996). Based on empirical observation of teachers, offers principles for faculty success, including specific suggestions about how to establish good communication in the classroom. See especially Boice's first principle.

Brookfield (2006). Chapter Ten, "Giving Helpful Evaluations," offers practical advice about grading and commenting within the context of a classic book about building trust and responsiveness in the classroom.

Palmer (1983, 1987, 1990, 1993, 2007). Inspiring work about being authentically present to one's self, one's students, and one's subject.

Paulsen and Feldman (1995). Reviews the literature and offers suggestions about communicating with students. (See the section titled "Listening to the Voice of Students," pp. 53–66, which focuses on collecting helpful written and oral student evaluations.)

Weimer (2002). Chapter Six, "The Purposes and Processes of Evaluation," discusses how faculty can shift their evaluation practices to be more learner centered.

Creating an Effective Syllabus

The well-wrought syllabus communicates enthusiasm for the discipline and welcomes the community of learners. It articulates what students will be able to know and do on successful completion of the course. The syllabus shows how the assignments and exams help students to learn and demonstrate their learning. It shows how in-class and out-of-class activities help students meet the standards for high-quality work. The syllabus is more than a content outline, time schedule, and list of the percentages that each piece of work will contribute to the final grade.

Articulate Connections Among Goals, Assignments, and Grades

A syllabus should make explicit the connections among goals, assignments, and grades. For example, a syllabus that Walvoord constructed for a course titled The Outsider in Modern American Fiction announced course goals on its front page, as "What You Can Learn in This Course":

- Familiarity with a body of well-known modern fiction
- The ability to analyze fiction orally and in writing using the tools of the discipline
- Particularly, the ability to analyze the role of the "outsider" in fiction
- Enjoyment of reading fiction as a life-long habit

Then, in a section labeled "How the Course Will Help You Learn These Things," a few paragraphs explained how the course was organized to help students achieve the learning goals.

In the part of the syllabus that contained the daily schedule of activities, each unit of the course announced the goals for that particular unit, all of which related to the general course goals. Under the unit title and goals was the daily schedule of events for the weeks within that unit, including preparation for class and a description of in-class activities (An excerpt is in Exhibit 9.1.)

Explain What Each Grade Represents

Within the context of this learning process, present the criteria and standards for grading student work on each assignment (see Chapter Four).

EXHIBIT 9.1

Portion of the Syllabus for Walvoord's Literature Class

Unit 2: First-Person Accounts by Outsiders

Goals

- To become familiar with some major American fiction that is written as a first-person account by an "outsider"
- To analyze this fiction orally and in writing, using the tools of literary analysis, particularly focusing on symbolism, plot, and allegory
- To analyze orally and in writing the role of the "outsider" in this fiction
- To enjoy reading, discussing, and writing

Day	Preparation	In Class
Tues 3/3	Read Prologue and Chapters 1–7 of Ellison's *Invisible Man* (2 hours). To help you analyze plot, symbol, and allegory, write the following (1 hour): [list of three questions about the novel]. Bring your writing to class for discussion. Hand in; pass-fail.	1. Manuel López: report on Tuskegee Institute. (5 min.) 2. Ruth Harrison: What is lobotomy? (1 min.) 3. Clear up basic questions about the novel. 4. Discuss plot, allegory, symbolism. 5. In-class freewrite: discuss your reactions to the novel so far. Share. (5 min.) 6. Discussion: What do you think will happen next in the novel? Why?

EXHIBIT 9.2

Walvoord's Syllabus Explanation of Grades

Because we are a learning community, in which everyone's contribution is important to construct our understanding of the literature, your final course grade will consist of two parts: one part for your written essays and one part for your class preparation and participation. Both parts are important. You cannot use excellence in class discussion to compensate for poor-quality written work or high-quality written work to compensate for poor class participation. The chart below presents the requirements for a course grade. [The handout includes a table similar to Table 8.1, showing what is required for course grades A, B, and so on.]

Explain How Course Grades Will be Calculated

The syllabus should contain an explanation of how course grades will be calculated and a rationale for the method you have chosen (see Chapter Eight). Walvoord had chosen the multiple category system explained in Chapter Eight. Her syllabus explains the calculation of the final course grade in terms of her philosophy (Exhibit 9.2).

Address Academic Honesty and Plagiarism

Your institution's policy on academic honesty and plagiarism should be included in your syllabus or course Web site. This can help guide your students and prevent problems later. O'Brien, Millis, and Cohen (2008) give examples of syllabus statements about academic integrity (pp. 87–90), as well as other kinds of information, such as disability policies, classroom rules for civility, and many other aspects of syllabus design.

Using Class or Online Discussion to Address Grading Issues

In addition to the syllabus and in-class review of the syllabus, you may want to hold classroom or online discussions with your students to establish healthy concepts of grading.

Compose a Plagiarism Contract

In the 300-level science writing course, Anderson feels that since she teaches students arriving from different institutions, different states, different countries, and different sciences, they should have a shared culture of experience in regard to plagiarism. Anderson asks her students to complete and sign a plagiarism contract. The first part of the contract asks students to complete the sentence, "Plagiarism is . . . " Anderson asks students to individually write in their answers and then asks several students to read their answers. The class formulates a working definition of plagiarism, and each student edits his or her answer. Then students talk briefly about how to answer the question, "To avoid plagiarism, I will cite . . . " Anderson synthesizes students' answers and instructs them to list the things they must cite: words, ideas, images of any kind, and patterns of organization. Then each student signs and dates his or her contract.

Later, students submit this contract with their library research position paper. Anderson finds that nonthreatening discussion, a group working definition, and the close proximity of this document have practically eliminated plagiarism on this paper.

Discuss the Roles of Grades

It pays to ask students how they think grades are useful to the classroom. Their answers will probably touch on some points mentioned in Chapter One: grades are an evaluation, a communication, a basis for motivation, a way of organizing the course, and a basis for reflection and self-analysis. Difficulty between teachers and their students over grades may arise from three additional roles that students often assign to grades but that teachers often resist:

- Reward for effort
- Ticket to upward mobility
- A purchased item that has been paid for

It does little good to deny or ignore these three roles because students' experience is that grades do function in these ways. We therefore suggest that teachers and students communicate about the roles they envision for grading.

Discuss Fairness

Difficulty may arise around the complex notion of fairness. You need to know what your students think fairness means and talk with them about how to achieve fairness for everyone (including you) in your classroom. One approach is to ask students toward the beginning of the course to describe a class they've had in the past where they thought the grading system was fair and helped them learn well; then they should describe a class in which the grading system was unfair and interfered with their learning. You will learn a lot this way about your students' definition of fairness and about how they think grades will contribute to their learning.

Responding to Student Work

When you get to the point of responding, orally or in writing, to students' work, the suggestions in Chapter Seven will help you make the responding process time-efficient. The suggestions in this chapter concern the tone and content of your discussion with students about their grades and their work.

Save Your Comments for the Teachable Moment

A teacher's response to early stages of an assignment often reaches the student in a more teachable moment than comments on a final paper do. When you're responding to work in progress, it's easier to nurture students' growth. You're trying to praise the student for making progress, indicate what yet needs to be done, and give advice to the student about how to do those things. By contrast, when you're responding to finished work, you can easily slip into the autopsy mode of describing why the paper is bad. You find yourself trying to justify the grade and to keep students' grade complaints out of your office.

Sometimes, however, response to the final, finished work can be motivating and applicable to the student. For example, Anderson holds individual conferences with the seniors in her class, using her rubric to go over their completed scientific research reports in detail—a process she believes is valuable to them because it forms a bridge to the work settings they will shortly enter as newly hired scientists, perhaps conducting similar kinds of experimentation.

Speak to the Learner, Not the Error

When we, as teachers, are sitting alone with a student's work in front of us, it's easy to imagine that our primary relationship is with the product, particularly with the errors in the product. We may imagine that our chief responsibility is not to let any errors pass our desk unmarked. In reality, the most important relationship is between us and the learner. The grade is a communication, and it must communicate to a person who can use it for learning. Our chief responsibility is to help this learner move forward. So ask yourself, *What does this learner need from me at this time?* Then shape your comments accordingly.

One common trap for teachers is to focus on justifying the grade. When justifying the grade, teachers tend to focus on describing how the paper is bad: it's poorly organized, lacks evidence, uses the wrong equation, and so on. The underlying message is, *Here's why this paper did not get a higher grade; please do not come to my office to ask me why you didn't get an A.* But when we keep in mind our aim to teach, we tend to focus on what the student has achieved and what might yet be achieved.

For example, consider a comment that Breihan made on a student essay draft in his history course on Western civilization (see Chapter Two). The assignment had asked students, based on their study of sixteenth- and seventeenth-century European governments, to recommend a form of government that would avoid anarchy and bloody revolution for a hypothetical country called Loyoliana. Before you read the actual comment, some background will set the scene. In this case, the student received back from Breihan the grading sheet in Exhibit 4.2 with a circle around the statement that best described the paper draft. In addition, Breihan gave the student the handwritten piece of scratch paper on which he had attempted to outline the draft as he read. If the outlining process broke down, there was clear evidence to the student that the teacher could not follow the organization of the essay. In addition to those two items, Breihan typed on his computer this comment to the student's draft:

Mr. Carter:

This essay puts forward a very clear thesis that a "strong government" is needed to end anarchy. After reviewing several alternatives, you end by saying that a mixed government on the English model would work best for Loyoliana.

What is missing here is argument and evidence in favor of the thesis that you state so clearly. Why would this system work so well? Have you any specific evidence? What about the arguments of Paine, Bossuet, etc.? What about the fact that the Hanoverian kings were not strong? That England had no written constitution?

In revising this, you should try to provide more evidence for your arguments and try to answer these counterarguments.

Notice that Breihan takes the time to reflect on and respond to what the student said. It is almost like a professional article, where the author begins by summarizing what other writers on the subject have said. Breihan's comment communicates his respect for the student as a person with a position on an issue rather than primarily a maker of errors. The comment acknowledges what has been achieved. Then Breihan suggests what the student can do to improve the essay.

Be the Transparent Reader

It is tempting to comment on students' work by adjectives that describe the work: *confusing, awkward, unclear, unsupported, illogical*. We call this the *judge role*—and we recommend that you consider a different approach. Long ago, Walvoord remembers, the Natural History Museum in Chicago exhibited a life-size woman's body made of transparent plastic, so the viewer could see inside to the beating heart, the alimentary canal, the lungs inflating and deflating. The *transparent reader* is a very useful role when you are responding to students' work. You can stick to the transparent reader alone or combine it with advice about how to affect the reader. Note in the following comments that the transparent reader describes her reading experience ("I got confused") and also explains why she had that experience:

Judge

"Confusing"

Transparent Reader

"I got confused here because I didn't understand how this paragraph related to the previous one."

"At this point, I thought about Huffington's work and wondered why you didn't reference it."

"Here, I didn't believe you because you made a claim without evidence."

"I felt irritated because of your consistent misuse of the apostrophe."

Transparent Reader Plus Advice Giver

"I got confused here because I didn't understand how this paragraph related to the previous one. You could state the relationship more clearly in the first sentence of the paragraph. Or perhaps the ideas in this paragraph belong on page 3 after the section on causes?"

Notice that even in the role of advice giver, the teacher may suggest more than one remedy for the problem, as in the example. The basic principle is that you should stay at the transparent reader level as much as possible. You are not fixing the paper; you are coaching the writer. You are working to build the student's abilities for self-critique and using reader response to move forward. (Further suggestions about responding to student work can be found in Anderson and Speck, 1998; Brookfield, 2006; and Speck, 2000.)

Communicate Priorities

When a student receives a draft on which the teacher has marked grammar and phrasing heavily in the margins and also written at the end that the draft is not well organized, needs better evidence, or some other large-scale concern, the student is receiving a contradictory message. Since students often revise by trying to fix the paper locally, they are tempted to ignore or underemphasize the final, global comment and instead revise by trying to fix the first passage the teacher has marked, then the second passage, and so on. They never fully deal with the global comment, which would require more reading or restructuring of the entire piece—which, in other words, would render many of the marginal comments irrelevant.

Our own study (Walvoord and Breihan, 1990) and that of others (Sommers, 1982) suggest that when a paper is in deep trouble with its conceptualization, organization, evidence, and similar global matters, teachers should communicate only those concerns and not confuse the learner with surface issues. Make clear to students, however, that issues such as phrasing, computation, labeling of graphics, grammar, and so on are crucially important and must be addressed at their proper time, even though at the moment you are not focusing on them.

Consider Face-to-Face Response

Do not assume that writing is the only medium for commenting. Consider face-to-face responses also. Teachers often believe that face-to-face comments will take too much time, and perhaps they will. But Walvoord and others can handle a draft of a five- to ten-page paper in a fifteen-minute student conference, which is about as much time as Walvoord would take at home to write comments on the paper.

One way to make time for face-to-face response is to hold individual or small-group conferences instead of class on a given week. Walvoord passes around in class (or places on the course's electronic bulletin board) an appointment sheet that lists enough fifteen-minute slots for all her students, plus a few extra slots. These slots include all the class hours, plus some additional hours, during a single week. Each student signs up for a time slot. The sign-up sheet is then posted on Walvoord's office door and the course's electronic bulletin board. Walvoord's policy is to tell students that if they do not come to their appointment on time, with the requisite draft, they will forfeit the right to turn in the revised paper, which results in an F paper. (Of course, in case of illness or emergency, new arrangements will be made.) The result of this policy is that students take the draft conference very seriously, and almost no one misses it.

During the week of conferences, Walvoord sits in her office seeing students in fifteen-minute slots (giving herself a ten-minute break every hour or so). If you try to read the drafts ahead of time and then hold the conference, you will perish under the workload. The only way to make this system work efficiently is to look at the draft right there on the spot, in front of the student who has brought the draft with her. The draft has to be word-processed, so

Walvoord can read it more quickly (typos are okay). Walvoord asks students to bring two copies of the draft: one for the student to write on during the conference and to take away at the end and the other for Walvoord to keep.

Walvoord's first move is to ask the student, "Where are you, and what do you think you need help with?" Students often have quite an accurate idea of where they are, and in this case, the conference may be short. If Sara, for example, knows what she needs to do, Walvoord can just reinforce her ideas and send her on her way. If Tim does not know where he is, Walvoord has a chance to read the paper and identify where the major problems lie. She doesn't comment on everything but identifies the problems that need immediate attention and gets the student working on them.

Make clear to your students, in writing, orally in class, and again in the conference, that this is not a conference where their papers will be fixed or where you will say everything there is to say. Rather, you are dipping in at a particular point in the growth of the paper to offer a few suggestions about where the student needs to go. Tell students you expect the paper to grow in ways you cannot predict.

Walvoord does not write on the drafts, but instead asks the student to take notes (have paper and pen ready for students who do not bring their own). After the conference, Walvoord jots for herself just a few phrases about what she suggested, so she will remember later what she said.

Hold back a few unpublished appointment times so that if a student needs more time or needs to come back, you can schedule that appointment. If there is a major problem, such as suspected plagiarism, and you don't want to handle it on the spot, it's perfectly okay to tell the student that you need more time to read and think about the paper and then to reschedule a later appointment.

Guide Peer Response

An alternative to the individual conferences is to have students meet with you in groups of four or five. In the group meeting, which lasts an hour or a class period, students read their work and receive responses from their classmates in addition to yours.

Some teachers have students respond to one another's work in small groups without the teacher present. The success of this method depends on four factors:

1. You have provided clear, written criteria and clear instructions for student response.

2. You are available for support if the students need you. Some of them will want your response no matter what the group says. Walvoord

offers to meet individually during her office hours with anyone who wants her response, but only after the group has responded.

3. Students have practiced and use the transparent reader approach, describing but not judging, what they see in each other's work. Exhibit 9.3 is a

---

EXHIBIT 9.3

Walvoord's Guidelines for Group Response to Drafts

1. Before handing out copies of the draft, the author reads aloud the first paragraph of the paper. The group then tells the author what they think the main point of the paper is and how they expect the paper to develop.
2. The author hands out copies of the draft to each group member.
3. The author reads the paper aloud.
4. Allow two to three minutes of silence for group members to digest the paper and gather their thoughts.
5. Group members then, in turn, voice their reactions to these questions:

- State the main point of the paper in a single sentence. Who do you think is the audience for the paper? What is the paper's purpose?
- What are the major subpoints for the paper? (In other words, outline it.)
- Which aspects did you like best about the paper?
- Were there any points at which you were confused about the subject or focus of the paper or its sections?
- Consider each section of the paper in turn. Is each developed with enough detail, evidence, and information?
- Is there material you think the author should add?
- Are the opening and concluding paragraphs accurate guides to the paper's theme and focus?
- Considering the paper paragraph by paragraph, what seems most vivid, clear, and memorable? Where does the language seem especially effective? Where did you find it awkward or unclear?
- What would an opponent of the author's position say? Has the author accurately represented and responded to the most telling points of the opponent?

Guidelines for the Writer

- Do not argue with the readers, and do not explain what you meant. You are gathering information about audience response, so simply gather it. If a particular response does not seem useful, you are free to ignore it in revising your paper. But for you to spend the group's time arguing and explaining is wasteful, and it can result in the group's getting focused on understanding what you meant rather than on reacting to what you wrote.
- It is usually productive for you to remain silent, taking careful notes about what the readers say.

   In addition, you may want to:
- Ask a reader to clarify or expand on a statement, so you understand it thoroughly.
- Ask readers to respond to an idea you have for improving some aspect of the paper they're unhappy with.
- Repeat back to the group what you think they're saying just to make sure communication is accurate.

guide that Walvoord uses for students in a first-year composition class to respond to one another's work.

4. Students have a chance to reflect on group process. For example, at the end of the group meeting, each person in the group might thank the classmate who gave him or her the most help. That strategy tends to make very clear to the group that writers often count explicit criticism as the most helpful feedback.

Communicating About Grade Challenges and Plagiarism

The conversations that every teacher dreads are those with students who contest their grades or get involved in plagiarism. The guiding principle for such conversations is to focus on what you want the student to learn. Events with high emotional content remain long in memory. Your student may remember for the rest of her life the tough conversations you have with her about grades and plagiarism. Stay calm and focused, and concentrate on the learning.

Students Who Contest Their Grades

If a student questions his or her grade, there are two issues: the grade and the learner:

- Should the grade be changed in order to preserve fairness?
- What is going on with this student, and what kinds of help might she or he really need?

You will be addressing both of these issues simultaneously, but with different tactics. When the student first complains about the grade, you can listen and observe the learner. Do not defend the grade or make a decision about it in this conversation; just gather information about the student. Is the student sober? Does he seem distressed? Are there situations in his life that may be leading him to this challenge? Try to find out why the student is questioning the grade—not why he thinks the grade is wrong, but why he is taking this step of coming to you. This is the first step in the conversation about the student.

The second step is about the grade, and it should be handled in writing. Ask the student to state formally in writing why she thinks her grade is not right, referring to your assignment sheet, rubric, or examples of good papers you have distributed. Thereafter, keep the discussion of whether the grade should be changed, and the reasons for the change, in writing between you and the student. That process slows things down, helps ensure that everyone's response is reasoned and calm, and gives you a chance to think about a response and, if needed, to consult with a trusted colleague or your department chair. Create a paper trail, and save it.

Meanwhile, you may also be talking with your learner about broader issues. Grades, like lightning rods, sometimes funnel strong emotions or serious troubles. You don't have to be a counselor; you can listen sympathetically ("um hm"), reflect back what the student says ("You're feeling really pressured with your job and your course load"), or suggest places to get help ("Are you talking with anyone else about this problem?" "Have you tried the counseling center?"). You can be sympathetic about the situation but unbending about the grade. Those are two different issues, two different negotiations. You may change a grade because you think your original grade was not accurate, but you don't have to give unmerited grades to students, even though their lives are very tough. If you believe your grade was fair, then everything you say should reflect that this is the student's grade, which she earned. It's not the grade you "gave" her. You can say, "I'm sorry that your work did not earn a higher grade," or "I know you are disappointed in the quality of your work."

In both conversations—about the learner and about the grade—be quick to talk to colleagues, your chair, or someone from counseling or student affairs. If the situation seems at all scary or puzzling or if there is any hint of violence (verbal or physical, threatened or actual), sexuality, or accusations about discrimination, favoritism, or sexual harassment, end the conversation at once, get yourself out of any private space where only the two of you are present, make thorough written notes about what was said or done, and get others involved.

Working with Teaching Assistants

If teaching assistants (TAs) are grading student work in your class, you can create an avenue for students to question the TA's grades. One professor who uses TAs for grading tells her students that they may send her any paper graded by a TA, along with a written explanation of why they thought they deserved a different grade. She herself will read the paper and make a decision. She may keep the grade the same or raise it, but she assures the student she will not lower the grade even if she thinks it deserves a lower grade. That makes the process of challenging the grade risk free for the student. She reports that in a class of two hundred, about fifteen students each semester challenge a TA's grade. She uses these challenges as a basis for discussion with her TAs, so they too encounter a learning experience.

Students Who Plagiarize

Giving clear instructions, warnings, and guidelines (for example, Anderson's plagiarism contract described earlier) is the first step in dealing with plagiarism. Then, if you ask to see a proposal, outline, or draft of a student's paper early in the writing process, it is much harder for that student to purchase, download, or copy someone else's work at the last minute. It's also much easier for you to head off a student's innocent misuse of sources.

If you are reviewing a draft you believe has made unethical use of sources, you can state your concerns as a reader's question: "When I read this passage, it doesn't sound like your voice sounds in the rest of the paper. I think a reader would wonder whether this is copied from another source. You never, ever want a reader to have that question, because it leads to suspicion of plagiarism. Let's talk about how you can help a reader trust your use of sources in the paper." If the cheating was intentional, such as using another student's paper or downloading a paper from the Web, you can issue stern warnings, but if it's still a draft, you can handle the situation by requiring the student to submit a revision of the paper, perhaps accompanied by a log of the paper's progress, copies of all sources cited, and a written statement by the student explaining, in her own words, what academic honesty means.

However, if you are reading a final paper, and you suspect it was plagiarized, you first have to try to determine whether it is plagiarized, either by checking the sources yourself or running the paper through an online plagiarism-checking service.

If you are not able to establish for sure that the paper was plagiarized, you can let the matter drop or hold an exploratory conversation with the student. Call him into your office, tell him that you are uneasy with the paper because you think it might have been plagiarized, and ask the student to tell you how the paper was generated. Some students admit their cheating right then. If the student denies plagiarizing, you can believe him, express your regret for any pain that your inquiry caused him, assure him that he will not suffer in any way in your class or in your esteem, and send him on his way. But if you don't believe the denial, you have ways to inquire further. A common technique is to select a passage of the paper, let the student reread it, and then ask some questions that someone who had written the passage himself would know. For example, you can ask for a definition of particular words or phrases. You can ask for further explanation of a particular statement. You can ask the student how he arrived at a particular conclusion. These inquiries may convince you that the paper is plagiarized, or they may elicit a confession from the student.

If you determine that the paper was plagiarized, check with your department chair or faculty handbook to be sure you know your institution's policies. Most likely, the student will receive an F grade, for either the paper or the entire course, and in some cases a report of plagiarism will be entered into the student's record, either temporarily or permanently.

Now you must communicate with the student. Consider the option of having someone else do it. Your chair, a counseling center staff member, or an ombudsperson may be able to request a conference with the student, tell the student what the penalty is, explain the options for grievance proceedings, and then move into a listening and counseling role to try to maximize the learning that occurs for the student. If you're out of the picture, the student cannot turn to presenting excuses or trying to talk you out of the penalty, but has to deal with the penalty as a given and then move forward.

If you decide to hold the conversation yourself, similar guidelines apply as for a student challenging a grade. Focus on what you want the student to learn. Stay calm. Keep the pace slow. If the student seems troubled, depressed, addicted, or desperate, urge her to go to the counseling center. If the student is verbally or physically threatening, end the conversation at once and move away from any place where you and the student are alone together. Be quick to seek help from your chair, a trusted colleague, the counseling center, or the student affairs office. Keep copies of the paper, the assignment, your syllabus statement about plagiarism, and any written exchanges with the student such as e-mails. Take thorough notes about any conversations with the student.

Grades and Student Evaluations

You might wonder whether giving higher or lower grades will affect your student evaluations. That correlation is one of the most highly researched areas of student evaluations. The bottom line is that a teacher cannot buy high student evaluations just by making the course easy or giving high grades. Much more important, it seems, is the way you communicate about the grading system and the respect with which you treat your students around all issues, including grades. The traits that correlate with high student evaluations are students' perceptions that the faculty member is fair, clear, well organized, accessible, friendly, and enthusiastic (Arreola, 2000; Cashin, 1988, 1995; Feldman, 1996).

If you have had a difficult exchange with one or a few students about grades in one of your classes and you are afraid that those students' disgruntled responses might lower your student evaluations, try to get a copy of the actual distribution of scores so that you know how many of your students rated you a 5, 4, 3, 2, or 1 on each survey item. If most students have rated you high, but just one or two have rated you very low, you can point out the disparity and offer an explanation to whoever is evaluating your teaching. (See Seldin and Miller, 2009, for advice about constructing a teaching portfolio.)

Ask for Student Feedback

You can ask students to write anonymously to you about how the grading and responding process helped their learning, what aspects of the process (not the grades themselves) might be changed, and what suggestions they have for you and for themselves. You can collect these responses and share them, in the aggregate, with the class ("Most of you thought that . . . "). This final step in the grading and responding process reinforces the central point: grading should enhance learning.

Activity

- Review the suggestions in this chapter, jotting down several ideas you can use in your own courses.
- Work out the details of one of your ideas.
- Review your plans with a colleague or students. Revise as needed.

Chapter 10

Using the Grading Process to Improve Teaching

"HMMM, THE STUDENTS did well on X, but not so well on Y. Maybe next semester I could . . . " What teacher hasn't said those words? Using the grading process to show you how to improve your teaching is natural. Being systematic can make that process even more productive. This chapter presents three ways, from pragmatic to publishable, that teachers can use course-embedded grading processes to inform and improve their own teaching and, if they wish, share their findings with others.

Divide and Conquer

When you find your students are not producing the kind of academic work you expected on assignments, a rubric can help you convert a big problem into one or more little ones. Anderson's colleague, Cindy Ghent, the coordinator for the 100-level, nonmajors general education biology course at Towson University, shared with Anderson early in 2004 that students did not seem to be improving at reading and interpreting graphic information in lab or lecture as the semester progressed. Ghent volunteered to construct a line graph on incidences of cancers in men and to design a quiz that could elicit the kinds of critical thinking and content application that she and the other instructors wanted.

Ghent gave the quiz, calculated what percentage of the items each student answered correctly, and returned the papers briefly to the sixty or so students. So far, she had a grade for each student and feedback to individual students about what they missed. But using a rubric could help her focus on specific learning goals for improvement. So she collaborated with Anderson. She gathered the papers back from the students, cut off the names, and gave them to Anderson, who scored each paper on a rubric (see example 14 Appendix A). Then they calculated the whole class score for each rubric item (Table 10.1). The average score for each rubric trait gives more detailed, diagnostic information than a pile of more than sixty numerical scores ranging from 51 to 93, the class average on the test, or the A through F grade distribution statistics for the assignment. The rubric scores

TABLE 10.1

Average Student Test Scores for Graphic Information, with 4.0 as the Highest Possible Score

Reading graphic information	3.21
Processing graphic information quantitatively	2.53
Interpreting graphic information	2.95
Making connections between graphic information and scientific issues	2.74

allow you to pinpoint where students are having problems. Considering Table 10.1, which aspect would you work on first?

Ghent and her colleagues saw that students needed to improve their skills in processing graphic information quantitatively. So the faculty who were teaching the course initiated changes such as copying a text graphic and asking students to write what they learned from it, giving practice graphics quizzes, going over the answers and having students calculate their own scores on each trait to see what they needed to work on, using more quantitative questions in lab, and having instructors go over those problems "in action," not just giving students the right answer. Student scores have improved. (Rubrics and data available on request at vanderson@towson.edu.) Most notably, in 2007, Ghent, Gasparich, and Scully published *Biology: The Science of Life Lab Manual.* In this manual, students select and construct their own graphics on blank graph paper pages rather than filling in prefabricated data charts and graphic formats.

The point of this case study is that examining student learning using rubrics can help faculty move from "they're not doing well on graphing" to "we need to work specifically on this particular aspect."

Put the Pieces Together

Using rubrics can help teachers track student performance over time in ways that test scores cannot. Mathematician Steven Dunbar at the University of Nebraska at Lincoln developed a system that allowed him to identify the strengths and weaknesses of his students, both individually and as a group, on specific goals over time (Table 10.2).

You can take any trait that you care about and lay out students' performance in a similar graph to identify whole-class weaknesses and strengths. Then use that analysis to guide your teaching.

TABLE 10.2

Dunbar's Graph of Student Progress in a Math Class

Goal 4: Solve and demonstrate an understanding of a dual problem and its meaning

	Exam 2, Q 14	Exam 2, Q 20	Homework 8, Q 7	Final Exam	Mean for Individual Student
Student 1	75	64	63	80	70
Student 2	64	48	44	74	56
Student 3	91	79	89	85	86
. . .					
Class mean for each question or problem	76	64	65	80	71

Dunbar reports that he has been able to refine the goals for the course and adjust the relative amounts of time spent on various goals based on the record from previous courses. For example, based on class performance records as in Table 10.2, students' averages were lower, and students had greater dispersion, on the problems related to modeling compared with the problems related to deriving the answer from a formulated model. So Dunbar recommended that in a large-enrollment course for senior math and actuarial science majors, more time be spent on mathematical modeling and less time on the algorithmic method used to derive answers from the models. By tracking the progress of individual students on the goals (along a row of the table), Dunbar can deduce whether individual students are having more or less trouble with topics of the course.

The point of this case is that the grading process can be tracked so as to allow the instructor to follow individual students' progress over time and also to identify classwide weaknesses, strengths, and progression.

Analyze Students' Difficulties

Let's flash back to Anderson's original science assignment in which students were to conduct and compose original science research. During the first two years that she taught this course, Anderson had not yet constructed a rubric for the research assignment. She was generally disappointed in the students' reports. She had worked hard to set the students up for success, using these strategies:

- The students had weeks to choose a product to test.
- Students had multiple opportunities to work on parts of the assignment and routine peer conferences in class.
- Earlier in the course, students had visited the library for two sessions to find primary research articles, use key word indexes, and discuss how important it was for scientists to use correct descriptors in their titles so that other researchers could find relevant work in the literature.
- The students had read five appropriately titled scientific journal articles with their abstracts cut off and had written abstracts for them. All of the articles that the students read demonstrated good "sciencing," good writing, and attention to audience, tone and format.

Anderson graded the students' papers holistically both years, using marginal comments, grammar marks, and occasionally end notes. She was much more prescriptive in her comments on the scientific method than in her writing suggestions. During the first two years that she used this assignment, Anderson was generally disappointed in the students' reports.

The next year, Anderson constructed a rubric for the science research assignment (the full rubric is in example 1 in Appendix A). Then she began to examine students' work and their rubric scores, as well as her own teaching methods, to discover why students were not performing better despite her hard work to help them.

Addressing Student's Difficulties with Scientific Titles

Why did Anderson's teaching methods—all the explanations, the reading of scientific articles, and the in-class peer response—result in a totally unscientific title such as "The Battle of the Suds" and other inappropriate titles listed in Chapter Four? Anderson realized that:

- Students were not using the titles they read as models for writing titles for their own research.
- Students were not using what they had learned about descriptors in the library to construct their own titles.
- Students seemed to have misconstrued Anderson's instructions "to write to an audience of your peers." Anderson thought of their peers as "scientists in training," but the students saw their peers as "college buddies" interested in sports, sex, and booze.

- Students appeared to be modeling titles after other disciplines or settings. "The Battle of the Suds," for example, might be an appropriately humorous title for a Speech 101 class. "Research to Determine the Better Paper Towel" might be like "Book Report on *Silas Marner*" for a high school English class.

In other words, constructing a rubric scale and examining student work in relation to each category in that rubric can help teachers diagnose exactly what is going wrong.

Next, Anderson had to figure out what would amend the situation. She did not want to spend enormous amounts of extra time on titling. Although titling is important to scientists because of their indexing systems, the title was not the most important feature of students' work. So Anderson set out to discover whether, within the same time constraints, she could improve her students' titles.

The key appeared to lie in helping students in three ways:

- Defining the appropriate audience
- Applying what they learned in the library and in their reading of scientific titles
- Applying Anderson's criteria when examining their own titles

Here is what Anderson did. After the library sessions and the abstracting of scientific articles were completed, Anderson called the students' attention to one of the articles they had abstracted: "Relative Climbing Tendencies of Gray (*Elaphe obsoleta spiloides*) and Black Rat Snakes (*E.o. obsoleta*)." She asked students how they would have felt about the author if the article had been titled "Do Snakes Get High?"

After the laughter, she asked them what they had learned about audience in their English composition classes and how it related to scientific writing. She asked them who they thought their audience was for the original research paper they were working on. They discussed the notion of peers, and she emphasized that she saw them as scientists in training rather than as party animals. As a class, they identified the words *high* and *snake* as descriptors in the title and discussed how little information these amusing title words would transmit in the keyword indexes in *BioAbstracts* or *Science Citation Index*.

The year after Anderson carried out this ten-minute exercise in class, 90 percent of her students scored 3.0 or better on her rubric for title, according to the scoring of two outside raters. In the year of "The Battle of the Suds," when Anderson had used the same amount of class time but did not have the specific data about students' strategies provided by the rubric, only

50 percent of the students had scored 3.0 or better on the title. (For more about these results, see Anderson and Walvoord, 1990.)

Constructing a rubric scale and examining student work in relation to it can help teachers engage in data-driven teaching strategies.

Addressing Students' Difficulties with Scientific Format

Anderson next turned her attention to helping her students with scientific format. Before she turned to constructing rubrics for grading, Anderson had used these strategies for teaching scientific format:

- Anderson told her students several times, verbally and in writing, that scientific research reports contain these sections: title, abstract, introduction, methods and materials, results, and conclusions and implications.
- Several sessions after her lecture on the scientific format, she asked her students to bring in three pages from their own methods and materials section. That was followed by a forty-minute peer-conferencing session in which students were free to address format or other concerns about their papers with each other.
- The students had read five appropriately titled scientific journal articles with their abstracts cut off and had written abstracts for them. All of the articles demonstrated use of scientific format.

What did students end up doing in their final reports? A few wrote papers with no sections at all. Some omitted sections. Some invented extra sections. And some organized material poorly within sections.

Clearly Anderson's strategies were not teaching students the correct format. A lecture and handout on the scientific format did not necessarily convey to students the information they needed to arrange their own material into the appropriate headings. Writing abstracts for scientific articles encouraged students to focus not on the "what-goes-where" in the scientific format but rather on the gist of the article. The peer conferences on their materials and methods sections might have helped students with organization of material within that section, but they did not help them conceptualize the entire report in terms of the format. Furthermore, Anderson's assignment to write the materials and methods section early in their experimental process initiated (or at least perpetuated) the erroneous idea that scientists write all of their work in sections. In fact, scientists write throughout the planning, piloting, and experimenting stages and not necessarily in the sequence they will eventually use to report their work to the scientific community.

After her rubrics allowed Anderson to separate out the components of poor format and diagnose more clearly how and why her students were going wrong, she used in-class time differently. She gave a fifteen-minute lecture on format this time, as before, but now she emphasized how she and other scientists wrote throughout the research process and then put their writing into the research report format later.

Next, she decided to use one of the articles students had already read and abstracted, but this time called students' attention specifically to format, which their abstracting task had not done. She cut up copies of one of the articles into separate paragraphs. In class, she put the students into small working groups and gave each group a handful of cut-up paragraphs, which they then had to reassemble into the complete article, with appropriate headings: introduction, methods and materials, and so on. Students had to justify why they placed each paragraph as they did. The activity took fifteen minutes.

At the end of class, Anderson asked students to bring to the next class three pages of text from their research. When they returned, she had the students assemble in the same small groups and work for fifteen minutes to decide into which scientific format sections the pieces of each person's own three pages of text would fit. As they had done for title, the scores of the class on scientific format improved substantially. Once again, Anderson was designing and testing data-driven teaching strategies to enhance student learning, one trait at a time. (See example 1 in Appendix A for the complete rubric and a fuller presentation of Anderson's class in Anderson and Walvoord, 1990.)

Careful analysis of students' work using rubrics, combined with careful analysis of how various pedagogical strategies are working in your classroom, can lead to substantial improvement in teaching and learning without necessarily increasing your time or workload.

The Scholarship of Teaching and Learning

If you are familiar with the scholarship of teaching and learning movement in higher education, you realize that is what we have been addressing here: faculty members investigating in their own classrooms how learning takes place and why, using that information for improvement, and sharing that information with others. Resource 10.1 offers more information.

Resource 10.1. The Scholarship of Teaching and Learning

Cambridge (2004). How campuses can support the Scholarship of Teaching and Learning.

Cross and Steadman (1996). A clear and helpful classic guide.

Hutchings (2000). Case studies and guiding principles for the scholarship of teaching and learning.

Huber and Hutchings (2005). Argues for the "teaching commons," in which faculty share their teaching and the findings of their classroom research, creating supportive communities, rather than isolated classrooms.

Reports by Carnegie CASTL Scholars from a wide variety of disciplines about their own investigations into their classrooms. www.carnegiefoundation.org.

International Society for the Scholarship of Teaching and Learning. Sponsors conferences, publications, and resources. www.issotl.org.

Activity

1. Take an aspect of your own students' performance that does not meet your expectations. Alone or with a colleague, explain as precisely as you can where their difficulties lie. Plan how you might help your students improve.

2. Try to articulate the models of learning and teaching that lie behind your proposed solutions in item 1. You might frame your response in the following ways:

   "The problem my students are having is . . ."
   "The problem is caused by . . ."
   "I might help them by . . ."
   "I think this strategy will work because . . ."
   Explaining why you think a strategy will work forces you to articulate your theories of student learning.

3. Pose a question about your students' learning that you believe would help you improve your teaching. Plan how you would gather data to answer your question. Discuss your plan with a colleague and revise if necessary.

Part Two

How Grading Serves Broader Assessment Purposes

Chapter 11

Assessment for Departments and General Education

IF WE AS TEACHERS can effectively assess students' work in our classrooms, we can collectively use those skills with our colleagues in our departments and programs, in general education, and throughout the institution. This chapter presents a guide to departmental and general education assessment, focusing on how to use students' classroom work as evidence of student learning. This chapter may be used along with other resources that explore how to establish an entire assessment system (Resource 11.1). Especially, this chapter is intended as a companion to Walvoord's *Assessment Clear and Simple* (2004; a new edition is in preparation).

Resource 11.1 Guides to Departmental and General-Education Assessment

---

Angelo (1999). Points true north. Don't lose sight of these principles. Angelo's writing is always brief, clear, and centered on human values.

Banta, Jones, and Black (2009). A judicious integration of guiding principles and many case studies showing how institutions have conducted assessment in sensible and useful ways. Emphasizes alternatives to using standardized tests as the sole measure of student learning.

Banta (2007b). Collection of essays from *Assessment Update* newsletter.

Palomba and Banta (2001). Organized as a manual of advice to practitioners; its 350 pages offer extensive details on many topics.

Suskie (2009). A 300-page guide to planning and conducting assessment, with many good ideas and illustrations.

Walvoord (2004). A short, clear guide in seventy-nine pages of text, plus appendixes. Opens with a chapter on assessment in general, followed by chapters intended for departments, general education, and institution-wide planners. (A new edition is in preparation.)

Other sources are guidelines and resources for assessment published by regional or disciplinary accrediting associations and sources for specific areas:

Community colleges: All of the above, plus Banta (2004), a collection of case studies; and Serban and Friedlander (2004), a practical guide.

General education: All of the above, plus two collections of case studies: Banta (2007a,) and Bresciani (2007); plus Leskes and Wright (2005), a practical guide.

Assessment in this context means the systematic collection of information about student learning, using the time, knowledge, expertise, and resources available to inform decisions about how to improve student learning. Guidelines from accreditors, boards, and legislatures generally ask institutions to follow three steps of assessment:

- Articulate the goals for student learning ("By the end of this program or course of study, students will be able to . . . ").
- Gather evidence about how well students are achieving the goals.
- Use that information for decisions in the department, program, general education, and institution.

Sometimes, a "curriculum mapping" step is added between goals and evidence: the department or program creates a matrix showing all its courses and the goals that each course addresses. This is not assessment per se, because it shows what is taught, not what is learned, but it can be very useful to a department or program.

Faculty evaluation of student classroom work can form an important part of an assessment system, along with other sources of information, such as student and alumni surveys or focus groups, employer input, standardized tests, and retention and placement data. Here are some brief examples:

- A department holds an annual two-hour assessment meeting for its undergraduate majors program. Faculty consider whatever evidence they have about how well their undergraduate majors are achieving the learning goals the department wants for them. During this meeting, faculty teaching the capstone course for undergraduate majors report on the strengths and weaknesses they observe in students' work on the penultimate assignment for that course. The department discusses that report, along with results from its senior student focus groups. By the end of the meeting, the department identifies one aspect of its students' achievement to celebrate and one action item by which it believes it can improve student learning.
- A general education program asks its faculty to submit brief written reports of the strengths and weaknesses they observe in student work in relation to the critical thinking and writing goals of the general education program. These reports are aggregated and used, along with results from standardized tests and student surveys, to inform decisions about the general education program.
- Another general education program works with student portfolios (a collection of one student's work across time). These portfolios are

evaluated by faculty readers to identify strengths and weaknesses in students' achievement of the general education goals. The readers' reports are used with other data to inform the general education program.

- A department is dissatisfied with the number of low grades and withdrawals in a service course it offers majors in its own and related disciplines. The grades themselves are too general for detailed analysis, but they serve as a warning flag. The department then analyzes students' classroom work and conducts student interviews to identify the factors contributing to students' problems. The department takes action.

- A department has for years been holding an annual meeting of its graduate faculty at which faculty review the progress of each doctoral student. To turn this meeting into department-level assessment, the department asks faculty dissertation advisors and faculty readers of qualifying exams to complete a written analysis of students' strengths and weaknesses in relation to the learning goals of the program. This information is aggregated to provide an overall view of student learning in the program as a whole, which can then serve as the basis for improvements to the program.

- A department asks outside experts to visit its campus once a year to hear student teams report on their senior projects. The outsiders judge student performances, award prizes, and give feedback to each student team. To turn this into department-level assessment, the department asks the external experts at the end of the day to evaluate the program as a whole and suggest improvements.

The next chapter presents fuller case histories of how departments, programs, and general education have used student classroom work for assessment. This chapter concentrates on principles and models. It explains in detail how evaluation of student classroom work can move from the classroom to wider arenas such as the department or general education.

Step 1: Establish Goals for Learning

The first step for any assessment program is to articulate goals (also called *objectives* or *outcomes*). The three terms are used confusingly within the assessment movement. Our advice is not to worry about the terminology. What you need are statements that begin, "When students complete this degree/major/certificate/, they will be able to . . . " These statements will be stated at different levels of generality. Course goals were discussed in

Chapter Two; department or program goals should be broad enough to encompass an entire course of study yet not so broad that they could apply to any discipline—for example, "Students will be able to design and carry out original scientific experiments." General education goals are often stated still more broadly—for example, "Students will think critically."

A department will need a set of goals for each distinct course of study—that is, each certificate program, each distinct track of the undergraduate major (for example music history and music performance), and each graduate degree. Of course, there will be overlap, so it's fine to say, "All our majors have these learning goals, and in addition, music performance has these, and music history has these." Three to ten goals are common, though departments accredited by disciplinary associations sometimes have many more goals or outcomes given to them for which they must be accountable. If you need models, go to the Internet. In addition, some professional organizations (such as the American Psychological Association) suggest learning goals for specific courses of study such as undergraduate majors.

General education programs need to establish specific goals derived from the general ones. For example, here is one institution's description of the general goal of mathematical thinking and quantitative reasoning:

Mathematical thinking and quantitative reasoning: Apply mathematics to analyze numerical relationships, solve problems, explain processes and interpret results.

Students will be able to:

- *Demonstrate knowledge of the basic theories and methods of mathematics.*

- *Use quantitative methods to test hypotheses and to construct quantitative solutions to problems.*

- *Apply mathematical skills and knowledge to their academic disciplines.*

- *Communicate quantitative ideas, both orally and in writing.*

Typically, general education goal statements will be used by departments to shape and assess general education courses and by general education committees to decide which courses will be accepted as general education requirements and to assess student learning in those courses.

The same principles apply to departments and general education as apply to individual courses discussed in Chapter Two. State your highest goals for your students, and then figure out how to get some indication about whether they are being met. Originality, ethical decision making, aesthetic sensibility, and mathematical intuition are all worthy goals. General education and liberal arts disciplines will find helpful the goal statements developed under the umbrella of the Association of American Colleges and Universities (www.aacu.org).

Step 2: Collect Information About Student Achievement of the Goals

To address step 2—gathering information about student achievement of the goals—the department or general education program should choose some combination of direct and indirect measures:

- *Direct measure*: Occurs when the student does something (takes a test, completes an assignment, interacts with a client, performs a musical composition or a laboratory procedure) that is directly observed and evaluated by someone else (faculty member, internship supervisor, external evaluator).

- *Indirect measure*: Occurs when there is another leap of inference between the student's action and the direct evaluation of that action. Indirect evidence includes:

  - Asking students or alumni what they thought they learned

  - Employer feedback

  - Retention, job placement, or career progress statistics

  - Awards won by students; student work accepted for publication or presentation

  - Admission into, and success in, further schooling

The most important principle is to collect only what you can fruitfully use for making improvements in student learning.

The basic no-frills plan is to use one direct and one indicted measure:

- *A direct measure.* Sometime shortly before students graduate, the department or general education program examines a sample of student work (not just their grades) to determine strengths and weaknesses and identify something to work on. This could be a sample of student classroom work that classroom instructors or a group of faculty readers evaluate (the latter part of this chapter is devoted to showing how this can be done). As relevant, a standardized test or certificate exam might be added as well.

- *An indirect measure.* An example is a survey or focus group of students held just before they graduate that asks them:

  - How well they thought they achieved each of the learning goals

  - What aspects of the program best helped them learn

  - What suggestions they have for improvement

If your department or program is collecting these two types of data and actually using the information for improvement, you will have a solid basis for reporting to accreditors.

In addition to measures that are used and analyzed within the individual departments or general education programs, the institution as a whole may gather data such as student and alumni questionnaires; retention and placement data; or standardized tests of writing, critical thinking, or other kinds of learning.

There is increasing pressure on institutions to use standardized tests of learning. Our recommendation is to first, or also, have a group of faculty examine student work—samples of work or portfolios. For a reasoned argument against the use of standardized tests as the sole measure of learning, see Banta's introductory essay in her edited collection on general education assessment (2007a). Banta is one of the key national figures in assessment, with years of experience in the field, including experience in systems that have used national standardized tests. She is a cogent and forceful voice for alternatives to standardized tests.

Using Student Classroom Work for Step 2

Three questions should guide the use of student classroom work for assessment:

- What information is needed, and by whom?
- Which student work will be assessed?
- Who will analyze student work, and who will establish criteria for the analysis?

We take up each of these questions in turn, showing how they apply to assessment in the department or program and in general education, whether in two-year, four-year, or graduate programs. There are differences among these various situations, but the three questions are basic to all.

Question 1: What Information Is Needed, and by Whom?

The first task is to identify the questions the program wants to ask. Some questions may arise from periodic review, perhaps spurred by a formal program review or upcoming accreditation:

- What are the strengths and weaknesses of student work measured against the learning goals established?
- What factors are affecting student learning?
- What actions on our part might improve student learning?

Sometimes a program's questions focus around a particular problem, issue, or situation:

- We have noticed a particular problem in student performance. What is going on, and how can we improve it?
- How can we do X [spend less faculty time, handle more students, adapt to new conditions, plan a new facility] in a way that will enhance student learning?

Once the questions are defined, the department or general education program will want to identify the sources of useful information about learning, including student classroom work, as well as other relevant evidence such as student and alumni surveys, interviews, focus groups, standardized tests, retention and placement data, and employer evaluations.

Question 2: Which Student Work Will Be Assessed?

If student classroom work appears to be a useful source of information for the question that is on the table, the department or general education program must ask, "Which student work?" In reporting their assessment, departments and programs sometimes make the mistake of listing all the tests and assignments in all their courses. It is true that in general, faculty members' knowledge of student work informs departmental and general education decisions, but it is impossible for the department or general education program to directly read all students' classroom work as a basis for program and institutional assessment. Thus, the department or general education program should choose a particular assignment or set of assignments that will best answer the questions they have posed and that will be considered by the department, not just by the individual instructor. Some common choices follow:

For the Undergraduate Major or Certificate Program, One or a Combination Of:

- One assignment or test within the capstone course (depending on the number of students involved, use the work of all the students or select a sample).

- If the program has no capstone course, choose a major assignment or test in one or more of the courses most students take near the end of their major or certificate program.
- Internship or clinical rotation in which students are expected to integrate what they know and apply it to real situations.
- Portfolios

For Professional or Graduate Degrees, One or a Combination Of:

- Qualifying exam or thesis
- Clinical or internship work in which students are expected to pull together what they know and apply it to real situations

For General Education

- A single assignment or test or a portfolio of student work:
  - In a key general education course or program such as composition, basic mathematics, first-year experience, learning communities, or a required course in religion or great books
  - In courses from many disciplines that address a particular general education goal, such as global awareness or oral communication
  - In all, or a sample, of general education distribution courses
- A senior capstone project. Some institutions ask senior capstone courses to be responsible for assessing not only the goals of the major but also the goals of the general education program. Thus, a penultimate assignment in a senior capstone course for majors may also assess general education goals such as writing, oral communication, critical thinking, or global awareness.

Choose some combination of courses, and assignments and tests, that is sustainable in terms of the available time and resources and will give useful information about the question on the table. Start small with a pilot study.

Portfolios

Portfolios that span the work of more than one class are usually more complex and labor intensive to collect and grade than single pieces of student work, because scorers must consider multiple pieces and because student work is read twice—by the original teacher for a grade and again by the portfolio scorers. So choose portfolios for departmental or general education assessment only when they confer benefits not available by assessing single pieces of student work. That said, portfolios may be powerful tools to assess these abilities:

- The consistency of a particular student performance in multiple situations
- A broad range of student skills
- The flexibility with which the student applies principles to varying situations
- The growth of the student's skills or knowledge over time
- The ability of the student to synthesize and reflect on his or her own work over time (this occurs when students review their own portfolios and write a reflection)

Resource 11.2 lists sources about using and scoring portfolios.

Resource 11.2 Using and Scoring Portfolios

Banta and Associates (2003). Articles chosen from *Assessment Update* illustrate how portfolios, including Web-based portfolios, have been chosen, scored, and used at various institutions to assess and improve programs in general education, the major, and advising, as well as overall institutional effectiveness.

Cambridge, Cambridge, and Yancey (2008). Helpful advice on electronic portfolios.

Zubizarreta (2009). Presents a rationale for portfolios and specific guidance, including sample assignment sheets, guidelines, criteria, evaluation rubrics, and other material for developing print and electronic portfolios. Emphasizes reflective practice. Focuses on using portfolios in classrooms, but material is adaptable for use by departments or general education programs.

Tests

Sometimes it makes sense to use a multiple-choice or short-answer test as a basis for departmental or general education assessment. This can be done in the following way:

- Choose a test that represents a penultimate aggregation of skills and knowledge: for example, a qualifying test, a test in a capstone course, or a test designed to measure knowledge and skills across the field.
- Administer the same test to students in multiple sections or classes. The purpose is not to discover whether one section or one instructor's students are doing better than another's, but rather to identify areas of weaknesses in students' performance and work together to devise ways to help students learn more effectively.
- Use different questions, depending on each faculty member's subject matter, but map the questions to the same rubric. For example, the rubric in example 14 in Appendix A could be used for questions on

reading graphics in a number of different disciplines. A table such as Table 4.1 could map test questions from several classes or disciplines onto the rubric for reading graphics to give an idea about how well students across disciplines are able to read and interpret graphic material.

Question 3: Who Will Analyze Classroom Work? Who Will Establish Criteria?

In addition to choosing the student classroom work to be analyzed, planners must decide who will analyze this classroom work. There are two options: the instructor or a group of external faculty readers (Figure 11.1). Each option has strengths and weaknesses, and each faces different challenges in establishing criteria.

Option 1: Instructors Evaluate Their Own Students' Work

One option is for instructors to evaluate their own students' work using a rubric or list of criteria. Instructors report the results of their evaluations to the department, general education committee, or other body, which then aggregates instructor reports and uses the information to improve

FIGURE 11.1

Evaluating Student Classroom Work: Two Options

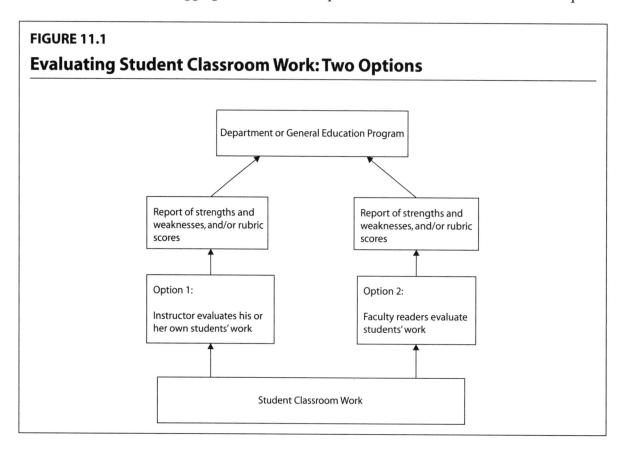

student learning. This system of instructor evaluation has both strengths and weaknesses.

Strengths

- Time-efficient. Faculty do the analysis along with their grading, and student work is read only once.
- Faculty buy-in. Faculty are analyzing their own classroom work and taking action or making recommendations based on their own analysis.
- Multiple sources of evidence. Faculty evaluators have student work on other assignments and student classroom feedback to help interpret results from a single assignment.

Weaknesses

- Analysis is conducted by the same faculty member who assigned and taught the material, thus creating a self-referencing, closed loop. Mitigate by (1) asking faculty to share their assignments, criteria, and rubrics with colleagues at the discussion, so the practices are public and open to conversation; or (2) organizing faculty into groups of two or three, and asking each to read, analyze, and score a few sample papers from the other's class. Share results among the small group.
- With many faculty working independently to evaluate student work, it is difficult to achieve interrater reliability (similar scores for the same piece of student work). Mitigate by (1) asking faculty to use the same rubric or some similar items on a rubric (see below for discussion of who establishes criteria); (2) holding sessions in which faculty practice evaluating sample student work and share their results; or (3) asking faculty to work in small groups to share evaluations of their students' work.

When faculty evaluate their own students' work for the purposes of the department or general education program, the question arises, at what level of generality will the general education program or department adopt common criteria or rubrics, and at what level will the instructors develop their own criteria or rubrics? In practices with the greatest instructor autonomy, the department or general education program supplies only the most general learning goals (for example, "Students will think critically") and asks individual instructors to construct an assignment and a set of criteria by which to evaluate critical thinking in whatever way seems relevant to the instructor. In practices with the greatest institutional or departmental guidance, the department or general education program, usually working through a faculty committee, may ask all instructors to make the same assignment, or at least the same type of assignment, address the same learning goals, and use a common rubric to evaluate that assignment.

Each approach has its strengths and weaknesses. Instructor-generated criteria may be closer to what was actually assigned and taught in the course, but reaching conclusions based on varying criteria or rubrics may be challenging for the department or general education committee. Nevertheless, it can be done. Even if six faculty teaching a certain course have different assignments, rubrics, and analyses of student work, let them each report to the department their assignment, rubric, and findings about students' strengths and weaknesses in reaching the learning goals. Then let the group discuss what they see, with the goal of identifying one item to celebrate and one item to work on.

When common assignments and rubrics are established by the department or general education committee, there may be more unanimity in the instructor reports, but instructors may feel that the common assignment or rubric does not match what they are actually doing in the classroom.

Much depends on the quality and specificity of the rubric. If the rubric's categories are vague, relying on broad adjectives (for example, "develops a superior argument," "develops a good argument," "develops a poor argument"), you have not specified anything about what makes a superior or good argument, so faculty will vary widely in how they rate student work. Furthermore, faculty are likely to rate most of their students' work in the "good" category, so the scores will not differentiate sufficiently to reveal anything. Chapter Four shows how to develop rubrics with greater specificity.

Option 2: Faculty Readers Analyze Portfolios or Samples of Student Work

An alternative to having faculty evaluate their own students' work is to have a group of faculty readers evaluate a sample of student classroom work. In this system, student work may be collected in several ways:

- Students submit assignments or portfolios. They may be paid to do so or required to do so as part of their general education, major, capstone course, or other requirement.
- Faculty submit student work from their own classes—for example.

  - A random sample of general education courses is chosen each semester by Institutional Research. Faculty teaching those chosen courses submit all the work that students did for a particular assignment that addresses a particular learning goal. These student works are scored by a group of faculty readers, who then make recommendations to the general education committee.

- In a college of business, instructors who assign written case studies in any of several upper-level courses submit a random sample of student case studies. These cases are scored by a college-wide group of faculty readers using a common rubric. The readers then make recommendations to the college.

There are established best practices for training and norming readers (White, 1994). To summarize, best practice suggests that the readers should meet together and be paid for their time. They should use a well-constructed rubric, accompanied by examples or so-called anchor pieces of student work that illustrate each level of scoring. Before beginning the actual scoring, readers should:

1. Discuss the rubric and examples.

2. Independently score the same samples of student work.

3. Discuss together any discrepancies or questions that have arisen during independent scoring. This may result in changes to the rubric or the anchor examples.

4. Repeat steps 2 and 3 until reasonable consistency in scoring is established. You don't necessarily need the same high levels of inter-rater reliability you would expect for published research. You are looking for enough commonality to give you indications about student work that can suggest strengths and weaknesses for follow-up action by the faculty.

5. Score student work. The usual practice is for two readers to score each paper independently. If the two scores are different, you can have the two readers discuss the paper to see whether they can agree, take the average of the two scores, or ask a third reader to read independently and then take the most common score.

If the raters are scoring many student works, they should repeat steps 2 and 3 at periodic intervals to prevent them from drifting apart in their scoring practices.

These are the strengths and weaknesses of faculty reader evaluation.

Strengths

- Student work is evaluated by someone different from the classroom teacher, bringing in other perspectives and avoiding possible instructor bias.

- Interrater reliability is potentially better because of the norming procedures.
- The rubric scores are easily aggregated because the group of readers must use a common rubric.

Weaknesses

- This evaluation is time-consuming and costly because student work that has already been graded must now be analyzed again by additional faculty readers.
- Because faculty are not analyzing their own students' work, they have less buy-in. They may believe that whatever report arises from the readers does not apply to their class.
- Readers may not understand the context of the writing: the assignment, what was taught, or what expectations were communicated to students.

These weaknesses can be mitigated in these ways:

- Very careful planning before portfolios and samples are launched, including the questions to be addressed by portfolio or sample analysis, content of the portfolio or sample, rubric for scoring, and a pilot in which the rubric is tested.
- Including information about the assignments in the portfolio or sample.
- Providing guidelines for faculty about how to construct appropriate and useful assignments and expectations
- Asking students to reflect on their own portfolios, explaining how the work was generated and what they thought they learned.

When a group of faculty readers examines student work, they must use common criteria, usually expressed as a rubric. Learning goals established at the departmental or general education level will be the broad guide, but if they are to achieve reasonable interrater reliability, faculty readers need a specific rubric for the work they are to read (see Chapter Four).

Step 3: Use Assessment Information for Improvement

The most important part of an assessment system is to use the information for improvement. Accreditors agree; they emphasize "closing the loop," and one of the most common critiques they make of assessment systems is that the department or institution is gathering data it never uses. So you need a system by which information about student learning can be aggregated, analyzed, interpreted, and used for decision making at all the sites of decision making that characterize a college or university, starting with faculty and moving up into institutional budgeting and strategic planning. We suggest the following sites for discussion and action based on assessment information:

- Departments, programs, and general-education units. Results are actions at that level or reports to other levels.
- Schools or colleges if relevant. Results are actions and reports.
- Committees such as the curriculum committee, general education committee, academic policies committee, or faculty senate. Results are actions and reports.
- Provost, officers, and president, who do strategic planning and budgeting. Results are actions and reports.

The initial forum, first in the list above, may be the most powerful and most important forum for change because it involves faculty members in small, cohesive units, examining data that in many cases they themselves have helped to gather, in which they feel invested, and on which they are willing to act. For that reason and because this book focuses on classroom information, this section describes the discussion of classroom work that occurs at the level of the department and in the general education unit.

Choosing a Forum for Initial Faculty Discussion

Choose a forum where faculty, in reasonably sized groups, can discuss the assessment information and take action or recommend action to others:

- For degree and certificate programs: the department or a subsection or committee of the department
- For general education: a unit that makes sense within the institution:
  - The department that sponsors general education courses
  - The program that administers a particular general education offering, such as the writing program, first-year seminar program, or learning communities
  - The group of faculty who share a common general education purpose or theme, such as all the courses that are writing intensive or help students fulfill the diversity requirement

A Structure for Discussion

The department, program, or relevant general education unit needs a structure of meetings in which to discuss its evidence and recommend actions.

Some departments or programs have annual retreats; some have a series of shorter meetings throughout the year; some place heavy responsibility in the hands of the chair or other department officer or a committee that may analyze the data and come to the department with recommendations. At a minimum, the department or general education unit might decide to hold one meeting of at least two hours each year. Some institutions designate an annual assessment day in which each department or program holds its meeting. The two-hour meeting should focus on only one degree or course of study or only on the department's general education courses. The department can take up a different program each year or address more than one program in a given year.

The Meeting

We suggest that the department, program, or general education unit institute the annual meeting immediately, no matter how inadequate or incomplete its student learning data are. Identify one action item, even if the first thing needed is to collect more information about that item.

Guidelines for the Meeting

- Time frame: At least two hours.
- Agenda: No other items except analysis of data on student learning.
- Take minutes: Who was present, the data presented, the conclusions drawn, the action item chosen, who was assigned responsibility, and suggestions made for strengthening the quality of the data next time.
- Purpose: To consider evidence, including evidence of student learning, that is relevant to the question on the table, but not for personnel review. Choose student work that asks students to pull together what they have learned within the program. Everyone takes responsibility for the learning that is revealed and the problems that show up.
- Evidence: The meeting considers all relevant evidence of student learning, including student classroom work, and also, as relevant or available, student surveys or focus groups, alumni surveys, certification exam pass rates, or student retention.
- By the end of the meeting:

    - Choose one action item based on consideration of the evidence
    - Assign responsibility and a time line
    - If needed, choose one way to strengthen the quality of data for next time

Agenda for a Two-Hour Annual Meeting

- Prior to the meeting: The chair, assessment person, or committee gathers and arranges the data in an understandable, usable form and distributes this information to members.
- First ten minutes: Reminder of purpose, guidelines, and agenda.
- Next sixty minutes: Review the data that have been distributed, answer questions, discuss issues, decide on an action item, and assign responsibility for follow-up.
- Next twenty minutes: Outline reports or recommendations that will be passed on to other decision-making bodies.
- Final minutes: If needed, decide on an action to strengthen quality of data for next time and assign responsibility for follow-up.

Preparing Assessment Data for the Meeting

The faculty forum needs information in a usable form. Here are common forms of data to present to faculty for discussion:

- Written summary of faculty evaluations of strengths and weaknesses in student work ("From faculty evaluations submitted to the committee, the three most commonly mentioned strengths were . . . and weaknesses were . . . ").
- Table of average scores for each item on a rubric (Tables 11.1 and 4.1).

TABLE 11.1

Rubric Scores Prepared for Departmental Discussion

Trait	Class Average Rubric Score (5 is high)
Title	2.95
Introduction	3.18
Scientific format	3.09
Methods and materials	3.00
Nonexperimental information	3.18
Designing the experiment	2.68
Defining operationally	2.68
Controlling variables	2.73
Collecting data	2.86
Interpreting data	2.90
Overall	2.93

Note: Based on a rubric used to score senior student research projects in a capstone biology course. See example 1, Appendix A.

- Summaries of findings from student surveys, retention, placement, and other materials.

Selecting an Action Item

When deciding on an action item, the department typically considers three questions:

- Which aspects of learning are most problematic?
- Which are most important?
- Which are we able to address?

If we apply these three questions to the rubric scores in Table 11.1, we see that the lowest scoring items are designing the experiment and controlling variables. Faculty in the department believe that these are among the most important skills that a scientist should have. At its meeting, the department might therefore focus on these two items, which are closely related. They might ask, "Can we take action that will help our students learn more effectively how to design experiments and control variables?" The annual assessment meeting might close with a decision to focus on these items, and the appointment of responsibility for follow-up.

Following Up and Taking Action

These follow-up moves are common:

- Examining the curriculum to see where students are being given instruction, models, practice, and feedback on designing experiments and controlling variables
- Looking at student work earlier in the curriculum to see whether students learned these skills but forgot them by their senior year or whether they never learned them
- Conducting surveys or focus groups of students to discover whether students are aware of these difficulties and what they think might help them learn more effectively

Among the common actions that can be taken in succeeding months are these:

- Change the curriculum. For example, the biology department might decide that courses 222 and 301 will more directly offer instruction, practice, and feedback in designing experiments and controlling variables.
- Offer faculty development. For example, the biology department might hold a series of brown-bag lunches where faculty can share

ideas about how to teach experimental design more effectively in their courses.

General Education

A department might meet to discuss its general education offerings just as it meets to discuss its major, certificate, or graduate programs. Or a general education unit might meet for the same purpose—for example, those teaching writing-intensive courses or courses that fulfill the diversity requirement.

Alternately, an institution-wide general education program might use a rubric that is sufficiently inclusive to apply to student work in multiple disciplines. For example, the criteria for Spanish journals in Exhibit 4.1 might apply to other languages as well; the rubric for reading and interpreting graphic information in Table 4.1 and example 14 in Appendix A might be used to match common rubric traits to student test answers in multiple disciplines; or a broad rubric for writing or critical thinking might be used to apply to students' essays in multiple disciplines (Facione and Facione, 2004). The common rubrics may be used by faculty members entering scores for their own students (a number of commercial and open source software programs are available to help with this task), or a group of readers may use the common rubric to evaluate a sample of work across disciplines (see Chapter Twelve for case examples of these strategies). Aggregated rubric scores would be presented to the general education committee. Based on the aggregated scores, the general education committee could decide on actions that might enhance students' achievement of general education goals.

The most common actions that result from such meetings include these:

- Change in curriculum or pedagogy in courses within the department or general education unit
- Faculty development: Workshops or Web-based resources to help faculty with problematic aspects such as designing tests and assignments that address course goals or teaching students how to deal with counterarguments and alternative positions

In addition, sometimes these meetings form an impetus for large-scale reform of the general education curriculum.

Reporting Classroom-Based Assessment

Having followed the three steps of assessment—articulating goals, gathering information about students' achievement of those goals, and using the information for improvement—the department or general education unit now needs to report its assessment processes to various audiences. There are typically two types of audiences for assessment reports and recommendations. Appendix B illustrates a sample report with two different end sections—one for each of the audiences described next.

Reports That Describe the Assessment Process

The first type of audience is accreditors or others who want to know that the department or program is assessing student learning. They will need a description of the process itself, not necessarily the specific data from any given year. Such audiences may include accreditors, boards, or systemwide administrative offices that require institutions to be conducting assessment.

The report in Appendix B, with its first ending, illustrates the kind of report a department would write for each of its degrees and programs, showing the process by which it conducts assessment. (If the same assessment process is used for more than one program, a single report can apply to both. If the process is primarily the same but differs in some respects, a single report can describe this branching. For example, the department might say that all of its programs are assessed with measures X and Y, and, in addition, the music performance track of the major includes measure Z). As the appendix example illustrates, the report should contain examples of actions the department has taken on the basis of its assessment data, but, again, the purpose of these examples is to illustrate that the department is acting on its assessment information.

Typically the institution will create a Web page that contains similar assessment reports for each department or program. Departments or programs themselves can access the Web site to share ideas about assessment, and the accreditors or state offices can see that departmental and program assessment are occurring at the institution. Such a Web page is often included as an appendix or resource in institutional self-studies for regional reaccreditation. Unless the actual process changes (for example, the department adds an alumni survey to its other methods of information gathering), this report remains the same from year to year. At some institutions, every three or four years, the provost asks all departments to update their reports, including new examples of actions they have taken. Thus, the Web page is always available and always reasonably up to date.

Reports for Program Review, Budget, and Planning

A second type of report focuses on the data from a particular year or assessment cycle, and its purpose is to recommend action and request support.

Audiences might include the provost or college dean. The report might be part of the department's annual review, periodic program review, or budget request. A strategic planning council or a curriculum revision committee might ask the department to contribute to an overall assessment of student learning. In Appendix B, the report with its second ending illustrates this type.

Both types of reports may be needed at most institutions. However, the most valuable is the second type, where assessment leads directly to planning and budgeting. If assessment is to have any real consequences for the department and program, it must lead to actions and resources. In the best of worlds, accreditors would not need separate assessment reports; instead, an institution would simply show the accreditor sample copies of its program reviews, budget appeals, and planning documents, all of which would clearly be based on assessment of student learning as a major source of information for decision making.

This chapter has explained the basic principles for using student classroom work. The next chapter presents case studies.

Chapter 12

Case Studies of Departmental and General Education Assessment

THIS CHAPTER PRESENTS four case studies illustrating how departments and general education programs in various types of institutions have used the grading process as part of their total assessment systems. In each case, there was a meaningful faculty forum for discussion and action. In sequence, the chapter presents:

- A university history department analyzing senior research papers and making curricular changes
- A university finance department constructing a new, common student assignment, analyzing student work on that assignment, and making curricular changes
- A community college allied health program analyzing student test results in a gateway course, identifying a correlation to students' reading scores, and taking action at the program level
- A community college general education program analyzing students' writing in multiple disciplines, using a common rubric, and taking action for faculty and student development

Case 1: Using Classroom Work to Assess Thinking and Writing in History Majors*

John C. Bean, David Carrithers, and Theresa Earenfight

The History Department at Seattle University had been concerned that not all its seniors were learning to think like historians: to learn how historians pose questions, conduct inquiry, gather and interpret evidence, and make historical arguments. When the faculty examined representative samples of history term papers written in senior-level courses, their anecdotally influenced preconceptions were confirmed. Many student papers were

---

*Adapted from Bean, Carrithers, and Earenfight (2005). Used by permission. A longer version of this case study was originally published in *The WAC Journal*.

narrative-based informational reports that addressed no clear problem or question, were uninformed by theory, and failed to answer readers' "so what?" questions about significance. The department's assumption that students would somehow learn these disciplinary thinking and writing skills through osmosis was called into question.

The department then turned its attention to two sophomore-level courses required of all majors: History 200 (Introduction to Historiography) and History 201 (Methods). An examination of syllabi and assignments showed that these courses did not focus on historical inquiry and argument. Taught largely through lecture with conventional term paper assignments, the courses seemed to be hodgepodges based on no guiding pedagogical principles. They did not explicitly introduce students to theory, teach interpretive practices, or coach the process of historical research and writing. Through ensuing discussion, the department established the following teaching goals for the two-course sequence: (1) to prepare students for upper-division course work in general and research seminars in particular; (2) to teach students how historians ask questions and how they develop theories of interpretation; (3) to provide a solid understanding of the major traditions and current trends of the discipline of history; and (4) to teach students how to conduct historical inquiry and present their conclusions to various audiences, whether in written or oral form.

The following year, coauthor Theresa Earenfight was assigned to teach the first of these courses, Historiography, with the explicit mission of redesigning it to fit these new department goals. She began by transforming the department's teaching goals into specific learning outcomes. By the end of the course, students should be able to (1) analyze and evaluate the theoretical assumptions in an historian's work; (2) articulate and defend their own theoretical assumptions; (3) do a close reading of primary sources; (4) interpret visual sources including maps; (5) assess oral sources; (6) evaluate quantitative materials; and (7) make their own historical arguments in the form of a research paper and an oral presentation. In place of the traditional term paper, Earenfight constructed a sequence of informal explanatory pieces, short papers, and a major final paper, all designed to teach the requisite knowledge and skills.

At the end of the course, Earenfight made copies of the students' final fifteen-page research papers and presented to the department her own analysis of students' strengths and weaknesses based on a rubric. In addition, five papers were randomly selected for scoring by the whole department. Finally, to see whether students could "talk like a history major," the department videotaped students' oral responses to readers' questions about their final papers. Throughout the process, the department tried to discover whether students were able to read different kinds of historical evidence critically and imaginatively, interpret a historical event in a reasoned format, and place the event in a historical context. The department also considered questions like these: Does the student use a sophisticated and specialized vocabulary? Does the student understand the differences among interpretive practices and the role of theory in writing history? Can he or she consider how to address a problem using the methods and approaches of a historian?

Use of Assessment Results. The department was impressed by how most of the sophomore students were able to synthesize complex and contradictory evidence and develop some sophisticated interpretations of a historical event. Of the sixteen students enrolled in the course, Earenfight identified nine papers as "strong," two as "good," and five as "weak." The department's discussion of the five randomly selected papers that all the faculty read showed considerable agreement about strengths and weaknesses.

The department's assessment procedures suggested that Earenfight's pedagogical approach helped students make progress toward more sophisticated historical inquiry and argument. The department then planned to extend the same procedures into the second of the two sophomore courses and ensure that students take the courses in sequence at the beginning of the major. In addition, faculty now seemed more confident in creating stringent research projects in upper-division courses. An unusually high number of recent history majors presented papers at undergraduate research conferences or won distinguished scholarships to graduate schools.

The case demonstrates that when a department takes the time to carefully examine its senior students' work, it can identify strengths and weaknesses that then can be used to reshape the curriculum at earlier points in the major. Such reshaping can significantly change how students learn.

Case 2: Using Classroom Work to Assess Critical Thinking in Finance Majors*

John C. Bean, David Carrithers, and Theresa Earenfight

The story of the undergraduate critical thinking assessment project in finance at Seattle University begins with faculty frustration at what instructors perceived as a lack of critical thinking skills among finance majors.

---

*Adapted from Bean, Carrithers, and Earenfight (2005). Used by permission. A longer version of this case study was originally published in *The WAC Journal*.

The frustration had been building for several years and often dominated departmental meeting discussions as well as informal faculty conversations. Led by coauthor David Carrithers, the department decided to conduct a pilot study of students' critical thinking skills using an embedded assignment.

To design the study, the department used Kurfiss's (1988) suggestion that critical thinking is triggered when people confront an "ill-structured problem"—that is, a problem that cannot be solved algorithmically to yield a single right answer. According to Kurfiss, an effective assessment of critical thinking would typically ask students to develop a best solution to an ill-structured problem and justify their proposed solutions, orally or in writing, with reasons and evidence appropriate to the discipline. Researchers could then study the processes by which students determined their solutions and developed supporting oral or written arguments.

The department's first task was to create an ill-structured finance problem that would evoke the kinds of critical thinking sought from students. Working as a committee of the whole, the Finance Department designed an ill-structured case problem in which the student, playing the role of an investment advisor, had to write a two-page memo offering advice to a husband and wife about two investment choices for the wife's retirement savings: plan A, taking a lump-sum payout of a 401(k) plan and buying a fixed-rate annuity, or plan B taking a lump-sum payout and investing it in a stock or bond fund. Of concern to the clients were the anticipated monthly income from each option, the long-range sustainability of that income, and the death benefit to survivors.

Numerous variables were built into the case—some crucial and some extraneous—to approximate a real-world ill-structured problem. Finance faculty hoped that students would get quickly to the heart of the problem by identifying the client's life span as the chief risk factor for plan A and the rate of return on the lump-sum investment as the chief risk factor for plan B. The students' task was to explain these risk differences to the clients and show them different scenarios. Faculty also expected students to construct audience-friendly graphics showing intersections between the two options under different variable conditions (different life spans and different rates of interest).

By designing a case centered on an ill-structured problem, the department conceptualized critical thinking in a dynamic, holistic way—as a total problem-solving and argumentative performance in response to a disciplinary problem. The department hoped to observe students' critical thinking abilities across several specific dimensions:

- The ability to determine appropriate analytical tools and finance methodologies to analyze each option
- The ability to determine relevant data, analyze and evaluate these data, apply the analysis to the client's problem, make good decisions, and create an argument justifying the decisions
- The ability to communicate ideas effectively in a professional situation to a nonfinance audience

The case assignment was administered in a 400-level course in finance taught by coauthor Carrithers. Students in the class tend to be graduating seniors who have satisfied the requirements of a finance concentration. The assignment was given as part of a take-home final examination. Students had approximately one week to analyze the problem, determine their solutions, and write their memos. Thirty-two student case analyses were submitted.

The case analyses were scored by seven finance faculty using norming and staff-grading processes well known by composition researchers (see, for example, White, 1994). The department developed a six-point scoring rubric specifying finance concepts and elements of communication the faculty felt should have been used in the analysis. (The rubric and a discussion of relevant methodological and epistemological issues are included in Carrithers and Bean, 2008.) After a norming session, the finance faculty staff-graded the case analyses giving each memo two independent readings with "splits" arbitrated by a third reader.

The most obvious and distressing result was that about half the finance students scored in a range that the faculty consider cause for concern, and even the students in the top half showed considerable critical thinking weaknesses. The faculty identified four kinds of frequently recurring critical thinking problems:

- Random rather than purposeful application of finance tools and methodologies
- Failure to address the client's problem and provide the requested financial counsel
- Inability to translate finance concepts and methods into lay language
- Failure to construct rhetorically useful graphics

Use of Assessment Results. In discussing the results of their assessment project, finance faculty quickly identified an underlying pedagogical problem: students were being asked to demonstrate skills they had never explicitly been taught. Typical homework assignments throughout the finance curriculum consisted of end-of-chapter problem sets in which students performed calculations in response to well-structured problems with right answers. The curriculum successfully taught students how to use sophisticated mathematical tools, but not when or why to use those tools in messy cases. With few exceptions, students were not asked to write professional arguments addressing messy problems within a rhetorical context. (For an example of an exception, see Robertson, Bean, and Peterson, 2004.) In addition, students were not taught to design graphics that extract information from spreadsheets to tell a relevant and significant story. In short, faculty realized that the design of the curriculum did not help students achieve desired learning outcomes in critical thinking and professional communication. (For further exploration of students' difficulties in this type of assignment and specific pedagogical suggestions, see Carrithers, Ling, and Bean, 2008.)

To address these problems, finance faculty redesigned the homework dimension of the finance curriculum. Although algorithmic problem sets were still a significant proportion of assigned homework, faculty created writing and speaking assignments that asked students to apply disciplinary knowledge to ill-structured finance problems. Through an assessment implementation grant funded by the provost's office, a research team also designed instructional modules to teach students how to create rhetorically effective graphics. A long-range goal for finance faculty is to develop a handbook for students on critical thinking within the discourse of finance and also a corresponding sourcebook for faculty containing examples of ill-structured finance problems writing assignments, grading rubrics, and a coordination plan for sequencing assignments within the finance curriculum.

The assessment model that the history and finance departments used is being adapted to almost all of the undergraduate majors under a $300,000 Teagle Foundation grant that Seattle University shares with Gonzaga University.

Case 3: Using Classroom Exams for Assessment in Health Sciences

Tara Eisenhauer Ebersole and Colette M. Schrank

The allied health faculty at Moraine Valley Community College in Palos Hills, Illinois, had recognized the need for a common exam for all sections of their gateway course, Medical Terminology (MRT 110). This course, primarily taught by adjuncts, laid the foundation for work in several allied health fields. To ensure that the course would be taught and assessed in the same manner, whether in a traditionally face-to-face setting, online, or hybrid, the faculty had already established a common final exam.

As the assessment process moved forward, a faculty team developed a set of stated learning objectives for the course. Then the faculty met to try to ensure that the exam measured what they wanted it to. They mapped the exam questions to the learning objectives and revised exam items, inviting widespread participation from faculty. They classified exam items as requiring lower-order thinking or higher-order thinking. The midterm exam, they decided, would have 70 percent lower-order questions and 30 percent higher-order questions, while the final exam would have a 40:60 ratio—twice as many higher-order questions. Faculty believed that in the second half of the course, students should develop the higher-order thinking required to apply medical terms to real-life situations and to lab and clinical procedures, and they should be able to answer questions relating to brief case studies. In sum, faculty collaborated to make the common final exam as valid and reliable as they could.

To use this common exam for assessment purposes at the department level, the faculty met regularly to review the exam results. One troubling finding was that students did more poorly on the higher-order exam items even in the last half of the semester. At one meeting, someone raised a question about a possible link between low student exam scores and low reading level and how that combination might affect student achievement.

To follow up on this reading question, faculty compared students' scores on a reading placement exam to their scores on the MRT 110 midterm exam. The midterm was selected in lieu of the final exam because the faculty were concerned that as a result of students withdrawing from the course after poor performance on the midterm exam, fewer students would be taking the final exam. The first comparison, limited to students of three MRT 110 sections, found that some students enrolled in the course were reading at a fourth- to seventh-grade level. The textbook the faculty had chosen, as well as several other textbooks in the field, were written at a tenth-grade level. Not surprisingly, the students who scored low in reading also scored low on their midterm exams. However, when a correlation study of the reading levels of all students versus midterm exam scores was completed, the correlation between the COMPASS reading test and the midterm was only 0.25 (based on the 156 students with both test scores). A second correlation study, however, showed that students who had completed a remedial reading course were significantly more successful on the MRT 110 exam than those who had not. These findings indicated the value of successfully completing the remedial reading course for success in MRT 110.

Using the Assessment Results. The faculty, in collaboration with the dean, took the following actions:

- Informed students about the importance of reading skills. The dean arranged to place a statement in the school mailer for MRT 110, advising students that they should be reading at a minimum of a tenth-grade level.

- Faculty placed in their syllabi the statement: "Students are expected to read at the tenth-grade level in order to succeed in this class."

- Faculty sought to determine what the successful students did to prepare for class and asked them to share their study strategies with others. As a result, faculty advise students clearly at the beginning of the course about study time requirements for the course, and they share other strategies that successful students have used, such as forming study groups.

- The department created a new learning environment that could optimize student potential and encourage engagement from the adjunct faculty:

  - They developed a set of PowerPoint slides and gave them to each MRT 110 instructor.

  - The publisher provided instructors with a desk copy of the text, instructor manuals, a medical dictionary, and wall charts.

  - The department chair secured a dedicated classroom for all sections of MRT 110 taught on campus and as a hybrid course. This classroom was equipped with a podium housing all the electronic equipment that an instructor could need, including access to the Internet. The institution purchased cabinets to store teaching materials. Each instructor was assigned a drawer for exams, handouts, and other teaching aids for easy access during class, thus enhancing organizational skills and time management.

  - A BlackBoard faculty resource site, fully accessible to each instructor, provided a resource where teaching suggestions, course information, and other items could be uploaded, stored, and shared.

Following these interventions, student scores rose between 2 and 5 percent in most categories of the exam. Heartened by this improvement, the faculty continued to work to ensure student success. The assessment process had provided a new level of collegiality to support this ongoing work.

Case 4: A Community College General Education Program Assesses Students' Writing Across Disciplines

Tara Eisenhauer Ebersole and Patricia Casey-Whiteman

Anne Arundel Community College in Maryland wanted to assess its students' written communication, one of the core competencies that had been established by the faculty senate. Rather than using a standardized test, they wanted to see what students were actually producing in classes across multiple disciplines. This goal involves methodological decisions that are more complex than the departmentally based assessment in the first three cases.

The faculty wanted to know (1) whether the writing met a standard of quality, (2) strengths and weaknesses in student writing, and (3) whether students who had taken the general education writing course performed better than those who had not. This third issue gets them into correlations and variables, a difficult task in real-life educational settings. They might have chosen pre/post-tests, comparing first-year writing with later writing, but at a community college, where students may be taking two, four, six, or more years to finish, pre/post-tests run the risk that any differences may be caused by factors such as work experience or maturation. Thus, a sample taken at a single point in time made sense. They chose a sample of eighty-three papers from seven disciplines, all completed within the same academic semester. Sample size was a compromise between the need for as large a number as possible and the limitations of faculty time and resources.

To address the three questions, the papers from different disciplines would need to be scored using a single rubric—a challenging task. The success of such an enterprise depends heavily on the care with which the rubric is created and the student work is scored. At Anne Arundel, an interdisciplinary team of six faculty, over two years, created a rubric (Exhibit 12.1).

The choice of traits and they way they are stated allow the rubric to be used for different assignments. Note that the paper is scored on how well it meets the needs of the assignment and the audience, no matter what those might be. The categories are defined not by the presence or absence of specific traits but by the balance between strengths and weaknesses. The trade-off for this wide applicability is that the rubric depends heavily on the reader's interpretation of what is appropriate for the assignment or what constitutes strengths and weaknesses within a particular category.

EXHIBIT 12.1

Rubric for Student Writing in Multiple Disciplines

Categories and Criteria	5. Few or no weaknesses found; writer satisfied the criteria with distinction	4. Strengths outweigh the weaknesses; writer shows sound under-standing of criteria	3. Strengths and weaknesses are about equal; writer shows aware-ness of criteria	2. Weaknesses outweigh strengths; writer shows limited under-standing of criteria	1. Weaknesses far outweigh strengths; writer does not show under-standing of criteria
1. CONTENT The paper fulfills the assignment and add-resses its audience's needs. Supporting evidence is developed and ana-lyzed sufficiently. The thesis is clear. Sources are appropri-ately documented.					
2. ORGANIZATION/STRUCTURE Introduction is fully developed and leads smoothly to thesis. Body paragraphs use topic sentences effectively. Paper is unified in relation to thesis. Conclusion provides insightful closure.					
3. WRITING STYLE/EXPRESSION Vocabulary and tone are appropriate to the assignment. The meaning of the sentences is clear. Sentence structure is varied. Transitions create smooth flow of ideas.					

Categories and Criteria	5. Few or no weaknesses found; writer satisfied the criteria with distinction	4. Strengths outweigh the weaknesses; writer shows sound understanding of criteria	3. Strengths and weaknesses are about equal; writer shows awareness of criteria	2. Weaknesses outweigh strengths; writer shows limited understanding of criteria	1. Weaknesses far outweigh strengths; writer does not show understanding of criteria
4. GRAMMAR/ MECHANICS Sentences are grammatically correct. Punctuation is correct. Spelling is correct (for example, homonyms used correctly). Paper format is correct. Column total					

A rubric such as this one, with latitude for reader judgment, puts a high premium on the quality of reader training and norming. One step the Anne Arundel faculty took was to include the rubric constructors on the scoring team to ensure consistency of interpretation (five additional faculty scorers were added). A second step was to train the readers. The eleven-member scoring team participated in a preassessment training session prior to the actual scoring session.

A scoring scheme needs a decision about the number of readers who will read each work and a way to settle differential scores. Anne Arundel decided to have two readers score each paper separately. Sixty percent of the scores agreed; for the other 40 percent, a third reader was engaged to determine the score. This rate of interrater reliability is not as high as one would expect for a publishable piece of research, but in these settings, where a single rubric, necessarily broad, is used by faculty to score papers from multiple classes, the institution is seeking information that can provide a reasonable basis for action.

Having arrived at scores, faculty addressed their first question—about quality—by establishing an internal benchmark of writing quality that was acceptable or not. To construct this measure, each category of the rubric was given equal weight. Since the maximum point value for the rubric was eighty points, fifty-six points, or 70 percent, was considered the level of written competency. This way of calculating the benchmark allows a paper weak in grammar but strong in thesis to score the same as a paper strong in grammar but weak in thesis. Nonetheless, the 70 percent benchmark offered a rough way to identify papers that were seriously deficient in a few areas or somewhat deficient in a number of areas. The payoff is that the college now has a rough idea of the percentage of its students who meet the writing benchmark, according to the scoring procedures.

The second question, about strengths and weaknesses, was addressed by analyzing students' scores in each of the rubric categories. The faculty assessors recommended help for students in citing sources, not plagiarizing, effectively integrating material from sources into their writing and checking their work against criteria set by instructors.

To address the third question, about the impact of the required courses, faculty found that 65 percent of students who had completed the general education composition and literature courses met the benchmark, while only 40 percent of students who had not yet taken those courses met the benchmark. The sample sizes and the possibility of other variables suggest caution in interpreting the results, but the study does suggest that students completing general education English courses may be producing better writing in their subsequent general education courses.

In addition, analysis by the faculty assessors suggested that faculty members might benefit from workshops on writing effective assignments, using the rubric, and infusing writing skills into their courses.

Use of Assessment Results. Outcomes of the assessment process have included the following:

- Fall faculty orientation workshops have focused on issues that appeared in the assessment of student work—for example, ethical expectations and plagiarism, information literacy, and standards for documentation in writing.
- Turnitin, a plagiarism detection service, has been highlighted, and the library has offered training to faculty.
- Additional workshops for faculty have been offered by the Office for Learning Assessment.
- Through the Office for Learning Advancement, all new faculty receive a mandatory forty-five-hour orientation across their first year of employment and are coached on fashioning syllabi and instructional modules that include how the college academic integrity policy applies in their courses and disciplines. Twice yearly, the part-time faculty receive an orientation session.

- An online quiz on academic integrity is included in the student orientation for online courses.
- The learner support services division includes discussion with students on academic integrity.
- Similar process models and templates have been used at the institutional level (for example, assessment of student speaking skills using a rubric developed by faculty), program level (for example, human services, physician assistant), and course level (for example, botany, legal studies).

Chapter 13

Assessment for Grant Proposals

FACULTY MEMBERS AT the Center for Biofilm Engineering at Montana State University (MSU) were preparing a new grant for a project that would produce a dynamic, Web-based resource for students to develop their science skills while learning about biofilms—slimy aggregates of microorganisms found in moist environments as diverse as our mouths or industrial water pipes. The three-year project would provide a source of interactive, direct instruction for undergraduates. Three content-skill levels would feature cutting-edge photomicrographs, streaming videos, research vignettes, teaching applets, links to current research, explicit laboratory instructions, and strategies to support independent student research investigations.

As the prospective co-principal investigators (co-PIs), Alfred Cunningham, Rockford Ross, and John Lennox, planned this project, they knew that the National Science Foundation (NSF) would be interested not only in the delivery of state-of-the-art scientific information and innovative learning technologies, but also in the impact this program would have on student learning: What would students be able to know and do when they finish using sections of *Biofilms: The Hypertextbook*?

It's easy to be intimidated as funding agencies tighten their requirements for assessment of student learning. But the principles of effective grading and assessment that we have discussed for classrooms, departments, and general education can be applied to any grant project that aims for student learning. And knowing how to design effective assessment can make a crucial difference. In this chapter, Anderson, the biologist, draws on her experience working with colleagues on eleven nationally funded external grants from agencies like the NSF, National Institutes of Health, and the Andrew W. Mellon Foundation.

This chapter is not a full discussion about all aspects of writing a good grant proposal. For that, go to the Foundation Center's open access "Proposal Writing Short Course" (http://foundationcenter.org/getstarted/tutorials/shortcourse/index.html). Our goal in this chapter is to inspire you to write a grant and show you how to plan and conduct assessment of learning within the grant.

Construct an Overall Assessment Plan

If you are seeking funding for a quality teaching or learning idea, don't let the language barrier stop you. Getting past the Program Announcement or Request for Proposals (RFP) is the hardest part because they are often written in the language of grants. If it says, "learning outcomes/goals/objectives," you need a "students will be able to" statement. (Direct and indirect evidence are defined in Chapter Eleven in this book.) The RFP may call for formative and summative assessment, defined, respectively, as ongoing assessment used for project improvement and assessment used for final evaluation of the project's success. If you need help with any aspect of the grant, ask a friend or mentor who has a grant, make an appointment with your school's grants officer, search for a grant Web site, talk to a grants program officer, or attend a workshop.

Address Four Questions

Grant instructions, no matter how long or complex, usually want you to address four questions that are familiar from other assessment contexts (see Chapter Eleven):

- What will participants be expected to be able to know and do at the end of the program?
- What experiences will facilitate their being able to do these things?
- What criteria and evaluative tools will be used to determine how well participants can do these things?
- What conclusions can be drawn from the quantitative and qualitative data collected in this experience, and how can those conclusions affect other learning experience?

Construct an Outcomes and Assessment Plan

Part of the grant planning is to list each learning outcome and show how that outcome will be assessed. You don't need a new measure for each outcome; one measure can serve for several outcomes.

Assessment measures for most grants fall into four categories:

- Student work evaluated by a rubric (direct measure)
- Students' behaviors, either self-reported or observed by faculty—for example, faculty observing how laboratory teams work together (direct measure if observed; indirect measure if self-reported)
- Questionnaires or interviews with students, alumni, or employers (indirect measure)

- Counting relevant aspects—for example, the graduate schools or jobs or awards or publications students achieve after the grant, the number of students who use one of the grant services or software projects, or the number of historically underrepresented groups recruited for the project (indirect measure).

In 2006, *Biofilms: The Hypertextbook* (http://www.biofilmbook.com), the project we described at the beginning of the chapter, was funded by the National Science Foundation.[1] The student learning outcomes and the assessment plan are shown in Table 13.1. Currently (2009) hundreds of students in a variety of science courses across the country, first-year to senior level, are piloting various sections of *Biofilms: The Hypertextbook*,

TABLE 13.1

Outcomes and Assessment Plan for *Biofilms: The Hypertextbook.*

Student Learning Outcomes for Each Skill Level and/or STEM Focus (STEM = science, technology, engineering, and mathematics)	Assessment Strategies Used to Provide Biofilms Formative (ongoing) and Summative (end point) Data
1. Develop a working knowledge of biofilms by acquiring selected vocabulary, concepts, principles, applications, laboratory techniques, and safety guidelines at one of the three cognitive levels in one the three STEM strands.	Written and performance tests (direct evidence) embedded in *Hypertextbook* and course-embedded tests Reflective learning journals Questionnaires (indirect evidence)
2. Demonstrate an enhanced proficiency in identifying, evaluating, and employing components of the scientific method, forming new research questions, and attending to ethical concerns/actions in planning biofilms research.	Student performance on pre/post-problem-based learning tests *Hypertextbook* responses Team and industry interviews
3. Exhibit the ability to utilize, the reflective willingness to value, and the propensity to continue finding and using primary literature to inform/document STEM research.	*Hypertextbook* monitoring of research hits Sample group observed technology skills tests Research Strategies Behavioral Checklist
4. Internalize that industrial, biomedical, environmental problems are complex and persistent, and that integrated STEM research actions and intellectual perseverance are needed.	Rubric analysis of reflective problem-solving research scenario One-year follow-up survey Team and industry interviews

---

[1] This material is based on work supported by the National Science Foundation under grant no. 0618744. Any opinions, findings, and conclusions or recommendations expressed in this material are those of the author(s) and do not necessarily reflect the views of the National Science Foundation.

and direct evidence of student learning is being collected and analyzed. Concurrently, the project is being assessed on its intellectual merit, capacity to infuse information about biofilms into the undergraduate curriculum, and the efficiency of the Web-based delivery system to do so.

You won't understand exactly what is meant by all the measures listed in the right-hand column, and you don't need to. Our point here is to illustrate how you can construct a table that shows outcomes and measures in relation to one another. The measures listed in the right-hand column may seem intimidating, but in fact, there are several repetitions, as a certain measure is used for multiple outcomes. Grant guidelines may call for multiple measures for each outcome, but that can be satisfied with a small total number of measures. Notice also that the measures fall into the four categories we listed earlier: student work, student behavior, questionnaires, and counting relevant aspects. It will be okay to modify the assessment measures as the grant project proceeds, provided you have good reasons for doing so, and you explain those reasons in your grant report.

Develop Assessment Tools

Once you have presented the overall picture of assessment, you need to develop, and explain to grantors, how you will implement each of the assessment tools listed in the overall plan (in the right-hand column of Table 13.1). Two of the more useful tools are rubric scoring of student tests or assignments and student behavioral checklists accompanied by interviews or focus group. We illustrate each of these in the following grant examples.

Gathering Evidence Through Assignments and Rubrics

Using rubrics to assess students' work can be a key assessment measure in a grant-funded project. An illustration of a fairly complex assignment-with-rubric measure, including a pre/posttest design, appeared in Towson University's summer 2007 grant project titled Research Experiences for Undergraduates (REU) in Biodiversity.[2] As part of their overall plan to assess student learning, the co-PIs, professors Don Forester and Larry Wimmers, decided on a pretest and posttest plan. They would compare and contrast the students' entering research skills with their exit skills ten weeks later.

First, the co-PIs formulated the learning outcomes:

---

[2]This material is based on work supported by the National Science Foundation under grant no. 0552654. Any opinions, findings, and conclusions or recommendations expressed in this material are those of the author(s) and do not necessarily reflect the views of the National Science Foundation.

The REU participant:

1. *Recognizes selecting a research topic as an integrative process that involves both scientific knowledge and informed decision-making.*

2. *Constructs an experimental design that is consistent with the research question and the inquiry standards, and that is adapted to the biodiversity context.*

3. *Recognizes the importance of a control group in experimentation.*

4. *Determines the characteristics of the experimental group that should be held constant or factored into the investigation in a given context.*

5. *Recognizes the significance of duration and replication to design.*

6. *Selects practical, appropriate research methodologies, and/or technologies.*

7. *Recognizes scientific research as both an individual and a collaborative human endeavor that may present diverse challenges.*

8. *Communicates effectively in writing*

Next, Forester designed an assignment that would test the learning outcomes. The assignment presented a scenario: students were to write a grant proposal in response to a hypothetical call from the Peruvian government asking researchers to design a study of biodiversity in a forested national park that was being fragmented by encroaching human development. This scenario grant-writing task would allow students to display their degree of mastery of the learning goals. As an example, we'll focus on two aspects of the task for students: (1) selecting a vertebrate species as the focus for their study and (2) designing the study, including selection of a site within the forest and selection of a control group to serve as a comparison of biodiversity.

To develop the rubric, both professors wrote out what they believed would be good answers to the assignment and discussed their answers. Wimmers then constructed an eight-point rubric. Routinely, an external evaluator will collect the student work, prepare it for blind scoring by the REU faculty, and tally the results. Exhibit 13.1 contains two items from that scoring rubric.

Students completed the scenario assignment near the beginning of the REU. In the ninth week, near the end of the project, the students completed a parallel scenario assignment (one that used the same skills in a new context). Both the process model of developing the parallel pre/post-scenario assessments scored by a single rubric and the pre/posttest rubric

---

EXHIBIT 13.1

Items from Scoring Rubric for Scenario Assignment

Trait: Recognizes that selecting a research topic is an integrative process that involves both scientific knowledge and informed decision making

_____ 4 Selects an appropriate vertebrate species and gives rationale for at least three factors (for example, mobility, generation time, and environmental limitations) influencing choice

_____ 3 Selects an appropriate vertebrate species and explains some factors that impacted that species selection

_____ 2. Selects an appropriate vertebrate species, but offers little insight into the process and/or fails to address obvious threats to design

_____ 1 Does not make an informed species decision.

Trait: Recognizes the importance of a control group in experimentation

_____ 4 Acknowledges the concept of a control group, selects an appropriate control group (for example, contiguous forest), gives rationale, and/or describes any aspect(s) of the control group

_____ 3 Selects an appropriate control group (for example, contiguous forest) and discusses any aspect(s) of the control group

_____ 2 Acknowledges the importance of a control, but does not select one

_____ 1 Ignores concept of control group

---

scores themselves were significant to the co-PIs and useful to the granting agency. We suggest that an assignment where student work is scored by a rubric can form a key measure for many grant projects that aim for student learning.

Gathering Evidence from Student Behaviors

A second assessment tool is a behavioral checklist with periodic interviewer corroboration. Our example comes from another project funded by the National Science Foundation (NSF) Research for Undergraduates—REU in Urban Environmental Biogeochemistry at Towson University with Ryan Casey as the PI.[3] Seven undergraduates and faculty from three different science departments participated in the summer 2008 institute. Students participated in interdisciplinary environmental research, an innovative project concept because such research is often stymied by rigid departmental approaches to funding and research.

To determine whether students were making progress in becoming researchers, a major goal of the NSF project, the PI and grant personnel

---

[3] This material is based on work supported by the National Science Foundation under grant no. 0754947 Any opinions, findings, and conclusions or recommendations expressed in this material are those of the author(s) and do not necessarily reflect the views of the National Science Foundation.

decided to measure certain key indicator behaviors with a before- and after-REU checklist. Combined with focus groups or evaluator interviews, this strategy can identify useful indirect evidence (Suskie, 2009).

As in this case, these behaviors are usually identified by groups of faculty or professionals who reflect on how "the "graduate of your dreams" would act. (Fink, 2003, also describes this reflective strategy process.) Quantitative data before and after the learning experience are easy to collect and useful in documenting whether affective change (change pertaining to attitudes, feelings, or values) has occurred in light of specific goal-oriented expectations.

Within the first full week of the project, the undergraduates were to respond orally yes or no to having participated in specific research-oriented behaviors. Periodically in the interview, Anderson, the evaluator, asked participants to describe some events more fully.

In the tenth week, Anderson duplicated the interview procedure. There were thirty items on the checklist. Some were distractors, asking about experiences with technologies, teaching, and volunteer interests, but fifteen were closely tied to the REU goal: to prepare students to engage in meaningful and authentic environmental research across disciplinary lines and to become better prepared to enter and excel in scientific careers or further education. The fifteen overt behaviors most closely linked to these REU outcomes are listed in Table 13.2.

Data collected showed that the average number of desired activities in which the seven members of the group had participated at their home institution before the REU was three of fifteen (20 percent). After attending the REU, the average number of desired activities in which the group had participated was thirteen of fifteen (87 percent).

This sample of seven students does not justify more rigorous treatment of these data. As the participant numbers grow over the next two years, the PI and the evaluator will explore correlation factors between the students' engagement in indicator activities and students' continued success: research presentations, publications, science-related employment, and graduate and professional school admissions. Granting agencies often require investigators to track such statistics for specified periods of time after a grant.

Conclusion

As these examples have illustrated, assessment of student learning within grant-funded projects can employ the principles of effective grading.

TABLE 13.2

Science-Valued Behaviors Used to Interview Student Researchers in the Urban Environmental Biogeochemistry at Towson University

Question Number and Brief Excerpt of Success Indicator
Each Statement Was Preceded By: Have You . . .

---

3. Attended seminar offered by two or more departments on integrated science topic

5. Attended professional science/research society meeting

8. Participated in a science internship, work study, or travel study course

10. Assisted a faculty member in collecting research data and/or samples

11. Presented at science seminar (not just as class assignment) to varied audience

12. Worked with science faculty in different fields to solve given research problem

14. Had ethnically diverse coworkers in your science lab or research group

18. Used more advanced scientific tools than those used in most science classes

19. Operated specialized computers or computerized tools to collect/analyze data

20. Operated pieces of scientific equipment and tools that crossed disciplinary lines in order to gather needed research data

25. Collected and examined biological, geological, chemical, *and* environmental samples to examine in lab concurrently

26. Collected and analyzed research data from biological, geological, chemical, and/or environmental samples and interpreted integrated research data

27. Composed an *original* research paper from science data you collected and analyzed

29. Presented an oral report/poster session to peers, faculty from several departments

30. Read two science articles (*not assigned*) from *scientific journals* in the last 3 months.

Grants usually require addressing four questions, constructing an overall plan showing outcomes and assessment measures, and then fleshing out the measures. Two of the most effective measures are student tests or assignments scored with a rubric and student behaviors evaluated through self-report and interview. To address the assessment requirement, use the principles of effective grading, which, as our own experience illustrates, can be brought from the classroom to the grant project and can be adapted across disciplinary lines. This chapter, like the rest of the book, has tried to demonstrate how we can use grading for every aspect of teaching and assessment. The "elephant in the classroom" need not be ignored or bemoaned; its strength can be directed for student learning.

Appendix A

Examples of Rubrics

Example 1: Biology: Original Scientific Experiment

Virginia Johnson Anderson

This rubric was used at Towson University, Towson, Maryland.

• • •

Assignment: Semester-long assignment to design an original experiment, carry it out, and write it up in scientific report format. Students are to determine which of two brands of a commercial product (such as two brands of popcorn) is better. They must base their judgment on at least four experimental factors. (For example, "percentage of kernels popped" is an experimental factor, but price is not, because price is written on the package.)

Title

5   Is appropriate in tone and structure to science journal; contains necessary descriptors, brand names, and allows reader to anticipate design.

4   Is appropriate in tone and structure to science journal; most descriptors present; identifies function of experimentation, suggests design, but lacks brand names.

3   Identifies function and brand name but does not allow reader to anticipate design.

2   Identifies function or brand name, but not both; lacks design information or is misleading.

1   Is patterned after another discipline or missing.

Introduction

5   Clearly identifies the purpose of the research; identifies interested audiences; adopts an appropriate tone.

4   Clearly identifies the purpose of the research; identifies interested audiences.

3   Clearly identifies the purpose of the research.

2   Purpose present in Introduction, but must be identified by reader.

1   Fails to identify the purpose of the research.

Scientific Format

5   All material placed in the correct sections; organized logically within each section; runs parallel among different sections.

4   All material placed in correct sections; organized logically within sections, but may lack parallelism among sections.

3   Material placed in proper sections but not well organized within the sections; disregards parallelism.

2   Some materials are placed in the wrong sections or are not adequately organized wherever they are placed.

1   Material placed in wrong sections or not sectioned; poorly organized wherever placed.

Materials and Methods

5   Contains effective, quantifiable, concisely organized information that allows the experiment to be replicated; is written so that all information inherent to the document can be related back to this section; identifies sources of all data to be collected; identifies sequential information in an appropriate chronology; does not contain unnecessary, wordy descriptions of procedures.

4   As in 5, but contains unnecessary information or wordy descriptions within the section.

3   Presents an experiment that is definitely replicable; all information in document may be related to this section; but fails to identify some sources of data or presents sequential information in a disorganized, difficult way.

2   Presents an experiment that is marginally replicable; parts of the basic design must be inferred by the reader; procedures not quantitatively described; some information in Results or Conclusions cannot be anticipated by reading the Methods and Materials section.

1   Describes the experiment so poorly or in such a nonscientific way that it cannot be replicated.

Nonexperimental Information

5   Student researches and includes price and other nonexperimental information that would be expected to be significant to the audience in determining the better product, or specifically states

nonexperimental factors excluded by design; interjects these at appropriate positions in text or develops a weighted rating scale; integrates nonexperimental information in the Conclusions.

4   As in 5, but is less effective in developing the significance of the nonexperimental information.

3   Student introduces price and other nonexperimental information but does not integrate them into Conclusions.

2   Student researches and includes price effectively; does not include or specifically exclude other nonexperimental information.

1   Student considers price and other nonexperimental variables as research variables; fails to identify the significance of these factors to the research.

Experimental Design

5   Student selects experimental factors that are appropriate to the research purpose and audience; measures adequate aspects of these selected factors; establishes discrete subgroups for which data significance may vary; student demonstrates an ability to eliminate bias from the design and bias-ridden statements from the research; student selects appropriate sample size, equivalent groups, and statistics; student designs a superior experiment.

4   As in 5, but student designs an adequate experiment.

3   Student selects experimental factors that are appropriate to the research purpose and audience; measures adequate aspects of these selected factors; establishes discrete subgroups for which data significance may vary; research is weakened by bias or by sample size of less than 10.

2   As above, but research is weakened by bias and inappropriate sample size.

1   Student designs a poor experiment.

Operational Definitions

5   Student constructs a stated comprehensive operational definition and well-developed specific operational definitions.

4   Student constructs an implied comprehensive operational definition and well-developed specific operational definitions.

3   Student constructs an implied (though possibly less clear) comprehensive operational definition and some specific operational definitions.

2   Student constructs specific operational definitions but fails to construct a comprehensive definition.

1   Student lacks understanding of operational definition.

Control of Variables

5   Student demonstrates, by written statement, the ability to control variables by experimental control and by randomization; student makes reference to or implies factors to be disregarded by reference to pilot or experience; superior overall control of variables.

4   As in 5, but student demonstrates an adequate control of variables.

3   Student demonstrates the ability to control important variables experimentally; Methods and Materials section does not indicate knowledge of randomization or selectively disregards variables.

2   Student demonstrates the ability to control some but not all of the important variables experimentally.

1   Student demonstrates a lack of understanding about controlling variables.

Collecting Data and Communicating Results

5   Student selects quantifiable experimental factors and defines and establishes quantitative units of comparison; measures the quantifiable factors and units in appropriate quantities or intervals; student selects appropriate statistical information to be utilized in the results; when effective, student displays results in graphs with correctly labeled axes; data are presented to the reader in text as well as graphic forms; tables or graphs have self-contained headings.

4   As in 5, but the student did not prepare self-contained headings for tables or graphs.

3   As in 4, but data reported in graphs or tables contain materials that are irrelevant or not statistically appropriate.

2   Student selects quantifiable experimental factors or defines and establishes quantitative units of comparison; fails to select appropriate quantities or intervals or fails to display information graphically when appropriate.

1   Student does not select, collect, or communicate quantifiable results.

Interpreting Data

5   Student summarizes the purpose and findings of the research; student draws inferences that are consistent with the data and scientific

reasoning and relates these to interested audiences; student explains expected results and offers explanations or suggestions for further research for unexpected results; student presents data honestly, distinguishes between fact and implication, and avoids overgeneralizing; student organizes nonexperimental information to support conclusion; student accepts or rejects the hypothesis.

4   As in 5, but student does not accept or reject the hypothesis.

3   As in 4, but the student overgeneralizes or fails to organize nonexperimental information to support conclusions.

2   Student summarizes the purpose and findings of the research; student explains expected results but ignores unexpected results.

1   Student may or may not summarize the results but fails to interpret their significance to interested audiences.

Source: Example 1 adapted from Anderson and Walvoord, 1991, Appendix A. Copyright 1991 by the National Council of Teachers of English. Reprinted with permission.

Example 2: Nursing and Occupational Therapy: Group Activities

Judith Bloomer, Occupational Therapy, and Evelyn Lutz, Nursing
This rubric was used at Xavier University, Cincinnati, Ohio.

• • •

Assignment: Group projects in occupational therapy and nursing.
Group Project: —————— Member being assessed: ——————
Instructions: Using the key that follows, circle the number that represents your opinion on the group member's performance on each item.

3	Outstanding
2	More than satisfactory
1	Satisfactory
0	Less than satisfactory
N/O	Inadequate opportunity to observe

Work-Related Performance

Comprehension: Seemed to understand requirements for assignment	0	1	2	3	N/0
Problem identification and solution: Participated in identifying and defining problems and working toward solutions	0	1	2	3	N/0
Organization: Approached tasks (such as time management) in systematic manner	0	1	2	3	N/0
Acceptance of responsibility: Shared responsibility for tasks to be accomplished	0	1	2	3	N/0
Initiative/motivation: Made suggestions, sought feedback, showed interest in group decision making and planning	0	1	2	3	N/0
Creativity: Looked at ideas from viewpoints different from the usual ways	0	1	2	3	N/0
Task completion: Followed through in completing own contributions to group project	0	1	2	3	N/0
Attendance: Attended planning sessions, was prompt, and participated in decision making	0	1	2	3	N/0

Work-Related Interactions with Others

Collaboration: Worked cooperatively with others	0	1	2	3	N/0

Participation: Contributed "fair share" to group project, given the nature of individual assignment	0	1	2	3	N/0
Attitude: Displayed positive approach and made constructive comments in working toward goal	0	1	2	3	N/0
Independence: Carried out tasks without overly depending on other group members	0	1	2	3	N/0
Communication: Expressed thoughts clearly	0	1	2	3	N/0
Responsiveness: Reacted sensitively to verbal and nonverbal cues of other group members	0	1	2	3	N/0

Add total score   Total: ____

Divide by number of items scored with a number   Average: ____

Comments (use back of paper):

Name of evaluator:

_____   Date: _____

Example 3: Economics: Analysis of a Proposed Law

Philip Way

This rubric was used at the University of Cincinnati, Cincinnati, Ohio.

• • •

Assignment: For your employer, a congresswoman, research and analyze a proposed law to raise the minimum wage.

Executive Summary

5   Clearly states the position of the researcher; summarizes the main reasons for this conclusion.

4   Clearly states the position of the researcher; provides information as to why the conclusion was reached.

3   Clearly states the position of the researcher.

2   Position of the researcher is present in the Summary but must be identified by the reader.

1   Fails to identify the position of the researcher.

Criteria

3   Student clearly and correctly defines the criteria used to assess the implications of the research question.

2   Student provides definitions of the criteria used to assess the implications of the research question, but the presentation is unclear or at least one definition is not factually correct.

1   Student fails to define correctly the criteria used.

Relative Weighting of Criteria

3   Student indicates the relative weighting (importance) of the criteria.

2   Student's weighting scheme, although present, is unclear.

1   Student fails to identify the relative weighting (importance) of the criteria.

Production Possibility Diagram

5   Student clearly presents and fully explains the impact of the proposed change in terms of a production possibility frontier (PPF) diagram. Graph is appropriately drawn and labeled. Discussion is in terms of identified criteria.

4   Student presents and explains the impact of the proposed change in terms of a PPF diagram. Either the explanation or the graph is less than clear, although they do not contain factual errors.

3   Student presents and explains the impact of the proposed change in terms of a PPF diagram, but the presentation contains some factual errors.

2   Student presents and explains the impact of the proposed change in terms of a PPF diagram. Presentation contains serious factual errors.

1   Student does not present the impact of the proposed change in terms of a PPF diagram.

Supply-and-Demand Diagram

5   Student clearly presents and fully explains the impact of the proposed change in terms of a supply-and-demand diagram. Graph is appropriately drawn and labeled. Discussion is in terms of identified criteria.

4   Student presents and explains the impact of the proposed change in terms of a supply-and-demand diagram. Either the explanation or the graph is less than clear, but they do not contain factual errors.

3   Student presents and explains the impact of the proposed change in terms of a supply-and-demand diagram, but presentation contains factual errors.

2   Student presents and explains the impact of the proposed change in terms of a supply-and-demand diagram. Presentation contains serious factual errors.

1   Student does not present the impact of the proposed change in terms of a supply-and-demand diagram.

Production Costs/Supply Diagram

5   Student clearly presents and fully explains the impact of the proposed change in terms of a production costs/supply diagram. Graph is appropriately drawn and labeled. Discussion is in terms of identified criteria.

4   Student presents and explains the impact of the proposed change in terms of a supply-and-demand production costs/supply diagram. Either the explanation or the graph is less than clear, but neither contains factual errors.

3   Student presents and explains the impact of the proposed change in terms of a production costs/supply diagram, but presentation contains factual errors.

2   Student presents and explains the impact of the proposed change in terms of a production costs/supply diagram. Presentation contains serious factual errors.

1   Student does not present the impact of the proposed change in terms of a production costs/supply diagram.

Supporting Data

5   Student provides an analysis of economic data that supports the student's position. Quantitative and qualitative information concerning the effect of the increase are presented accurately; differences of opinion are noted where they exist.

4   Student provides an analysis of economic data that support the student's position. Either quantitative or qualitative information concerning the effect of the increase is presented accurately; differences of opinion are noted where they exist.

3   Student provides an analysis of economic data that support the student's position. However, the discussion is unclear or contains factual errors.

2   Student provides an analysis of economic data that support the student's position. However, the discussion is very unclear or contains serious factual errors.

1   Student fails to provide an analysis of economic data that supports the student's position.

Integration

3   Student provides a clear link between the theoretical and empirical analyses and the assessment criteria.

2   Student provides some link between the theoretical and empirical analyses and the assessment criteria.

1   Student does not provide a link between the theoretical and empirical analyses and the assessment criteria.

Conclusions

3   Student's conclusion is fully consistent with student's analysis.

2   Student's conclusion is generally consistent with student's analysis.

1   Student's conclusion is not consistent with student's analysis.

Original Thought

3   Paper shows evidence of original thought: that is, analysis is not simply a summary of others' opinions or analyses but rather an evaluation of the proposals in light of the criteria and weighting scheme chosen by the student.

2   Paper shows some evidence of original thought but is mostly a summary of others' opinions or analyses rather than an evaluation of the proposals in light of the criteria and weighting scheme chosen by the student.

1   Student's paper fails to show evidence of original thought.

Miscellaneous

5   Student appropriately cites sources. The paper is word-processed, neat, and easy to read.

4   The student's paper is generally professional and includes citations, but it contains minor stylistic errors.

3   The paper is legible and includes some citations. However, it contains serious stylistic errors.

2   The student's paper lacks citations and is sloppy or otherwise unprofessional.

1   The student's work is not professionally presented.

Example 4: Art History: Hypothetical Newspaper Article

Christine Havice, Director, School of Art, Kent State University

This rubric was used at the University of Kentucky, Lexington, Kentucky.

• • •

Assignment: For a hypothetical "newspaper" in the ancient Assyrian empire, write a news report on the unveiling of the palace relief titled *Ashurnasirpal II at War*.

Criteria for Evaluation (Possible Fifteen Points)

14–15   Describes work concisely

Relates message to artist's choices and use of various devices

Develops how message affects beholder

Considers audience in writing

Clearly organized and presented

Well imagined

Legible

No problems with mechanics, grammar, spelling, or punctuation

11–13   Good description

Relates message to artist's choices and use of various devices

Some consideration of effect on beholder

Considers audience

Perhaps could be better organized or presented

Adequately imagined

Legible

Few problems with mechanics, grammar, spelling, or punctuation

8–10   Adequate description

Less thorough analysis of how artist conveys message and devices

Audience not necessarily kept in mind

Needs significant improvement in organization or presentation

Needs better imagination

Problems with legibility, mechanics

6–7   Lacking substantially in either description or analysis

Problems with audience, organization, presentation, or mechanics interfere with understanding

0–5   Substandard on more than two of these: description, analysis of choices and devices, effects on beholder

Major problems with audience, organization, presentation, or mechanics

Example 5: Career Planning: Field Observation

Cheryl Cates

This rubric was used at the University of Cincinnati, Cincinnati, Ohio.

• • •

Assignment: Students research a career field they are interested in and write a report. Assignment includes conducting an interview with a professional employed in the field of students' interest.

Content/Format

5   Report offers information that relates to the assignment and leads the reader through the information in a logical and interesting way.

4   Report covers many of the content issues required by the assignment but is not arranged in a format that provides for interesting reading.

3   Information is incomplete, confusing, and arranged in such a way that it is difficult to judge how it relates to the assignment.

2   Information does not relate to the assignment.

1   Information is absent.

Research

5   Report sufficiently answers most of the questions listed in the assignment through both secondary library research and formal interview.

4   Student answers at least half the questions through both secondary research and informational interview.

3   Student makes an attempt through secondary research and informational interview.

2   Student conducts no secondary research and does little to address questions asked in the assignment.

1   Student has in no way answered the relevant questions (no secondary research and no interview).

Interview

5   Student conducts a formal in-person interview with someone the student considers to be a potential employer.

4   Student conducts an informal or telephone interview with someone that the student considers to be a potential employer.

3   Student conducts a formal interview with another (senior) student in the same discipline.

2   Student conducts an informal interview with another student (for example, the student catches a senior after co-op information night and asks a few quick questions).

1   Student did not conduct a personal interview for the project.

Example 6: Education: Poster Presentation

Suzanne Wegener Soled, Professor and Chair, Department of Teacher Education and School Leadership, Northern Kentucky University

This rubric was used at the University of Cincinnati, Cincinnati, Ohio.

• • •

Assignment: Students asked to develop a poster to illustrate how they have demonstrated certain themes in their internships.

Distinguished

_____ A variety of multiple intelligences are addressed in the poster.

_____ Creativity is evident; you explain why you chose to present the way y ou did.

_____ Risk taking is evident; includes explanation of what worked, what didn't, and why.

_____ You clearly and concisely explain how you used assessment materials.

_____ You meet the needs of diverse learners.

_____ Statistical concept included, and its use clearly and concisely explained.

_____ Reflection provides explicit documentation of the theme.

_____ Reflection is written in professional language; no convention errors.

Proficient

_____ Several multiple intelligences addressed in poster presentation.

_____ Some creativity evident; some explanation of why you chose to present the way you did.

_____ Some risk taking evident; includes explanation of what worked, what didn't, and why.

_____ How you used the assessment materials is clearly explained.

_____ Meeting the needs of diverse learners is fairly evident.

_____ Statistical concept is included and its use clearly explained.

_____ Reflection provides fairly clear documentation of the theme.

_____ Reflection written in professional language; one convention error.

Apprentice

_____ Multiple intelligences addressed minimally in poster presentation.

_____ Creativity partially evident: partial explanation of why you chose to present the way you did.

_____ Minimal or no risk taking evident. Does not include explanation of what worked, what didn't, and why.

_____ How you used assessment materials partially explained.

_____ Meeting the needs of diverse learners partially evident.

_____ Statistical concept included and its use partially explained.

_____ Reflection provides partial documentation of the theme.

_____ Reflection written with some errors in professional language; some convention errors.

Example 7: Business Management: Team Project

Lawrence D. Fredendall

This rubric was used at Clemson University, Columbia, South Carolina.

• • •

Assignment: Student teams work with a firm to identify problems and offer recommendations. To be completed by members of the business firms in which student teams work, this sheet is given to students and to members of the firm from the very beginning of the project.

Team's Customer Satisfaction Skills		
Punctuality Some team members missed appointments or did not return phone calls. 0 1 2 3	All team members arrived on time for appointments and returned all phone calls promptly. 4 5 6 7	All team members were early. 8 9 10
Courtesy Some team members were not respectful of some firm employees. 0 1 2 3	All team members were always courteous and respectful of all firm employees. 4 5 6 7	All employees felt that the team members were very respectful and courteous and fully elicited their ideas. 8 9 10
Appearance Sometimes some team members were inappropriately dressed. 0 1 2 3	All team members were always appropriately dressed. 4 5 6 7	All team members adjusted their attire to match the attire used in our firm. 8 9 10
Enthusiasm Some team members did not seem interested in the project. 0 1 2 3	All team members appeared enthusiastic and eager to work on the project. 4 5 6 7	The enthusiasm of the team members to complete the project was contagious and inspired others at our firm. 8 9 10

Communication		
Some team members did not communicate clearly during meeting or phone calls.	The team members always communicated clearly with employees during meetings and phone calls.	The team members always made an extra effort to make sure they understood us and that we understood them during meetings and phone calls.
0 1 2 3	4 5 6 7	8 9 10

Team's Project Management Skills

Plan Awareness		
No team member ever presented a plan to the firm about how to complete the project.	The team presented a plan, but some team members did not seem to follow it.	All the team members seemed to be aware of the plan and following it.
0 1 2 3	4 5 6 7	8 9 10

Problem Definition		
The team's definition of the problem was absent or vague.	The problem was clearly defined. Data were provided measuring the scope of the problem.	The problem's importance and relationship of the firm's goals were clearly stated.
0 1 2 3	4 5 6 7	8 9 10

Plan Feasibility		
The plan that was presented was not feasible.	The plan that was presented was feasible but needed improvement.	The plan was feasible and was regularly updated as necessary during the project.
0 1 2 3	4 5 6 7	8 9 10

Plan Presentation		
A written plan was not presented.	A clear plan with a Gantt chart was presented.	The team was able to explain clearly why it collected certain data and did not collect other data.
0 1 2 3	4 5 6 7	8 9 10

Team's Data Analysis

Data Collection		
The team did not use any apparent method to determine which data to gather.	The data were gathered in a systematic manner.	The team was able to explain clearly why it collected certain data and did not collect other data.
0 1 2 3	4 5 6 7	8 9 10

Collection Method The team's data collection method was haphazard and random.	The team has a clear plan they followed to collect the data.	The data collection methods simplified the data analysis.
0 1 2 3	4 5 6 7	8 9 10
Analysis Tools The team used no tools to analyze the data, or the tools seemed to be randomly selected.	The team used all the appropriate tools for data analysis.	The team fully explained why it selected certain tools and did not use others for data analysis.
0 1 2 3	4 5 6 7	8 9 10
Results Analysis The team did no evaluation of the validity of its data analysis results.	The team validated its results by checking with the appropriate staff for their insight.	The team validated its results by conducting a short experiment.
0 1 2 3	4 5 6 7	8 9 10

Team's Recommendations

Clarity The team had no recommendations, or they were not understandable.	The team's recommendations were reasonable given the problem examined.	The recommendations logically emerged from the problem statement and data analysis.
0 1 2 3	4 5 6 7	8 9 10
Impact The impact of implementing the recommendation was not examined or was completely wrong.	The recommendations are specific enough to serve as the basis for decisions by management.	The recommendations include an implementation plan that is feasible to implement.
0 1 2 3	4 5 6 7	8 9 10

Qualities of Team's Paper

Executive Summary There was no executive summary.	The executive summary was well written and captured key goals, problems, analysis, steps, and recommendations.	The executive summary is as good as those usually presented in our firm.
0 1 2 3	4 5 6 7	8 9 10

Organization The paper is difficult to follow. 0 1 2 3	The paper is easy to follow and read. 4 5 6 7	All relationships among ideas are clearly expressed by the sentence structures and word choice. 8 9 10
Writing Style The paper is sloppy, has no clear direction, and looks as if it was written by several people. 0 1 2 3	The format is appropriate with correct spelling, good grammar, good punctuation, and appropriate transition sentences. 4 5 6 7	The paper is well written and is appropriate for presentation in the firm. 8 9 10

Team Members' Personal Skills

Self-Confidence Some team members' mannerisms made them look as if they were not confident of their abilities. 0 1 2 3	All the team members always seemed confident. 4 5 6 7	All team members were confident and would be able to lead in this organization. 8 9 10
Knowledge Some team members did not seem to understand what they were doing. 0 1 2 3	All team members seemed to have adequate knowledge or ability to learn the necessary material. 4 5 6 7	All team members were proactive about identifying skills they needed and obtaining them in advance. 8 9 10
Reliability Some team members did not follow through with their commitments. 0 1 2 3	All team members fulfilled all commitments they made to staff here. 4 5 6 7	The work the team completed more than met my expectations. 8 9 10

Your Satisfaction with the Product

Project Completion The team did not do a reasonable amount of work on the project. 0 1 2 3	The team completed a reasonable amount of work on the project. 4 5 6 7	The work the team completed more than met my expectations. 8 9 10

Project Recommendations		
The recommendations provide no insight.	The recommendations are useful and will be examined in detail by our firm.	The recommendations will be implemented in full or in part.
0 1 2 3	4 5 6 7	8 9 10
Satisfaction		
We are not satisfied.	We are completely satisfied.	We are more than satisfied; we are delighted with the team's work!
0 1 2 3	4 5 6 7	8 9 10

Your name: _____

Would you sponsor another team project? _____

What do you recommend that the department do to improve the project?

Example 8 Architecture: Architectural Program

Cara Carroccia

This rubric was used at University of Notre Dame, Notre Dame, Indiana.

• • •

Assignment: To construct an architectural program.

Program: Plan

4 The assigned program is carefully analyzed and developed. The architect has not omitted any portion of the program and has in fact added to the program.

3 The architect provides some insight or depth of understanding to the assigned program. However, the internal logic and character of the work need to be more clearly established and developed.

2 The development of the program is generalized and lifeless. Mainly surface relationships are provided. The program has not been developed much beyond the level of bubble diagram.

1 The architect communicates no real understanding or development of the assigned program.

Clarity of Concept and Design Objectives

4 The architect's concept is organized and unified and has logical transitions between the urban and intimate scale.

3 The design objective is mainly clear to the viewer because the architect has tried to order the objectives. The link between the urban and architectural realms is not fully explained graphically.

2 Although there may be some attempt at presenting design objectives in a thoughtful manner, the work is confused and disjointed.

1 The project has no discernible concept.

Style

4 The architect demonstrates a quality of imagination and rigor that results in a distinctive project. The work shows a personal exploration.

3 The architect includes refining details, but a portion of the work remains general. The overall composition is pleasing.

2 The architect does not invest himself or herself into the work. The style seems bland, guarded, flat, and not very interesting.

1   The architect demonstrated no recognizable individualistic or historic style.

Development of the Small Scale; Detailed Information

4   Character, detail, and scale are clearly expressed in plan and section.

3   Some details are thoughtful and vivid. However, the character of the plan or section is not developed.

2   Simplistic details are used in a typical way. Repetition of these details distracts from the work. The plan and section together describe a reasonable, believable building, but little information about or attention to detail is developed.

1   Development of the character of the plan or section is limited and immature.

Development of the Urban Scale

4   The development of the urban scale shows a confident control of the project and communicates a clear parti. The work "reads" smoothly from urban scale to the intimate scale. Coherent development at this level makes the project clear and easy to understand.

3   The architect shows some control in the development of an urban parti, and has only a few elements at the urban scale that are awkward or perfunctory.

2   The architect has definite problems with parti: in simplistic terms, the big idea. Most of the urban plan is simplistic in conception and immature in its development.

1   There is no discernible urban idea. All is perfunctory.

Knowledge of Construction

4   There are no obvious errors in construction. The architect shows familiarity with the building materials and their appropriate use.

3   A few errors in construction practices appear in the project, showing the architect is still learning about the building materials that were chosen. These errors do not substantially detract from the overall impression of the work.

2   Errors or omissions in the use of the chosen building materials are so numerous that they are distracting to the viewer.

1   Errors or omissions in standard building practices are serious enough and frequent enough to interfere with meaning.

Graphic Presentation

4   The project is presented in a complete and compelling manner.

3   The project is compelling but incomplete.

2   Required drawings are missing, and the presented work is not legible due to the lightness of the drawings or the haphazard method of presentation.

1   Little effort was invested in the graphic communication of the assigned project.

Example 9: Statistics: Statistical Investigation

William Marsh

This rubric was used at Raymond Walters College of the University of Cincinnati, Cincinnati, Ohio.

• • •

Assignment: Conduct a statistical investigation, including identifying a problem, developing an hypothesis, obtaining a random sample, measuring variables, analyzing data, and presenting conclusions.

Methodology

5   Correct statement of problem with accompanying null and alternative hypothesis. Well-defined population with appropriate random sample. Data collection is free of bias or contamination.

4   One part of the 5 level is not as high as it should be, and overall the quality of the methodology is just slightly lower than the highest level.

3   All the necessary parts of the methodology are present, but the quality level is only adequate.

2   There is a serious deficit in the methodology in the form of poorly performed tasks or some portions simply omitted. The results are compromised and may be unusable.

1   There is total failure to understand the task. The results will be invalidated because the methodology is erroneous.

Data Analysis

5   Uses appropriate statistical test with correct results. Provides an interval estimation of the values of the parameter. Includes a hypothesis test and gives accompanying *p*-level stating probability of type 1 error.

4   Provides most of level 5, but one of the characteristics is missing or unclear.

3   Uses correct statistical test, but estimation or interpretation is omitted.

2   Uses correct statistical test, but there are errors in calculation and other work.

1   Incorrect statistical test: data are erroneous or missing.

Conclusions

5　　A complete presentation of results with conclusions, estimations, and p-levels for type 1 errors. Identifies possible threats to the study and also any areas in need of additional study.

4　　As in 5, but one characteristic could be improved.

3　　The presentation is only adequate. Conciseness and clarity are lacking.

2　　Conclusions are vague and inaccurate. There has been an effort by the student, but there is an obvious lack of understanding and thoroughness.

1　　A failure to make the necessary conclusions and implications.

Example 10: Office Administration: Spreadsheet

Maureen Margolies

This rubric was used at Raymond Walters College of the University of Cincinnati, Cincinnati, Ohio.

Introduction				
5	4	3	2	1
Identifies the purpose of the application, who will be the primary user, how the application will be used.	Identifies the purpose of the application and how it will be used.	Identifies the purpose of the application.	Purpose of the application is unclear.	Fails to identify the purpose of the application.
Construction of Spreadsheet				
5	4	3	2	1
Based on chosen application, student constructs a spreadsheet in a logical, clearly understood format using appropriate labels, values, and formulas, including two or more logical and statistical functions and a data table or lookup table.	Based on chosen application, student constructs a spreadsheet in a logical, clearly understood format using appropriate labels, values, and one logical or statistical function.	Based on chosen application, student constructs a spreadsheet in a logical, clearly understood format using basic mathematical formulas and functions.	Based on chosen application, student constructs a spreadsheet in a logical, clearly understood format using basic mathematical formulas and functions.	Spreadsheet is not based on application, or is it logically or clearly understood by the reader or other user.
Application of Formulas and Functions and Testing for Accurate Results				
5	4	3	2	1
Student works through the application, testing formulas	Student works through the application, testing formulas	Student works through the application, testing formulas	Student works through the application, testing formulas	Student fails to test the application or correct any

and functions for accurate results. Debugs if necessary and corrects. Makes decisions about changing formulas or functions to achieve desired results.	and functions for accurate results. Debugs if necessary and corrects.	and function for accurate results. Corrects obvious mistakes but fails to debug.	and function for accurate results; but no corrections are made.	miscalculations for formulas.

Data Analysis, Reporting, and Summarizing

5	4	3	2	1
Creates three graphs from the spreadsheet that compare, contrast, or show percentage of the whole to help analyze the data. Queries the spreadsheet to extract data that would be used in a planning report.	Same as 5, except creates only two graphs.	Creates two graphs from the spreadsheet that compare, contrast, or show percentage of the whole to help analyze the data, or queries the spreadsheet to extract data that would be used in a planning report.	Creates one graph from the spreadsheet that compares, contrasts, or shows percentage of the whole to help analyze data.	Creates a graph but fails to show how it compares, contrasts, or shows a percentage of the whole.

Analysis of Purpose, Findings, and Conclusions

5	4	3	2	1
Summarizes purpose and findings, draws conclusions on usefulness in fulfilling user goals, explains results, and offers explanations.	Summarizes purpose and findings, draws conclusions on usefulness in fulfilling user goals, but fails to explain results or offer explanations.	Summarizes purpose and findings but fails to draw conclusions on usefulness.	Vaguely summarizes the purpose of findings and fails to draw conclusions.	Summary statement either does not summarize purpose or findings and is merely a restatement of purpose, or there is no summary at all.

Example 11: Mathematics: Journals

Bob Drake and Linda Amspaugh developed this list of items to illustrate the kinds of criteria that might be used for journal entries.

Criteria	5	4	3	2	1
Thoroughness of comments: Are the comments just superficial, or do they demonstrate deeper processing? Do your writings appear to be a restatement of someone else's words, or an interpretation in your own words? Have you mentioned applications or relationships to other material?					
Completeness: Have all important points been discussed? Are there omissions of information?					
Understanding: Are the ideas correctly understood? What evidence illustrates that understanding?					
Personal connections: Is the information connected to your personal observations and experiences?					
Growth: Is there evidence that your understanding has increased? Did you learn something that you didn't know before?					
Inquiry: Have you thought of other questions? Have you asked any additional questions not yet answered?					
Problem completion: Does it appear that problems have been attempted, or have they merely been skimmed over?					
General quality: What is the overall quality of your work in this journal?					

Reprinted by permission from Drake, B. M., and Amspaugh, L. B. "The Write to Learn Mathematics." *Literacy: Issues and Practices*, 1993, 10, 28–34

Example 12: Business Management: Case Analysis

Daniel Singer, Professor of Finance, Towson University, Towson, Maryland

This rubric was used at Loyola College in Baltimore, Maryland.

• • •

Assignment: Students write a case analysis.

Part One of the Paper: Strategic Statement

1. The following four elements are present: (1) analysis of the firm's goals, (2) resources, (3) environment, and (4) past, present, or planned strategy.   1 2 3 4 5

2. The analysis of the firm's goals:

The statement about goals is consistent with the material in the case.   1 2 3 4 5

The writer presents sufficient and clearly organized evidence for the summary of the firm's goals.   1 2 3 4 5

The writer has chosen the most important or primary goals.   1 2 3 4 5

The goals are stated specifically enough to be the basis for decisions by management.   1 2 3 4 5

3. The analysis of the firm's resources:

The statement about resources is consistent with the material in the case.   1 2 3 4 5

The writer presents sufficient and clearly organized evidence for the summary of the firm's resources.   1 2 3 4 5

The writer has chosen the most important or primary resources.   1 2 3 4 5

4. The analysis of the firm's environment:

The statement about environment is consistent with the material in the case.   1 2 3 4 5

The writer presents sufficient and clearly organized evidence for the summary of the firm's environment.   1 2 3 4 5

		1	2	3	4	5
	The writer has chosen the most important or primary environmental features.	1	2	3	4	5
5.	The analysis of how the firm expects to achieve its goals:					
	The statement about how is consistent with the material in the case.	1	2	3	4	5
	The writer presents sufficient and clearly organized evidence for the summary of the how.	1	2	3	4	5
	The writer chose the actual strategies rather than being misled by what an individual in the firm may think is the how.	1	2	3	4	5

Part Two of the Paper: Strategic Fit

6.	The writer analyzes the fit and the appropriateness of the firm's present and planned strategy in light of the firm's goals. The writer tells how probable it is that the firm will achieve its goals by those means.	1	2	3	4	5
7.	The writer supports the analysis of strategic fit by logical reasoning and by evidence from the case.	1	2	3	4	5

Part Three of the Paper: Recommendations

8.	The recommendations grow logically out of the first two sections of the paper.	1	2	3	4	5
9.	The recommendations are specific enough to serve as the basis for decisions by management.	1	2	3	4	5
10.	The recommendations are clearly stated and explained.	1	2	3	4	5

Part Four: Qualities of the Entire Paper

11.	Within the paper is a clear statement of the writer's thesis (the summary of the main ? that guides the entire analysis).	1	2	3	4	5
12.	The voice of the writer is appropriate for a consultant addressing a board of directors.	1	2	3	4	5

13.	The paper is interesting and fresh.	1	2	3	4	5
14.	The relationships among ideas are clearly reflected in sentence structure and word choice.	1	2	3	4	5
15.	Important ideas are given appropriate emphasis.	1	2	3	4	5
16.	The word choice is precise.	1	2	3	4	5
17.	The paper is economically written: every word pulls its weight.	1	2	3	4	5
18.	Paper is accurate in spelling.	1	2	3	4	5
19.	The writer properly punctuates sentence boundaries.	1	2	3	4	5
20.	The writer correctly uses apostrophes and plurals.	1	2	3	4	5
21.	The writer observes "standard English" forms of noun-verb agreement and pronoun-antecedent agreement.	1	2	3	4	5
22.	The writer observes "standard English" forms of verbs, pronouns, and negatives.	1	2	3	4	5
23.	The writer correctly uses other punctuation such as commas within sentence boundaries, colons, semicolons, quotation marks, capitals, and so on.	1	2	3	4	5

Example 13: First-Year Composition: Essay

Barbara E. Walvoord

This rubric was used at Loyola College, Baltimore, Maryland, and the University of Notre Dame, Notre Dame, Indiana.

• • •

Assignment: To write an essay that explores an idea or insight. Students are to use external sources as needed, but this is not a term paper.

A Range

Originality of thesis: The author develops an authentic, fresh insight that challenges the reader's thinking. The paper shows a complex, curious mind at work.

Clarity of thesis and purpose: The thesis and purpose are clear to the reader.

Organization: The essay is organized in a way that fully and imaginatively supports the thesis and purpose. The sequence of ideas is effective, given the writer's thesis and purpose. The reader always feels that the writer is in control of the organization, even when the organizational plan is complex, surprising, or unusual. The subpoints serve to open up and explore the writer's insight in the most productive way.

Support: The writer offers the best possible evidence and reasoning to convince the reader. No important pieces of available evidence and no important points or reasons are omitted. It is clear that the writer is very well informed, has searched hard and effectively for appropriate evidence, and has thought about how evidence may be used for the argument. Evidence presented is always relevant to the point being made. Through telling detail, the writer helps the reader to experience what the writer is saying.

Use of sources: The writer has used sources to support, extend, and inform the ideas but not to substitute for the writer's own development of an idea. The writer has effectively combined material from a variety of sources, including, as relevant and needed, personal observation, scientific data, authoritative testimony, and others. (This is not to say that the writer must use a certain number or type of sources. Need and relevance should be the determining factors.) The writer uses quotations to capture a source's key points or turns of phrase but does not over-use quoted material to substitute for the writer's own development of an idea. Quotations, paraphrase, and citation are handled according to accepted scholarly form.

Ethos: The writer creates a "self" or "ethos" that sounds genuine, that is relevant to the writer's purpose, and that is consistent throughout the essay.

Style: Language is used with control, elegance, and imagination to serve the writer's purpose. The essay, when read aloud, pleases the eye and ear.

Edited Written Standard English (ESWE): Except for deliberate departures (the quoted speech of a person, a humorous purpose, and so on), the writer uses ESWE forms of grammar, punctuation, spelling, and syntax.

Presentation: The essay looks neat, crisp, and professional.

B Range

Falls short of the *A* range in one or more ways.

C Range

Originality of thesis: The thesis may be obvious or unimaginative.

Clarity of thesis and purpose: The thesis and purpose are clear to the reader.

Organization: The essay is organized in a way that competently supports the thesis and purpose. The sequence of ideas is effective, given the writer's thesis and purpose. The reader almost always feels that the writer is in control of the organization, even when the organizational plan is complex, surprising, or unusual. The subpoints serve to open up and explore the writer's insight in a productive way.

Support: The writer offers solid evidence and reasoning to convince the reader. No important pieces of available evidence and no important points or reasons are omitted. It is clear that the writer is well informed and has thought about how evidence may be used for the argument. Evidence presented is usually relevant to the point being made.

Use of sources: The writer has used sources to support, extend, and inform the ideas but not to substitute for the writer's own development of an idea. The writer uses quotations to capture a source's key points or turns of phrase but does not overuse quoted material to substitute for the writer's own development of an idea. Quotations, paraphrase, and citation are handled with reasonable consistency, according to accepted scholarly form.

Ethos: The writer creates a "self" or "ethos" that sounds genuine, that is relevant to the writer's purpose, and that is generally consistent throughout the essay.

Style: Language is used competently, though it may be awkward at times. There are few or no sentences that confuse the reader or are incomprehensible.

Edited Written Standard English (ESWE): Except for deliberate departures (the quoted speech of a person, a humorous purpose, and so on), the writer generally uses ESWE forms of grammar, punctuation, spelling, and syntax. There are no more than an average of two departures from ESWE per page in any combination of the following areas: sentence boundary punctuation, spelling and typos, use of apostrophe and plural, ESWE verb and pronoun forms, ESWE agreement between subject-verb and pronoun-antecedent.

Presentation: The essay looks neat, crisp, and professional.

Any one of the following may result in a *D* or *F*:

D–F Range

The thesis is obvious, cut-and-dried, trite.

The reader cannot determine the thesis and purpose.

The organization is not clear to the reader.

The organizational plan is inappropriate to the thesis; it does not offer effective support or explanation of the writer's ideas.

The writer offers little or no effective support for the ideas.

The writer has neglected important sources that should have been used.

The writer has overused quoted or paraphrased material to substitute for the writer's own ideas.

The writer has used source material without acknowledgment. (This may also result in the kinds of penalties attached to plagiarism. See Student Handbook.)

The language is so muddy that the reader is frequently at a loss to understand what the writer is trying to say.

The use of ESWE falls below the standard established above for a C.

Example 14: All Sciences: Reading and Interpreting Graphic Information

Virginia Anderson, Biological Sciences, Towson University, Towson, Maryland

Use this rubric to assess the student and/or class proficiency at reading and interpreting information in a line graph.

Reading Graphic Information

4   Accurately describes the function of the graph; identifies points and ranges

3   Partially identifies the functions of the graph; identifies points and ranges

2   Identifies points OR ranges only

1   Lacks competency

Processing Graphic Information Quantitatively

4   Computes, extrapolates, employs quantitative reasoning needed for all tasks

3   Computes and extrapolates accurately

2   Computes OR extrapolates only

1   Lacks competency

Interpreting Graphic Information

4   Draws conclusions from and recognizes limitations of the graphic information

3   Draws conclusions accurately from most (70% to 85%) data statements

2   Draws conclusions accurately at a limited but passing level (60% to 69%)

1   Lacks competency

Making Connections Between Graphic Information and Scientific Issues

4   Makes most relevant content, concept, and ethical connections

3   Makes some relevant content, concept, and ethical connections.

2   Makes content and concept connections, but does not respond to ethical issues.

1   Superficial, biased, irrelevant, or no stated connections made.

Appendix B

Example of Departmental Assessment Report

This is a biology department report for undergraduate majors. Similar reports would be produced for certificate and graduate programs in the department.

Learning Goals for Majors

- Describe and apply basic biological information and concepts.
- Conduct original biological research and report results orally and in writing to scientific audiences.
- Apply ethical principles of the discipline in regard to human and animal subjects, environmental protection, use of sources, and collaboration with colleagues.

Web site and/or other avenues by which these are readily available to students, prospective students, and faculty _____

Measures and Use of Information

Measures	Goal 1	Goal 2	Goal 3	Use of the Information
Standardized test given to all seniors AND Final exams of three basic biology courses required of all majors	X			Data are reported to the department annually by the standardized exam committee and the instructors of the three basic courses. The department supports and encourages the instructors, takes any appropriate department-level actions, and reports meeting outcomes to dean or other body which has resources to address problems, and to those composing reports for accreditation or other external audiences. All data are reviewed as part of program review every seven years.
In senior capstone course, students complete an original scientific experiment, write it up in scientific report format, and also make an oral report to the class. The instructor(s) use explicit criteria to evaluate student work.	X	X	X	Annually, the senior capstone instructor(s) share students' scores with the department. The department takes action as above.
Alumni survey asks how well alumni/ae thought they learned to conduct and communicate scientific research, what aspects of the program helped them learn, and what suggestions they have for improvement in the program.	X	X	X	Data reviewed annually by department for action, as above.
Sample of regional employers gathered two years ago to reflect how well our majors are doing and give advice to dept.	X	X	X	Data reviewed annually by department for action, as above.

Recommendations for Improving Assessment Processes

The standardized national test is costly and time-consuming to administer, has low student motivation in its current format, and results are difficult to map to our curriculum. The committee should review the usefulness of the national test.

[From this point on, the report might have either of two possible final sections, depending on its audience and purpose.]

Final Section for Report on Assessment Process

[If the report is intended for audiences such as accreditors who need to know that the department is conducting assessment, the final section would demonstrate that the department has been using assessment information for change.]

- Two years ago, our advisory council of regional employers said that our majors had a good level of biological knowledge but needed stronger skills in conducting biological research. Data from the alumni survey also mentioned this problem. We instituted the required capstone course, which requires students to conduct original scientific research, and we asked the instructor(s) annually to report to the department on student research and communication skills demonstrated by their capstone projects. In three years, when several cohorts of majors have passed through the capstone, we will again survey alumni and employers to see whether student skills have increased, and we will review data from all years of the capstone projects.

- The capstone instructor(s) last year reported low graphing skills in seniors; we arranged with the mathematics department for greater emphasis on graphing and better assessment of graphing in the required math course. The capstone instructor(s) will report next year whether graphing skills are stronger. Prof. Jones is currently developing a rubric to assess graphing skills more systematically in the capstone.

Alternate Final Section for Program Review, Planning, or Budget Request

[If the assessment report is part of program review, planning, or budgeting cycles, it would have a final section that moves from assessment methods (above) to current findings, actions, and budget requests. The sections would address findings from analysis of data, planned actions to improve learning, and budget requests.]

References

Achacoso, M. V., and Svinicki, M. D. (eds.). *Alternative Strategies for Evaluating Student Learning*. New Directions for Teaching and Learning, no. 100. San Francisco: Jossey-Bass, 2004.

Adelman, C. (ed.). *Signs and Traces: Model Indicators of College Student Learning in the Disciplines*. Washington, D.C.: U.S. Department of Education, 1989.

Anderson, L., and others. *Taxonomy for Learning, Teaching, and Assessing: A Revision of Bloom's Taxonomy of Educational Objectives*. (Abridged ed.) Needham Heights, Mass.: Allyn & Bacon, 2001.

Anderson, R. S., Bauer, J. F., and Speck, B. W. (eds.). *Assessment Strategies for the On-Line Class: From Theory to Practice*. New Directions for Teaching and Learning, no. 91. San Francisco: Jossey-Bass, 2002.

Anderson, R. S., and Speck, B. W. *Changing the Way We Grade Student Performance: Classroom Assessment and the New Learning Paradigm*. New Directions for Teaching and Learning, no. 74. San Francisco: Jossey-Bass, 1998.

Anderson, V. J. "Authentic Assessment: A Microbiology Mandate." *Focus on Microbiology Education Newsletter*, 67, Winter 2001. www.microbelibrary.org/edzine/details.asp?id=1073&Lang=.

Anderson, V. J., and Walvoord, B. E. "Conducting and Reporting Original Scientific Research: Anderson's Biology Class." In B. E. Walvoord, L. P. McCarthy, and others, *Thinking and Writing in College: A Naturalistic Study of Students in Four Disciplines*. Urbana, Ill.: National Council of Teachers of English, 1990.

Angelo, T. A. "Doing Assessment As If Learning Matters Most." *AAHE Bulletin*, 1999, *51*(9), 3–6.

Arreola, R. A. *Developing a Comprehensive Faculty Evaluation System: A Handbook for College Faculty and Administrators on Designing and Operating a Comprehensive Faculty Evaluation System*. (2nd ed.) San Francisco: Anker/Jossey-Bass, 2000.

Astin, A. W. "Involvement in Learning Revisited: Lessons We Have Learned." *Journal of College Student Development*, 1996, 37(2), 123–134.

Baer, J., and Kaufman, J. C. "Creativity Research in English-Speaking Countries." In J. C. Kaufman and R. J. Sternberg (eds.), *The International Handbook of Creativity*. Cambridge: Cambridge University Press, 2006.

Bain, K. *What the Best College Teachers Do*. Cambridge, Mass.: Harvard University Press, 2004.

Banta, T. W. (ed.). *Community College Assessment: Assessment Update Collections*. San Francisco: Jossey-Bass, 2004.

Banta, T. W. (ed.). *Assessing Student Achievement in General Education: Assessment Update Collection*. San Francisco: Jossey-Bass, 2007a.

Banta, T. W. (ed.). *Assessing Student Learning in the Disciplines: Assessment Update Collections*. San Francisco: Jossey-Bass, 2007b.

Banta, T. W., and Associates (eds.). *Portfolio Assessment Uses, Cases, Scoring, and Impact: Assessment Update Collections*. San Francisco: Jossey-Bass, 2003.

Banta, T. W., Jones, E. A., and Black, K. E. *Designing Effective Assessment: Principles and Profiles of Good Practice*. San Francisco: Jossey-Bass, 2009.

Barkley, E., Cross, K. P., and Major, C. H. *Collaborative Learning Techniques: A Handbook for College Faculty*. San Francisco: Jossey-Bass, 2005.

Barnet, S. *A Short Guide to Writing About Art*. (3rd ed.). Glenview, Ill.: Scott, Foresman, 1989.

Barnet, S. *A Short Guide to Writing About Art*. (9th ed.) Upper Saddle River, N.J.: Pearson, 2008.

Bates, A. W., and Poole, G. *Effective Teaching with Technology in Higher Education: Foundations for Success*. San Francisco: Jossey-Bass, 2003.

Bean, J. C. *Engaging Ideas: The Professor's Guide to Integrating Writing, Critical Thinking, and Active Learning in the Classroom*. San Francisco: Jossey-Bass, 1996.

Bean, J. C., Carrithers, D., and Earenfight, T. "Transforming WAC Through a Discourse-Based Approach to University Outcomes Assessment." *WAC Journal*, 2005, *16*, 5–21.

Black, L., Daiker, D. A., Sommers, J., and Stygall, G. (eds.). *New Directions in Portfolio Assessment: Reflective Practice, Critical Theory, and Large-Scale Scoring*. Portsmouth, N.H.: Boynton-Cook, 1994.

Bloom, B. S. (ed.). *Taxonomy of Educational Objectives*. New York: McKay, 1956.

Bloom, B. S., Hastings, J. T., and Madaus, G. F. *Handbook on Formative and Summative Evaluation of Student Learning*. New York: McGraw-Hill, 1971.

Blumberg, P. *Developing Learner-Centered Teaching: A Practical Guide for Faculty*. San Francisco: Jossey-Bass, 2009.

Boice, R. *First-Order Principles for College Teachers: Ten Basic Ways to Improve the Teaching Process*. San Francisco: Anker/Jossey-Bass, 1996.

Boice, R. *Advice for New Faculty Members: Nihil Nimus*. Needham, Mass.: Allyn and Bacon, 2000.

Boud, D., Dunn, J., and Hegarty-Hazel, E. *Teaching in Laboratories*. New York: Open University, 1986.

Bransford, J., Brown, A., and Cocking, R. *How People Learn: Brain, Mind, Experience and School*. Washington, D.C.: National Academies Press, 1999.

Bresciani, M. J. (ed.). *Assessing Student Learning in General Education*. San Francisco: Anker/Jossey-Bass, 2007.

Brookfield, S. D. *The Skillful Teacher: On Technique, Trust, and Responsiveness in the Classroom*. (2nd ed.) San Francisco: Jossey-Bass, 2006.

Brookfield, S. D., and Preskill, S. *Discussion as a Way of Teaching*. (2nd ed.) San Francisco: Jossey-Bass, 2005.

Cambridge, B. L. *Campus Progress: Supporting the Scholarship of Teaching and Learning*. Washington, D.C.: American Association for Higher Education, 2004.

Cambridge, D., Cambridge, B. L., & Yancey, K. (Eds.) *Electronic Portfolios 2.0: Emergent Findings and Shared Questions*. Sterling, VA: Stylus, 2008.

Camp, M. B., and Middendorf, J. "Using JiTT to Motivate Student Learning." In S. P. Simkins and M. H. Meier (eds.), *Just in Time Teaching: Across the Disciplines and Across the Academy*. Sterling, Va.: Stylus, forthcoming.

Carey, L. M. *Measuring and Evaluating School Learning*. (2nd ed.) Needham Heights, Mass.: Allyn and Bacon, 1994.

Carrithers, D., and Bean, J. C. "Using a Client Memo to Assess Critical Thinking of Finance Majors." *Business Communication Quarterly*, 2008, *71*(1), 10–26.

Carrithers, D., Ling, T., and Bean, J. C. "Messy Problems and Lay Audiences: Teaching Critical Thinking within the Finance Curriculum." *Business Communication Quarterly*, 2008, *71*(2), 152–170.

Cashin, W. E. *Improving Essay Tests*. Manhattan: Kansas State University, Center for Faculty Evaluation and Development, 1987. www.theideacenter/IDEAPapers.

Cashin, W. E. *Student Ratings of Teaching: A Summary of the Research*. Manhattan: Kansas State University, Center for Faculty Evaluation and Development, 1988. www.theideacenter.org/IDEAPapers.

Cashin, W. E. *Student Ratings of Teaching: The Research Revisited*. Manhattan: Kansas State University, Center for Faculty Evaluation and Development, 1995. www.theideacenter.org/IDEAPapers.

Chickering, A. W., and Gamson, Z. F. "Seven Principles for Good Practice in Undergraduate Education." *AAHE Bulletin*, 1987, *39*(7), 3–7.

Clegg, V. L., and Cashin, W. E. *Improving Multiple Choice Tests*. Manhattan: Kansas State University, Center for Faculty Evaluation and Development, 1986. www.theideacenter.org/IDEAPapers.

Comeaux, P. (ed.). *Assessing Online Learning*. San Francisco: Anker/Jossey-Bass, 2005.

Conrad, R., and Donaldson, J. A. *Engaging the Online Learner: Activities and Resources for Creative Instruction*. San Francisco: Jossey-Bass, 2004.

"A Course Redesign That Contributed to Student Success." *Teaching Professor*, 2009, *23*(1), 6.

Covington, M. V. "A Motivational Analysis of Academic Life in College." In R. P. Perry and J. C. Smart (eds.), *The Scholarship of Teaching and Learning in Higher Education: An Evidence-Based Perspective*. New York: Springer, 2007a.

Covington, M. V. "Update on Educational Policy, Practice, and Research from a Self-worth Perspective." In R. P. Perry and J. C. Smart (eds.), *The Scholarship of Teaching and Learning in Higher Education: An Evidence-based Perspective*. New York: Springer, 2007b.

Cross, K. P., and Steadman, M. H. *Classroom Research: Implementing the Scholarship of Teaching*. San Francisco: Jossey-Bass, 1996.

Dabbagh, N., and Bannan-Ritland, B. *Online Learning: Concepts, Strategies, and Applications*. Upper Saddle River, N.J.: Pearson Education, 2005.

Davis, B. G. *Tools for Teaching*. (2nd ed.) San Francisco: Jossey-Bass, 2009.

Entwistle, N. "Promoting Deep Learning Through Teaching and Assessment." In L. Suskie (ed.), *Assessment to Promote Deep Learning*. Washington, D.C.: American Association for Higher Education, 2001.

Erikson, B. L., Peter, C. D., and Strommer, D. W. *Teaching First-Year College Students*. San Francisco: Jossey-Bass, 2006.

Facione, P. A. *Critical Thinking: A Statement of Expert Consensus for the Purposes of Educational Assessment and Instruction*. 1990. (ED 315 423)

Facione, P. A., and Facione, N. C. "Holistic Critical Thinking Scoring Rubric." 2004. Retrieved Jan. 16, 2009, from www.insightassessment.com.

Feinberg, L. "Multiple-Choice and Its Critics: Are the 'Alternatives' Any Better?" *College Board Review*, 1990, *17*, 12–17, 30.

Feldman, K. A. "Identifying Exemplary Teaching: Using Data from Course and Teacher Evaluations." In M. Svinicki and R. Menges (eds.), *Honoring Exemplary Teaching*. New Directions in Teaching and Learning, no. 65. San Francisco: Jossey-Bass, 1996.

Fenwick, T., and Parsons, J. *The Art of Evaluation: A Handbook for Educators and Trainers*. Toronto: Thompson Educational, 2000.

Fife, J. D. "Student Responsibility and Student Motivation." *National Teaching and Learning Forum*, 1994, *4*(1), 1–3.

Fink, L. D. *Creating Significant Learning Experiences*. San Francisco: Jossey-Bass, 2003.

Flower, L. S. "The Role of Task Representation in Reading-to-Write." In L. S. Flower and others (eds.), *Reading-to-Write: Exploring a Cognitive and Social Process*. New York: Oxford University Press, 1990.

Garrison, D. R., and Vaughan, N. D. *Blended Learning in Higher Education: Framework, Principles, and Guidelines.* San Francisco: Jossey-Bass, 2008.

Geisler, C. *Academic Literacy and the Nature of Expertise: Reading, Writing, and Knowing in Academic Philosophy.* Mahwah, N.J.: Erlbaum, 1994.

Ghent, C., Gasparich, G., and Scully, E. *Biology: The Science of Life Laboratory Manual.* Dubuque, IA: Kendall Hunt, 2007.

Gilbert, R. *Living with Art.* (3rd ed.) New York: McGraw-Hill, 1992.

Gilbert, R., and McCarter, W. M. *Living with Art.* (2nd ed.) New York: Knopf, 1988.

Ginsberg, M. B., and Wlodkowski, R. J. *Diversity and Motivation: Culturally Responsive Teaching in College.* (2nd ed.) San Francisco: Jossey-Bass, 2009.

Golub, J. N. (ed.). *More Ways to Handle the Paper Load on Paper and Online.* Urbana, Ill.: National Council of Teachers of English, 2005.

Gray, T. (2005). *Publish and Flourish: Become a Prolific Scholar.* Las Cruces: Teaching Academy, New Mexico State University, 2005.

Haladyna, T. M. *Developing and Validating Multiple-Choice Test Items.* Mahwah, N.J.: Erlbaum, 1994.

Halpern, D., and Hakel, M. (eds.). *Applying the Science of Learning to University Teaching and Beyond.* New Directions for Teaching and Learning, no. 89. San Francisco: Jossey-Bass, 2002.

Hill, W. F. *Learning Through Discussion.* Thousand Oaks, Calif.: Sage, 1982.

Hobson, E. *Getting Students to Read: Fourteen Tips.* IDEA Paper, no. 40. Manhattan, KS: The Idea Center, 2004. www.theideacenter.org/IDEAPapers.

Huba, M. E., and Freed, J. E. *Learning-Centered Assessment on College Campuses: Shifting the Focus from Teaching to Learning.* Needham Heights, Mass.: Allyn & Bacon, 2000.

Huber, M. T., and Hutchings, P. *The Advancement of Learning: Building the Teaching Commons.* San Francisco: Jossey-Bass, 2005.

Hunt, L. L. *Writing Across the Curriculum.* Spokane, Wash.: Whitworth College, 1992.

Hutchings, P. (ed.). *Opening Lines: Approaches to the Scholarship of Teaching and Learning.* Stanford, Calif.: Carnegie Foundation for the Advancement of Teaching, 2000.

Innes, R. *Reconstructing Undergraduate Education: Using Learning Science to Design Effective Courses.* Mahwah, N.J.: Erlbaum, 2004.

Jacobs, L. C., and Chase, C. I. *Developing and Using Tests Effectively: A Guide for Faculty.* San Francisco: Jossey-Bass, 1992.

Johnson, W. B., and Mullen, C. A. *Write to the Top: How to Become a Prolific Academic.* New York: Palgrave Macmillan, 2007.

Kalman, C. S. *Successful Science and Engineering Teaching in Colleges and Universities.* San Francisco: Anker/Jossey-Bass, 2007.

Kantz, M. *Shirley and the Battle of Agincourt: Why It Is So Hard for Students to Write Persuasive Researched Analyses.* Berkeley: University of California, Berkeley, and Pittsburgh, Pa.: Carnegie Mellon University, Center for the Study of Writing, 1989.

Klauser, H. A. *Write It Down, Make It Happen: Knowing What You Want and Getting It.* New York: Fireside, 2001.

Knowles, M. J. *Using Learning Contracts: Practical Approaches to Individualizing and Structuring Learning.* San Francisco: Jossey-Bass, 1986.

Kuh, G. D., and others. *Piecing Together the Student Success Puzzle: Research Propositions, and Recommendations.* ASHE Higher Education Report, vol. 32, no. 5. San Francisco: Jossey-Bass, 2007.

Kurfiss, J. G. *Critical Thinking: Theory, Research, Practice, and Possibilities.* ASHE-ERIC Higher Education Report, no. 2. San Francisco: Jossey-Bass, 1988.

Lage, M. J., and Platt, G. "The Internet and the Inverted Classroom." *Journal of Economic Education,* 2000, *31*(1), 11.

Lage, M. J., Platt, G. G., and Treglia, M. "Inverting the Classroom: A Gateway to Creating an Inclusive Learning Environment." *Journal of Economic Education,* 2000, *31*(1), 30–43.

Laing, D. "Nurturing Discussion in the Classroom." In K. Smith (ed.), *Teaching, Learning, Assessing: A Guide for Effective Teaching at College and University.* Oakville, Ontario: Mosaic Press, 2007.

Leskes, A., and Wright, B. *The Art and Science of Assessing General Education Outcomes: A Practical Guide.* Washington, D.C.: Association of American Colleges and Universities, 2005.

Linn, R. L. *Educational Measurement.* Phoenix, Ariz.: Oryx, 1993.

Lloyd-Jones, R. "Primary Trait Scoring." In C. Cooper and L. Odell (eds.), *Evaluating Writing: Describing, Measuring, Judging.* Urbana, Ill.: National Council of Teachers of English, 1977.

Lowman, J. "Assignments That Promote and Integrate Learning." In R. J. Menges, M. Weimer, and Associates, *Teaching on Solid Ground: Using Scholarship to Improve Practice.* San Francisco: Jossey-Bass, 1996.

Lowman, J. *Mastering the Techniques of Teaching.* (2nd ed.) San Francisco: Jossey-Bass, 2000.

McManus, D. A. *Leaving the Lectern: Cooperative Learning and the Critical First Days of Students Working in Groups.* San Francisco: Anker/Jossey-Bass, 2005.

Mezeske, R. J., and Mezeske, B. A. (eds.). *Beyond Tests and Quizzes: Creative Assessments in the College Classroom.* San Francisco: Jossey-Bass, 2007.

Michaelsen, L. K., Knight, A. B., and Fink, L. D. (eds.) *Team Based Learning: A Transformative Use of Small Groups in College Teaching.* Sterling, Va.: Stylus, 2004.

Middle States Commission on Higher Education. *Student Learning Assessment: Options and Resources.* (2nd ed.) Philadelphia: Middle States Commission on Higher Education, 2007.

Miller, G. A. "The Magical Number Seven, Plus or Minus Two: Some Limits on Our Capacity for Processing Information." *Psychological Review,* 1994, *101*(2), 343–352.

Millis, B. *Enhancing Learning-and More! Through Cooperative Learning.* Manhattan, Kans.: Kansas State University, Center for Faculty Evaluation and Development, 2002. www.theideacenter.org/IDEAPapers.

Millis, B. J., and Cottell, P. G. Jr. *Cooperative Learning for Higher Education Faculty.* Phoenix, Ariz.: Oryx, 1998.

Myers, C. B. "Divergence in Learning Goals Priorities Between College Students and Their Faculty: Implications for Teaching and Learning." *College Teaching,* 2008, *56*(1), 53–58.

National Center for Education Statistics. *National Assessment of College Student Learning: Identifying College Graduates' Essential Skills in Writing, Speech and Listening, and Critical Thinking.* Washington, D.C.: U.S. Department of Education, 1995.

Neff, R. A., and Weimer, M. (eds.). *Classroom Communication: Collected Readings for Effective Discussion and Questioning.* Madison, Wisc.: Atwood, 2002.

Nilson, L. B. *Teaching at Its Best: Research-Based Resource for College Instructors.* (2nd ed.) San Francisco: Anker/Jossey-Bass, 2003.

Novak, G. M., Patterson, E. T., Gavrin, A. D., and Christian, W. *Just-in-Time Teaching: Blending Active Learning with Web Technology.* Upper Saddle River, N.J.: Prentice Hall, 1999.

O'Brien, J. G., Millis, B. J., and Cohen, M. W. *The Course Syllabus: A Learning-Centered Approach.* (2nd ed.) San Francisco: Jossey-Bass, 2008.

Pagano, N., and others. "An Inter-Institutional Model for College Writing Assessment." *College Composition and Communication,* 2008, *60*(2), 285–320.

Palmer, P. *To Know As We Are Known.* New York: HarperCollins, 1983.

Palmer, P. J. "Community, Conflict, and Ways of Knowing." *Change,* 1987, *19*(1), 20–25.

Palmer, P. J. "Good Teaching: A Matter of Living the Mystery." *Change,* 1990, *22*(1), 11–16.

Palmer, P. J. "Good Talk About Good Teaching: Improving Teaching Through Conversation and Community." *Change,* 1993, *25*(6), 8–13.

Palmer, P. J. *The Courage to Teach: Exploring the Inner Landscape of a Teacher's Life.* (10th anniversary ed.) San Francisco: Jossey-Bass, 2007.

Palloff, R. M., and Pratt, K. *Lessons from the Cyberspace Classroom: The Realities of Online Teaching.* San Francisco: Jossey-Bass, 2001.

Palomba, C. A., and Banta, T. W., (eds.). *Assessing Student Competence in Accredited Disciplines: Pioneering Approaches to Assessment in Higher Education.* Sterling, Va.: Stylus, 2001.

Pascarella, E. T., and Terenzini, P. T. *How College Affects Students. Vol. 2: A Third Decade of Research.* San Francisco: Jossey-Bass, 2005.

Paulsen, M. B., and Feldman, K. A. *Taking Teaching Seriously: Meeting the Challenges of Instructional Improvement.* ASHE-ERIC Higher Education Report, no. 2. San Francisco: Jossey-Bass, 1995.

Perry, R. P., Menec, V. H., and Struthers, C. W. "Student Motivation from the Teacher's Perspective." In R. J. Menges, M. Weimer, and Associates (eds.), *Teaching on Solid Ground: Using Scholarship to Improve Practice.* San Francisco: Jossey-Bass, 1996.

Petrosino, A., Martin, T., and Svihla, V. (eds.). *Developing Student Expertise and Community: Lessons from How People Learn.* New Directions for Teaching and Learning, no. 108. San Francisco: Jossey-Bass, 2007.

Pintrich, P., and Schunk, D. *Motivation in Education: Theory, Research and Applications.* Upper Saddle Ridge, N.J.: Merrill Prentice Hall, 2002.

"A Plan for Effective Discussion Boards." *Online Classroom*, May 2007, pp. 1, 3.

Robertson, D. R. *Making Time, Making Change: Avoiding Overload in College Teaching.* Stillwater, Okla.: New Forums Press, 2003.

Robertson, F., Bean, J. C., and Peterson, D.. "Using Federal Reserve Publications in Institutions and Market Courses: An Approach to Critical Thinking." *Advances in Financial Education*, 2004, 2, 15–25.

Rock, D. A. *Development of a Process to Assess Higher Order Thinking Skills for College Graduates.* Washington, D.C.: National Center for Education Statistics, 1991. (ED 340 765)

Sayre, H. M. *Writing About Art.* Upper Saddle River, N.J.: Prentice Hall, 1989.

Sayre, H. M. *Writing About Art.* (6th ed.) Upper Saddle River, N.J.: Prentice-Hall, 2009.

Schwegler, R. A., and Shamoon, L. K. "The Aims and Process of the Research Paper." *College English*, 1982, 44, 817–824.

Seldin, P. *The Teaching Portfolio: A Practical Guide to Improved Performance and Promotion/Tenure Decisions.* (3rd ed.) San Francisco: Jossey-Bass, 2003.

Seldin, P., and Miller, J. E. *The Academic Portfolio: A Practical Guide to Documenting Teaching, Research, and Service*. San Francisco: Jossey-Bass, 2009.

Serban, A. M., and Friedlander, J. (eds.). "Developing and Implementing Assessment of Student Learning Outcomes." New Directions for Community Colleges, no. 126. San Francisco: Jossey-Bass, 2004.

Sher, B., and Gottlieb, A. *Wishcraft: How to Get What You Really Want*. New York: Ballantine, 2003.

Simonson, M., Smaldino, S., Albright, M., and Zvacek, S. *Teaching and Learning at a Distance: Foundations of Distance Education* (4th ed.) Upper Saddle River, N.J.: Pearson Education, 2009.

Sommers, N. "Responding to Student Writing." *College Composition and Communication*, 1982, *33*(2), 148–156.

Speck, B. W. *Grading Students' Classroom Writing: Issues and Strategies*. ASHE-ERIC Higher Education Research Report, vol. 27, no 3. San Francisco: Jossey-Bass, 2000.

Speck, B. W. *Facilitating Students' Collaborative Writing: Issues and Recommendations*. ASHE-ERIC Higher Education Report, vol. 28, no. 6. San Francisco: Jossey-Bass, 2002.

Stein, R. F., and Hurd, S. *Using Student Teams in the Classroom*. San Francisco: Anker/Jossey-Bass, 2000.

Stevens, D. D., and Levi, A. *Introduction to Rubrics*. Sterling, Va.: Stylus, 2005.

"Structuring the Case Method for Asynchronous Online Learning." *Online Classroom*, June 2004, pp. 1–2.

Subiño Sullivan, C. S., Middendorf, J., and Camp, M. E. "Engrained Study Habits and the Challenge of Warmups in Just-in-Time Teaching." *National Teaching and Learning Forum*, 17(4), 2008, 5–8.

Suskie, L. *Assessing Student Learning: A Common Sense Guide*. (2nd ed.) San Francisco: Anker/Jossey-Bass, 2009

Svinicki, M. D. *Learning and Motivation in the Postsecondary Classroom*. San Francisco: Anker/Jossey-Bass, 2004.

Svinicki, M. D. "Student Goal Orientation, Motivation, and Learning." IDEA Paper, no. 41. Manhattan, Kans.: Kansas State University, Center for Faculty Evaluation and Development, 2005. www.theideacenter.org/IDEAPapers.

Theall, M. (ed.). *Motivation from Within: Encouraging Faculty and Students to Excel*. New Directions for Teaching and Learning, no. 78. San Francisco: Jossey-Bass, 1999.

Thiell, T., Peterman, S., and Brown, M. "Assessing the Crisis in College Mathematics: Designing Courses for Student Success." *Change*, July–Aug. 2008, pp. 44–49.

Thiell, T., Peterman, S., and Brown, M. "A Course Redesign That Contributed to Student Success." *Teaching Profession*, 2009, *23*(1), 6.

Tobias, S. "The Contract Alternative: An Experiment in Testing and Assessment in Undergraduate Science." *AAHE Bulletin*, 1994, *6*(6), 3–6.

Tobias, S. "In-Class Exams in College-Level Science: New Theory, New Practice." *Journal of Science and Technology Education*, 1996, *5*(4), 311–320.

Trajkovski, G. (ed.). *Diversity in Information Technology Education: Issues and Controversies*. Hershey, Pa.: Information Sciences, 2006.

Walvoord, B. E. *Helping Students Write Well: A Guide for Teachers in All Disciplines*. (2nd ed.) New York: Modern Language Association, 1986.

Walvoord, B. E. *Assessment Clear and Simple: A Practical Guide for Institutions, Departments, and General Education*. San Francisco: Jossey-Bass, 2004.

Walvoord, B. E. *Teaching and Learning in College Introductory Religion Courses*. Malden, Mass.: Blackwell, 2008.

Walvoord, B. E., and Breihan, J. "Arguing and Debating: Breihan's History Course." In B. E. Walvoord, L. P. McCarthy, and others, *Thinking and Writing in College: A Naturalistic Study of Students in Four Disciplines*. Urbana, Ill.: National Council of Teachers of English, 1990.

Walvoord, B. E., McCarthy, L. P., and others. *Thinking and Writing in College: A Naturalistic Study of Students in Four Disciplines*. Urbana, Ill.: National Council of Teachers of English, 1990.

Walvoord, B. E., and Robison, S. M. "Using Social Science to Help Oneself and Others: Robison's Human Sexuality Course." In B. E. Walvoord, L. P. McCarthy, and others, *Thinking and Writing in College: A Naturalistic Study of Students in Four Disciplines*. Urbana, Ill.: National Council of Teachers of English, 1990.

Walvoord, B. E., and Sherman, A. K. "Managerial Decision Making: Sherman's Business Course." In B. E. Walvoord, L. P. McCarthy, and others, *Thinking and Writing in College: A Naturalistic Study of Students in Four Disciplines*. Urbana, Ill.: National Council of Teachers of English, 1990.

Walvoord, B. E., and Williams, L. *Making Large Classes Interactive*. Cincinnati, Ohio: University of Cincinnati, 1995. Videotape.

Weaver, C., 1996. *Teaching Grammar in Context*. Portsmouth, N.H.: Boynton/Cook, 1996.

Weimer, M. *Learner-Centered Teaching: Five Key Changes to Practice*. San Francisco: Jossey-Bass, 2002.

Weimer, M. E. "Poorly Designed Group Work." *Teaching Professor*, 2008, *22*(7), 3.

White, E. M. *Teaching and Assessing Writing*. (2nd ed.) San Francisco: Jossey-Bass, 1994.

Wiggins, G. *Educative Assessment: Designing Assessments to Inform and Improve Student Performance.* San Francisco: Jossey-Bass, 1998.

Wlodkowski, R. J. *Enhancing Adult Motivation to Learn: A Comprehensive Guide for Teaching All Adults.* (3rd ed.) San Francisco: Jossey-Bass, 2008.

Yelon, S. L., and Duley, J. S. *Efficient Evaluation of Individual Performaânce in Field Placement.* East Lansing: Michigan State University, 1978.

Wulff, D. H. (ed.). *Aligning for Learning: Strategies for Teaching Effectiveness.* San Francisco: Anker/Jossey-Bass, 2005.

Zubizarreta, J. *The Learning Portfolio: Reflective Practice for Improving Student Learning.* (2nd ed.) San Francisco: Jossey-Bass, 2009.

Zull, J. E. *The Art of Changing the Brain.* Sterling, Va.: Stylus, 2002.

Index